THE GLOBAL MANAGEMENT SERIES

Research Methods for Accounting and Finance

A guide to writing your dissertation

Audrey Paterson, David Leung, William Jackson, Robert MacIntosh and Kevin O'Gorman

(G) **Goodfellow Publishers Ltd**

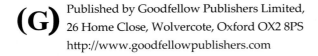

Published by Goodfellow Publishers Limited,
26 Home Close, Wolvercote, Oxford OX2 8PS
http://www.goodfellowpublishers.com

Published 2016

British Library Cataloguing in Publication Data: a catalogue record for this title is available from the British Library.
Library of Congress Catalog Card Number: on file.

ISBN: 978-1-910158-89-0

 Design and typesetting by P.K. McBride, www.macbride.org.uk

Cover design by Cylinder

Printed by Marston Book Services, www.marston.co.uk

Contents

Firstly ... nothing exists;
secondly ... even if anything exists, it is incomprehensible by man;
thirdly .., even if anything is comprehensible, it is guaranteed to be inexpressible and
incommunicable to one's neighbour.

Gorgias 500 BC, quoted in Aristotle, *De Melisso Xenophane Gorgia* 980a:19–20

Acknowledgments

The genesis for this text book arose from the perceived the need for a resource that reflected the broad research interests of faculty members, which could stimulate students' curiosity about research within the accounting and finance disciplines and, at the same time, also provide essential advice and guidance on the research process.

There is an extensive source of accumulated knowledge within the School of Management & Languages at Heriot-Watt University, in the form of both faculty members and PhD students alike. We decided to put this resource to good use by utilising this shared knowledge to produce a textbook that reflects the wide variety of research projects that have been and can be undertaken within the field of accounting and finance, regardless of where you are based in the world. While there were a few stressful moments, the execution of this project has been very collegiate and a lot of fun, and certainly beats working in seclusion!

We owe gratitude to a number of supporters of this project, to whom we wish to give our thanks. First, to our colleagues at Heriot-Watt University, who were badgered for information and advice. Second, to our colleagues at Goodfellow Publishers, who have provided support and advice on the deliverable aspects of this complex project. We are also indebted to Amber Jasmine Jackson for her proofreading and copy-editing of the manuscript and the speed and accuracy of her work. Finally, we would like to thank our families who have provided encouragement, enthusiasm and endless cups of tea throughout the duration of this project.

Audrey, David, William, Robert and Kevin

Biographies

Nana Abena Kwansa is a finance PhD candidate at Heriot-Watt University, Edinburgh. Her research focuses on capital structure of multinational companies and how markets value international growth opportunities. She received a MSc in Finance from University of Strathclyde in 2014 and a Bachelor of Commerce from University of Cape Coast in 2012. Prior to joining the PhD programme she worked for an investment banking firm in Ghana which specialises in debt and equity issue and financial advisory.

Norin Arshed is an Associate Professor and the Programmes Director for Leadership and Organisational Performance suite of postgraduate programmes in the Department of Business Management at Heriot-Watt University. She is an economist by background with professional experience both in the public and private sectors. Her research concentrates on exploring and understanding the enterprise policy process by applying institutional theory as the theoretical lens. She is involved with numerous stakeholders which involve government institutions, think tanks and the private sector.

Nigel Caldwell is a Reader at Heriot Watt School of Management and Languages. He has worked at Bradford, Plymouth and Bath Universities. Prior to his academic career, he worked at a leading UK automotive manufacturer. His research today explores the fields of Operations and Supply Management. Nigel publishes in journals such as *International Journal of Operations & Production Management* and *Industrial Marketing Management*. He has generated research income approaching three quarters of a million pounds from the UK Engineering and Physical Research Council.

Ross Curran is a final year PhD candidate at Heriot-Watt University, Edinburgh, where he is a member of the Intercultural Research Centre. His primary research interests focus on nonprofit marketing and volunteer management practices, as well as authenticity and heritage in tourists' experiential consumption. He has published research in journals including *Nonprofit and Voluntary Sector Quarterly*, *Tourism Management*, and the *International Journal of Tourism Research*.

Mike Danson is Professor of Enterprise Policy at Heriot-Watt University and has worked widely on issues about urban and regional economic development, island and rural economies and enterprises, demographic change, volunteering, Gaelic, microbreweries and poverty. He has published 14 edited books and 250 papers. He has advised parliaments, governments, and such organisations as the OECD, European Commission, Scottish Enterprise. Mike graduated with the first DLitt from the University of the West of Scotland in 2012. He is Treasurer of the Academy of Social Sciences.

Mercy Denedo is a PhD student in the School of Management and Languages at Heriot-Watt University, Edinburgh. Her research interests focus on interdisciplinary studies on accountability and governance in the context of human rights, corporate social responsibility, counter accountability, stakeholders' engagement and sustainable development. Her current research explores counter accountability, human rights accountability and sustainable development in Africa, especially in Nigeria using a qualitative and interpretive research approach. Additionally, she is a teaching assistant on a number of accounting courses at Heriot-Watt University.

Thomas Farrington is a Post-Doctoral Research Associate in Management and Organisation at Heriot-Watt University. His research examines contemporary issues in business and management through a lens of critical theory. Thomas has taught at South East European University in Tetovo and at the University of Edinburgh, from which he received his doctorate. His work has most recently appeared in the *Journal of American Studies*, *Research in Hospitality Management* and the *Journal of Marketing Management*.

Anees Farrukh is a PhD student in the School of Management and Languages at Heriot–Watt University. His PhD aims to shed light on the accountability of NGOs in Pakistan to address the question of transparency that has emerged with a massive increase of public, international and private funds. The research focal point is the educational crises in Pakistan, with emphasis on the role of NGOs in establishing social justice, change and equality in a society.

Keith Gori is a doctoral researcher in the School of Management and Languages at Heriot-Watt University. His doctoral research engages with Consumer Culture Theory, identity and consumer narratives in the context of the British Home Front during World War Two, and more widely he is interested in consumer culture and marketing history. He teaches on global management and marketing courses in the Department of Business Management.

Emma Hill is a PhD student in the department of Languages and Intercultural Studies at Heriot Watt University. She holds a BA(Hons) in English Studies from the University of Exeter and a MA in English Literary Studies from the University of York. Her current research is focused on the ways in which migrant peoples have themselves heard in both the public and private spheres, particularly with reference to the Somali population in Glasgow. More generally, her interests include topics concerning migration, identity, memory, place and text.

Amber Jasmine Jackson is a freelance proof-reader and copy-editor. Amber holds a MSc in Late Antique, Islamic and Byzantine Studies from the University of Edinburgh and a MA in Classics from the University of Cambridge. She currently operates as International Projects Editor in the International Reversioning team of a company that develops digital educational resources for use in around 60 countries throughout the world, in languages such as Brazilian Portuguese, Slovenian and Malay.

William (Bill) Jackson is Head of the Department of Accounting, Economics and Finance at Heriot-Watt University and holds a PhD from the University of Edinburgh. Bill's research interests are primarily in the history of accounting, particularly where accounting interfaces with medical practice. Other interests are in the more contemporary interface between accounting and medical practice, the history of accounting and popular culture, management accounting practices in non-Anglo-Saxon contexts and the gendering of the accountancy profession.

Darren Jubb is a PhD student at Heriot-Watt University, Edinburgh. His primary research interest is considering the role that accounting plays in shaping popular culture, with a current emphasis on how accounting influences the cultural practice of record production. Darren received an MA Hons in Accountancy from Heriot-Watt University in 2010 before working in professional accountancy practice for a number of years. During this period he qualified as a Chartered Accountant with the Institute of Chartered Accountants Scotland.

Christian König is a PhD student in the School of Management and Languages at Heriot-Watt University, Edinburgh. He is an active member of the Logistics Research Centre and his primary research interests focus on the outsourcing strategies of focal firms and the continuous development of service providers. In his doctoral thesis, he investigates the role of systems integrators in the logistics industry using an exploratory approach Christian received an MSc. in Logistics and Supply Chain Management with distinction from Heriot-Watt University in Edinburgh in 2012.

Anthony Kyiu is a PhD student and tutor in Finance at Heriot Watt University. His research examines how ownership structure affects the reaction of stock prices to corporate information in selected common law African countries. He holds an MSc in Investment Analysis (distinction) from the University of Stirling, UK (2014), and a Bachelor of Commerce from the University of Cape Coast, Ghana (2012). He is also a graduate of the Institute of Chartered Accountants, Ghana and an Associate Fellow of the Higher Education Academy (UK).

David Leung is an Associate Professor in Accounting at Coventry University. David is a qualified accountant and worked as a financial controller and consultant in a number of sectors including biotechnology, printing, financial services, tourism and retail before joining academia. He gained his MBA at Durham University and his MSc. by Research in Science and Technology Studies, and PhD in Social Studies of Finance at the University of Edinburgh. He is the author of *Inside Accounting: The Sociology of Financial Reporting and Auditing*.

Sean Lochrie is an Assistant Professor in Management at Heriot-Watt University, Dubai. His primary research interest focuses on the creation of custodianship behaviours within World Heritage Site management. Recent publications have explored stewardship and local community engagement in World Heritage Site management. He has published research in journals including the *Journal of Marketing Management*, and the *International Journal of Contemporary Hospitality Management*.

Robert MacIntosh is Professor of Strategy and Head of School at Heriot-Watt University. His research focuses on strategy development and organizational change using methods that include ethnography, video diaries and action research. He has consulted extensively with public and private sector organizations and sits on the board of the charity Turning Point Scotland.

Dr Andrew MacLaren is Assistant Professor of Marketing, Heriot-Watt University. His main research interests focus on the service industry and he is also CEO of Vuzii, Scotland's fastest growing technology platform. His outlook is international and he works throughout Europe, the USA, the Middle East and India. He has published widely in the field on multiple topics, contributing in the domains of theory, method and industry practice.

Gavin Maclean is a PhD Student in the School of Management and Languages at Heriot-Watt University. His PhD thesis examines the work of professional musicians in terms of labour process theory and Pierre Bourdieu's theory of practice. More widely he is interested in sociological study of work and employment and 'symbolic' forms of work, particularly cultural production, public sector work and multilingualism in the workplace. He teaches on Human Resource and Critical Approaches to Management courses.

Bridget Efeoghene, Ogharanduku (ACA) is a doctoral student at Heriot Watt University. Her primary research interest focuses on understanding women's experiences within the accountancy profession from a non-western context. She holds an MSc in Accounting and Financial Analysis (Distinction) from Anglia Ruskin University where she was awarded the Anglia Trust Scholarship for graduating as the best international student on the MSc programme. Bridget obtained her Bachelors in Accounting (First Class Honours) from Delta State University Nigeria. She teaches on the Research Methods in Accounting course.

Kevin O'Gorman is Professor of Management and Business History in Heriot-Watt University. He trained in Glasgow, Salamanca and Rome as a philosopher, theologian and historian. His research interests have a dual focus: Origins, history and cultural practices of hospitality, and philosophical, ethical and cultural underpinnings of contemporary management practices. Using a wide range of methodological approaches, he has published over 100 journal articles, books, chapters, and conference papers in business and management.

Angeliki Papachroni is a Research Associate in Strategic Management at Heriot-Watt University. Her research focuses on issues around dual strategies, strategy implementation, paradox management and organizational tensions. She holds a PhD in Strategy and Organizational Ambidexterity from Warwick Business School. Her work on paradoxes and organizational ambidexterity is published in *Journal of Applied Behavioral Science & Human Relations*. Other contributions include strategic teaching case studies on leading companies published in strategy books and chapters on qualitative research published in research methods books.

Audrey Paterson is an Associate Professor in Accounting at Heriot-Watt University and holds a Bcom (Hons), MSc in Social Science Research and a PhD from the University of Edinburgh. Audrey is currently involved in several research networks including the Institute of Public Sector Accounting Research (IPSAR) and is the founder of the Accounting for Society and the Environment (ASE) research network which meets annually. Audrey is currently responsible for the management of the PhD programme within the Department of Accounting, Economics & Finance.

Rodrigo Perez Vega is an Assistant Professor in Marketing in the School of Management and Languages at Heriot-Watt University Dubai Campus. He has experience doing qualitative and quantitative research in online environments. Prior to finishing his PhD, Rodrigo had marketing experience in several digital marketing and brand management roles within FMCG and service industries.

Catherine Porter is an Assistant Professor in the Department of Accountancy, Economics and Finance at Heriot-Watt University. In the past she has been a British Academy Postdoctoral Fellow, and worked for the public sector. She is an economist, specialising in the economics of developing countries. She has been involved in the design and fieldwork of several large-scale quantitative surveys in Ethiopia, India, Peru and Vietnam. Her research involves the statistical analysis of such quantitative surveys to measure poverty.

Stephen Rae is a PhD student in the School of Management and Languages at Heriot-Watt University, Edinburgh. His primary research interests lie in how and why companies release information. He received an MA in Accounting and Finance in 2010 and an MRes in the same in 2011, both from Heriot-Watt University. He has a further research interest in quantitative methodologies and their uses following an earlier degree in Statistics, awarded in 2007 from the same institution.

James Richards is an Associate Professor in HRM in the School of Languages and Management in Heriot-Watt University, and an Academic Member of the CIPD. James has published research in HRM journals, edited book collections and consultancy-based reports. James' early research projects looked at employee use of social media for misbehaviour and resistance. More recent research looks at hidden disabilities in the workplace and in-work poverty. James is the Research Ethics Officer for the School of Management & Languages.

Roza Sagitova is a PhD student at Heriot-Watt University, Edinburgh. Her research focuses on corporate environmental responsibility. Roza's thesis examines disclosure of greenhouse gas emission information by Russian companies, motivations for environmental activities and motivations for (non) disclosure of this information. Her research combines quantitative and qualitative approaches. Roza is a teaching assistant on the Research Methods course for the Accountancy and Finance disciplines. She holds an MSc in Accounting and Finance with distinction from Heriot-Watt University.

Ahmed Salhin is a PhD student at Heriot-Watt University, Edinburgh. His research interest mainly focuses on behavioural finance and asset pricing. Ahmed's PhD thesis investigates the relationship between investor sentiment and stock returns in the UK. He assists in the teaching of Managing Corporate Value, Financial Market Theory, and Derivatives courses in the Department of Accountancy, Economics and Finance at Heriot-Watt University. Ahmed received a MSc in Finance with distinction from Heriot-Watt University in 2011.

John Sanders is an Associate Professor in Management in the School of Management and Languages at Heriot-Watt University. He teaches strategic management courses to both undergraduate and post-graduate students. In addition, he teaches a small business management course to final year undergraduate students. Strategic fit within a University setting was the subject of his PhD. His past research efforts have focused on Internet portals, website quality, social networks and the market reach of rural small firms in Scotland.

Katherine Sang is an Associate Professor of Management in the Department of Business Management. Using feminist theory, her research examines how gender inequality is maintained in male dominated professions, including the creative industries and academia. In addition, Kate is researching gender and in-work poverty and supervising PhDs exploring organisational culture, gender and behaviour change. Kate chairs the Feminist and Women's Studies Association UK & Ireland.

Mo Sherif is an Associate Professor of Finance. He received his PhD from the University of Manchester, Manchester Business School, UK. He is an interdisciplinary finance researcher whose initial contributions to the finance literature are in entrepreneurial and behavioural finance, stock trading strategies and asset pricing fields. He is a fellow of the Higher Education Academy in the UK and a member of American Finance Association in the USA. He is currently the Director of Postgraduate Taught Programmes in Finance (AEF) at SML at Heriot-Watt University.

Rafał Sitko is a Ph.D. student in Business and Management at Heriot-Watt University with research interests primarily in diversity management and inclusion. His work focuses on explaining intersections of privilege and oppression in a workplace and their effects on migrants' work experience. Rafał received an MSc from Queen Mary, University of London (2012) and a BA in Psychology and Management (2011) from University of Bradford. During student exchange programs Rafal also studied at Hosei University in Tokyo (2010) and Vrije Universiteit in Amsterdam (2009).

Babak Taheri is an Associate Professor in Marketing at the School of Languages and Management, Heriot-Watt University. His research has a dual focus: 1) unpacking and theorising cultural consumption experiences; 2) services marketing management. He has published over 50 articles, book chapters and conferences papers in these areas. His recent work has appeared in *Annals of Tourism Research, Tourism Management, Nonprofit and Voluntary Sector Quarterly, International Journal of Hospitality Management, Journal of Travel & Tourism Marketing, Journal of Marketing Management* and *Consumption, Markets & Culture.*

Vera Tens has an engineering degree in Wood science and technology from a German university and an MBA from Edinburgh Napier University. She is currently in the process of finishing her doctoral research at Heriot-Watt University on the subject of future generations in family firms, considering it from a stakeholder perspective. Her general research interests are in family businesses and the implications for practitioners, policy development and education.

Alastair Watson is Assistant Professor of Management in the School of Management and Languages, at Heriot-Watt University Dubai Campus. His primary research interest is the commitment and motivation of staff in the UK hospitality industry, and the application of Goffman's theory of Total Institutions. Other areas of interest include employee and organisational spirituality and commitment, and further understanding people's desire, as opposed to their need, to work.

Nikolaos Valantasis-Kanellos is an Assistant Lecturer in Logistics, in the National Institute for Transport and Logistics, Dublin Institute of Technology. His research draws upon contemporary developments in operations management, and the value creation within business networks. He currently researches the formation of Service led Strategies of ports and intermediaries. Nikolaos received an MSc in Logistics and Supply Chain Management from Heriot-Watt University (with distinction) and a BA in Economic and Regional Development from the Panteion University, Athens.

Lakshman Wimalasena PhD is an Assistant Professor of Management, in the School of Management and Languages, Heriot-Watt University and obtained his PhD in Management also from Heriot-Watt University. He is a graduate in human resource management, and also holds an MBA and a postgraduate diploma in social research methods. His main research interests are the meaning of work, social inequality, diversity, agential reflexivity, habitus and critical issue in human resource management. His doctoral study explores the MoW within a postcolonial society, Sri Lanka.

Lubaina Zakaria is a PhD student at Heriot-Watt University, Edinburgh. Her research interest lies within critical discourse of narrative reporting and specifically focuses on how organisations use symbolic discourse via social media in crisis situation. Lubaina received MSc in International Accounting and Management with distinction from Heriot-Watt University in 2013. Prior to that, she had eight years of working experience with Petronas, a Malaysian oil and gas company.

Preface

The primary purpose of this book is to provide some insights into the practice and experience of doing research. It is aimed primarily at accounting and finance students undertaking research for the first time. The book aims to demystify the research process by providing the novice researcher with a guide through all of the stages of the research process from identifying a research topic to the finished project. The book has adopted an accessible writing style and utilises a variety of methods to carefully link the subject matter and topics. The text is supplemented with appropriate examples and reflective exercises to support your skills and knowledge development. Each chapter includes a useful reference list and suggested further readings. While the book is predominantly targeted at accounting and finance students the subject matter covered is also applicable to interdisciplinary research and is thus suitable for those undertaking a research project in other social science subjects.

The book opens with an exploration of the nature and scope of research within the disciplines of accounting and finance; various aspects of the research process and the more specific skills required when conducting a research project within these subject groups. Following this, we provide some ideas and insights into how to identify a suitable research project and stress the importance of understanding and contextualising your research ideas within prior literatures in order to create a space for your research topic. The research process invariably involves reading and synthesising a large volume of academic literature. In Chapter 3 we highlight the importance of the literature review as the underpinning of the research project. The various approaches to conducting a literature review, the importance of critically analysing the literature and presentation of logical and coherent arguments that relate to your project are emphasised.

While there are some distinct traditions within accounting and finance research, there is no single 'right' way to conduct research. Indeed, as will be exemplified within various chapters of this text book, accounting and finance research has many philosophical traditions, data gathering approaches and methods of analysis. Bearing this in mind, Chapter 4 will arm you with the insights required to choose which type of research you will undertake and with the vocabulary to locate your choice amongst the wider set of available research traditions.

The various areas of accounting and finance research have different traditions for conducting research, which will have a direct impact on the researcher's choice of data collection method. As such it is necessary to consider a number of factors such as validity, reliability and generalisability of the data intended for use within your research project. These are neatly outlined within Chapter 5.

Two broad approaches to the collection of qualitative data: historical research and the utilisation of the internet and social media as a social research tool are addressed in Chapter 6. Both historical sources and the presence of online resources offer a diverse range of approaches to the collection of data during your research project. However, collecting this material alone does not offer you the opportunity to infer conclusions or answer your research questions. Consideration also has to be given to the appropriateness and suitability of the analytical techniques employed for your study. Thus, Chapter 7 discusses some common approaches to qualitative research methods as outlined in the Methods Map presented in Chapter 4 and the issues that must be considered with their application.

Qualitative research often generates a large amount of data that is of varying quality and usefulness. The process of navigating through this vast amount of data can be overwhelming for even the most experienced researcher. Moreover, interpreting your findings can be time consuming and difficult. Chapter 8 provides a useful guide on how to transcend beyond describing what participants have said or what you have observed or discovered in documents, to actually analysing and engaging with the data. Some of the most common approaches to analysing qualitative data are discussed. Potential challenges you may encounter are highlighted. Suggestions are made where each approach is considered more appropriate for a particular research area or data.

Much of the research conducted within accounting and finance is concerned with analysing and solving problems. These problems come in many forms, can have common features and often include numerical information. It is therefore important that researchers who are interested in researching such problems develop competency in the use of a range of quantitative data gathering and analysis methods. Thus Chapters 9 and 10 focus on methods of collecting quantitative data, and tools for conducting statistical and quantitative analysis.

Research is essentially about the production of knowledge but in the pursuit of generating this knowledge we must also take into consideration that the research community has a responsibility, not just to pursue knowledge or objective truth but also to the subject of their enquiry and its participants. Keeping this in mind, it is therefore important when conducting any research project to review the ethical position regarding your study and to be aware of and adhere to ethical and professional codes of conduct. Ethical issues and research codes of practice are thus outlined in Chapter 11.

For many people, their dissertation or research project represents the largest piece of written work they will have had to produce. Academic writing is quite different to other kinds of writing, however, as with any other form of writing, academic writing also relies on a strong narrative thread. As such sufficient time and effort should be applied to writing up your project as logically, coherently and precisely as possible. Advice on the writing process is therefore provided in Chapter 12.

Finally, while research is often presented as a logical flow, the reality is that as you progress through your project you often have to visit each of the stages more than once triggering the need to reflect and refine your thoughts and interpretations on the associated issues along the way. Whilst you may feel anxious about the prospect of conducting a research project, the advice and examples used in this book will help you to break this large piece of work down into a set of interrelated tasks in a way that will also allow you to bring them back together into a coherent whole. Having set the scene, you are now ready to work your way through the book gathering skills, techniques and insights as you go.

We wish you luck and enjoyment on your research journey!

Audrey, David, William, Robert and Kevin

1 The Nature of Accounting and Finance Research

Audrey Paterson, William Jackson, Moh Sherif, Robert MacIntosh and Nigel Caldwell

Students in the latter stages of their programme of study are commonly required to complete a research-based project, dissertation or thesis, which typically represents the longest piece of writing that you will have to undertaken. This is a challenging task for many students, who encounter common issues in the course of their project. For the remainder of this chapter, any such extended piece of research-based work will be referred to as a research project. To prepare and submit a research project, you must first conduct a piece of original research. This can be an intimidating prospect and is often seen as a rite of passage during your studies. The primary purpose of this book is to provide some insights into the practice and experience of doing research into accountancy and finance related topics. It offers structured and clear advice for those at the start of the journey from blank page to completed research project, and is aimed primarily at students undertaking research for the first time.

Textbooks and courses in research methods are often unpopular with students, either because the prospect of undertaking a research project seems daunting or because they do not recognise the relevance or benefits of the practice of research to their future career. We argue, however, that learning more about research methods will allow you to both broaden and deepen your knowledge of key research processes and the various methods that can be utilised therein. Such courses and books are designed to ensure that students understand the variety and merits of the techniques that are used in modern social science research and which are available to them as they undertake their own research project. In addition, the study and use of research methods facilitates the development of transferable professional skills, which will be invaluable in future careers in accountancy and finance.

The majority of graduates from accountancy and finance programmes take up employment in the financial services industry, typically with organisations operating in global markets. Within this industry, key employability skills include the ability to analyse various data using a range of quantitative and qualitative techniques, alongside the possession of a critical understanding of contemporary accounting, finance and business issues and related ongoing debates. Furthermore, graduates undertaking professional training in accounting or finance must develop problem-solving skills applicable to the areas of accounting, finance and business, using advanced research tools, to assist in the development of strategic financial plans, procedures, etc., and to research and communicate these in a structured and comprehensible manner. Engagement in a research project towards the end of your studies therefore provides you with an opportunity to develop your skillset and thereby positively influence your future career.

In this introductory chapter we begin by considering what constitutes research, following by a general discussion of knowledge production and the skills required of accounting and finance researchers. Novice researchers are often bamboozled by the variety of research methods, methodologies and philosophical pathways open to them; moreover, terminology can often be inconsistent, which adds further confusion. In order to minimise confusion, we have included an overview of the philosophical traditions of accounting and finance research. We then address the nature of accounting and finance research more broadly, highlighting topical areas of research, before turning our attention to various aspects of the research process and the specific skills required when conducting a project in this area.

What is research?

Research can have many labels: 'academic', 'scientific', 'fundamental' and 'applied' are just four examples (Ryan *et al*, 1992). At its heart, research is about discovery; we engage in research in order to learn more about something. When we have a question or a problem we want to resolve, we research it. We may already think we know the solution and, furthermore, we may consider the answer to be obvious or common sense; however, until we have subjected the problem to rigorous scrutiny, our 'knowledge' remains effectively guesswork or intuition. Research has therefore been defined as the 'systematic investigation into and study of materials, sources, etc., in order to establish facts and reach new conclusions. It is an endeavour to discover new or collate old facts etc. by the scientific study of a subject or by a course of critical investigation' (*Oxford Concise Dictionary*). However, while this definition is useful, it is only a starting point in understanding research; the greater challenge is understanding both what research is and what it is not.

The term 'research' features frequently in everyday life. For example, when engaging with digital or printed news, documentaries and debates, we often find the term 'research' being used to validate the information presented (Saunders *et al*, 2003). Politicians similarly justify their political decisions with research findings, while some companies use opinion polls as an advertising strategy. These examples demonstrate how the term 'research' is ubiquitously applied in everyday contexts.

However, while this use of the word 'research' may be grammatically valid, Walliman (2001) argues that it is often semantically incorrect and creates a misleading impression. For example, while information and data collection is part of the research process, its outputs are of limited value and not considered to be academically rigorous unless it is systematic and with a clear purpose. Reports may contain a lot of data and reference additional sources of data; however, unless the data has been collected with reference to a systematic methodology and analysed and interpreted accordingly, it does not advance knowledge and cannot, therefore, constitute research. Thus, Walliman (2001) argues that, although the term 'research' can be used to instil confidence or respect in a specific idea or product, more information should be sought about the research process and type of analysis used. In many cases, the research process and type of analysis are either fudged or inaccessible, which inevitably invalidates the 'research' as a form of knowledge production. Good research seeks to expand knowledge by acquiring specialised and detailed information in a focused and systematic way, while providing a basis for analysis and highlighting observations on the subject of investigation (White, 2000).

■ Knowledge production

As the above discussion demonstrates, academic research is fundamentally concerned with the production of new knowledge. Chapter 2 discusses how ideas for new research projects originate. First, however, we set the scene by introducing a distinction between two different approaches to knowledge production. Michael Gibbons and colleagues (see Gibbons *et al.* 1994) argue that recent decades have seen the emergence of a new approach to research, which they call 'mode 2 knowledge production'. To contextualise this, it is necessary to explain that mode 1 represents the traditional, some would say ancient, approach to discovery.

Consider some historical figures who made breakthrough discoveries. In the cases of both Galileo's radical suggestion that the earth moves around the sun and Newton's 'discovery' of gravity, new insights produced new theories. In the terminology of Gibbons, the traditional approach to research is theory-led.

We first review our understanding of a particular phenomenon then design a piece of research that is intended to broaden our understanding by scientifically confirming our theoretical hunch. There are few better examples of this than the development of the Large Hadron Collider at CERN to confirm the existence of the Higgs Boson. Peter Higgs speculated on what was only a theoretical possibility in 1964. It required huge capital investment to create the apparatus necessary to prove his theoretical insight, and the joint award of a Nobel Prize to Higgs and François Englert in 2013 represented the culmination of a long, theory-led journey.

During the Renaissance there existed far fewer universities than today, and many great thinkers were polymaths with knowledge of biology, astronomy, physics and chemistry. As academic opportunities opened up and focusing on a specific discipline became the norm, universities began to produce specialists. An unintended consequence of this, particularly in the natural sciences, was the emergence of a scientific method that placed heavy emphasis on theory and experimental design. In Chapter 5 we problematize the notion that there is a single 'scientific' approach to research. For now, it is sufficient to highlight the observation that traditional (mode 1) approaches to research are firmly grounded in theory.

Considering mode 2, we can see that, although it was originally an offshoot of mode 1, it is becoming increasingly distinct.

> "our view is that while Mode 2 may not be replacing Mode 1, Mode 2 is different from Mode 1 – in nearly every respect ... it is not being institutionalised primarily within university structures ... (it) involves the close interaction of many actors throughout the process of knowledge production ...(it) makes use of a wider range of criteria in judging quality control. Overall, the process of knowledge production is becoming more reflexive and affects at the deepest levels what shall count as 'good science.'"

(Gibbons *et al*, 1994, p.3)

Thus the traditional, theory-led approach to the development of research projects has been joined by a second approach to research, with five distinguishing characteristics.

1   In mode 2-style projects knowledge is produced in the context of application. Knowledge production is organised around a specific real-world problem where a firm or industry is struggling to achieve particular outcomes. There is an imperative to be practically useful, rather than theoretically curious, when framing a new research project and research is therefore produced under "continuous negotiation" (Gibbons *et al* 1994, p. 3) with practitioners.

1

2 Mode 2 research is transdisciplinary, as the real-world problem that forms the focus of the research may best be addressed by a combination of skills, expertise and theories from various disciplines. This prompts an interesting return to the Renaissance-style mix of disciplines and theories which fell out of favour as scientific specialisation became the norm. In the case of accounting and finance research, phenomena such as decision making have been viewed through the lenses of psychology, sociology, and economics; however, the boundaries between these approaches are increasingly elided, with hybrid approaches emerging. The suggestion that utilising a combination of disciplines offers the best strategy may seem obvious, but it introduces the challenge of ensuring that researchers genuinely reach a shared understanding and are not simply talking past each other (Pfeffer, 1993). Furthermore, the particular mix of disciplines required may not be evident at the outset; mode 2 research is therefore characterised as "problem solving capability on the move" (Gibbons *et al*, 1994, p5).

3 Mode 2 research is more reflexive than mode 1. This is the only way to offset the tendency to talk past each other. Multi-disciplinary teams of experts and practitioners are drawn together around a particular problem and must engage in open communication, continually considering the research from the standpoint of other participants in the ongoing process of negotiation. In mode 1 research, teams of specialists with common viewpoints, methods and theories can survive without the need to engage in highly reflexive dialogue about the nature of the problem at hand.

4 In mode 2 research the composition of the research team is more heterogeneous and organizationally diverse; that is, the research will not exclusively occur within the traditional boundaries of the university sector. Firms like Google, Apple and Microsoft increasingly spend vast sums of money on research and development and, in many areas, may be ahead of the development curve relative to their academic peers. That said, mode 2 research tends to feature collaboration between industry and academia, creating problem-solving teams composed of diverse individuals and experiences.

5 The final difference between mode 1 and mode 2 research is the wider range of quality controls present in mode 2. The quality of knowledge produced in a mode 2 project is assessed by a substantially broader interested community (i.e. both academic peers and practicing managers). Mode 1 research is typically evaluated by academic peer review of the type whose highest accolade would be a Nobel Prize or equivalent award, such as the Fields Medal in mathematics. In mode 2 research such academically oriented assessments of quality would sit alongside many other considerations, such as the practicality, ethics and financial viability of proposed solutions to the problem under investigation.

While your own research project may be unlikely to win a Nobel Prize (at least in the short term), it is worth considering the research tradition within which your work will sit. Is your proposed project led by the observation of a practical difficulty facing an organization or industry? For example, how to allocate operating costs in a fluid and collaborative partnership between two organisations. Or is your project founded on a theoretical problem that you wish to test? For example, the application of institutional theory could be utilised to understand the relatively slow pace of change in some particular aspect of accounting regulation. Both styles of research are valid, but will be assessed in their respective ways in order to confirm that you have completed your research project.

■ Knowledge production and skills development

The creation of knowledge through research is not achieved by chance. It comes from mastering a set of skills that empower the researcher to engage in activities that will advance existing knowledge and expose new avenues of academic enquiry. The types of skills required vary according to the preferred methodology of the researcher. For instance, research into finance or market-based accounting requires strong knowledge of econometric techniques, and these and other forms of research are likely to require knowledge of specialist software packages for data analysis. However, some skills apply to most research projects, such as staying abreast of current research and literature within your research area, and the ability to understand and recognise not only research problems for investigation, but also problems that may obstruct your own research. The assimilation and interpretation of complex research content is another important skill for researchers, alongside the ability to identify and evaluate the contribution to knowledge made by your research. The ability to critically evaluate evidence and conduct thorough analyses of the constituent parts of your research will advance your research goals. Finally, the ability to clearly document, report, communicate and defend your research to interested parties is another essential skill that will serve you well in the future. The skills described above aid in the production of excellent research, but equally important is an understanding of the research traditions to which you will contribute. The following section outlines the background of accounting and finance research.

The subject matter of accountancy and finance research

It is easy to view the subject matter of accounting and finance as intrinsically connected with the modern world – and it is, without doubt. However, the practice of accounting has an ancient pedigree and is rooted in our social and cultural heritage. Research by accounting historians has shown that accounting techniques can be traced back at least 7,000 years to ancient civilisations such as Mesopotamia, where evidence of recording expenditures and goods traded and received has been uncovered (Robson, 1992). Others have observed that proto-cuneiform, the earliest known writing system, is essentially a form of bookkeeping, and that accounting existed even earlier in a system of clay tokens (Mattessich, 1989). There is also evidence of the counting and recording of money and early auditing systems in such geographically diverse contexts as the writings of ancient Egypt and Babylon (Oldroyd and Dobie, 2008) and the scriptures of the Indian Maurya dynasty (322–185 BCE). During the Roman period, Emperor Augustus had access to detailed financial information, as evidenced by his *Res Gestae*. This text provided a record of the empire's public expenditure during about 40 years of Augustus's reign, including an account of subsidies to the treasury, awards of land or money to army veterans, expenditure on building projects, theatrical shows, gladiatorial games and financial distributions to the people (Oldroyd, 1995). Through the chronological and geographical breadth of these examples we can see that accounting as a practice is hard to separate from the known roots of modern civilisation.

More modern conceptions of accounting began to emerge within Europe when, in 1494, Luca Pacioli (often called the Father of Accounting) published a book, *Summa de Arithmetica, Geometria, Proportioni et Proportionalita*, containing a treatise on double-entry bookkeeping as a means of recording debits and credits (Sangster *et al*, 2007), a method which remains largely unchanged today. The development of joint-stock companies around 1600 necessitated the production of accounting information for users like investors. Slightly earlier than this an early commodity market emerged in Antwerp, which was the model for the 1571 opening of the Royal Exchange (an early stock market) in London. Stock markets subsequently opened around the world and developed into other forms, such as futures and options exchanges. The increasing sophistication of markets and company forms brought a need for increased regulation, as scandals and failures rocked the financial system. In the middle of the nineteenth century professional associations of accountants began to form in Scotland; the idea quickly spread across the UK and elsewhere. Legislation began to require formal audit of companies, and different types of accountancy became increasingly recognised, such as the provision of information for internal (management accounting) and external (financial accounting) purposes, alongside increasing specialisation in audit and tax. By the second half of the twentieth century it was possible to identify most of the features of finance and accounting that we would recognise today, therefore a significant point to note is that the practices that we consider central to these disciplines are as old as human history and may even be essential to the functioning of complex societies.

■ Research traditions in accounting and finance

Throughout history much has been written about accounting and finance. Until relatively recently, such writings tended to be largely descriptive, institutionally orientated and atheoretical (Ryan *et al.*, 1992, p30). This changed as increasingly sophisticated economic theory began to find applications elsewhere. About 60 years ago we witnessed significant developments within finance research as the Markowitz model for portfolio risk (1953) and Modigliani and Miller's (1958) analysis of capital structure offered the two main precursors of change in finance research. Both models created opportunities to conduct more sophisticated research across the field. The introduction of other analytical tools within the discipline, such as Sharpe's (1964) capital asset pricing model (CAPM) and Fama's (1970) paper on efficient market hypothesis, generated a considerable amount of empirical research. Continued experimental refinements, such as the application of continuous time mathematics to pricing under conditions of risk and uncertainty and the development of the Black and Scholes (1973) option pricing model, represented further significant theoretical developments within the field.

Following these developments in finance, accounting researchers also adopted such positive methodologies. This took off with the seminal works of Ball and Brown in the late 1960s and led to a significant expansion in theoretically orientated accounting research. The positivist tradition discussed here in relation to both finance and accounting is more closely examined in Chapter 4, but is essentially concerned with finding 'laws' that explain the working of the social world. Researchers develop hypotheses from theories and test them using large sample data; typically, analysis of the findings leads to theoretical revisions, which seek to improve the explanatory power of the original. This central tradition of research in finance is paralleled by an equivalent ongoing stream in accounting, especially in the US. The first two decades of positive accounting research were nicely synthesised by Watts and Zimmerman (1986); however, by then accounting researchers were already exploring alternative methodologies and had substantially expanded the accounting research arena.

Broadly parallel to the development of positivism in finance and (mostly financial) accounting, an alternative tradition was developing in relation to management accounting. Initially led by the mid-1960s work of Robert Anthony at Harvard Business School, this was a normative tradition; heavily influenced by theoretical developments within economics, it differed from positivism in that it sought to deliver technical models of practice based upon what was deemed the 'correct' approach. Modern management accounting textbooks utilise this approach, describing techniques according to the theoretically best method, with limited reference to what happens in practice. Normative approaches survive, but they suffer from heavy critiquing of their underlying assumptions, which are typically drawn from economic theory. In response to the perceived narrow perspectives of economic-based theorisations, in the 1970s and 80s accounting researchers sought alternative explanations for accounting practice.

There has been significant, although arguably fairly limited, engagement with psychology in accounting; however, more major developments might be identified in the adoption of a range of sociological theories and research approaches. This chapter will not describe the range and breadth of these, as this is covered in subsequent chapters. Suffice it to say that they have been responsible for the transformation of the research agenda, expanding accounting research from a narrow focus on what accountants do, to a consideration of the breadth and complexity of the effects of accounting practice on society, and vice-versa. Differing perspectives have highlighted the highly political nature of financial accounting and reporting, and the politicised process of regulation. Behavioural, organisational and social dimensions have been introduced into the discipline of management accounting research, and interpretative techniques adopted which facilitate a clearer understanding of accounting as a social practice. The application of critical theory to the structures, including accounting, that underpin society and social practice has created opportunities for social change by revealing significant social imbalance and injustice. Over three decades, these developments have radically changed the landscape of accounting research; meanwhile, the finance research agenda has experienced much less expansion. Perhaps because of the central focus on financial markets and the endurance of the efficient markets hypothesis and similar theoretical positions, finance research has only relatively recently adopted alternative approaches.

In recent years, some researchers have critiqued the traditional approach to finance research, which has led to the emergence of behavioural finance, in parallel with the field of behavioural economics. The similarities between these areas of finance research are in some ways slight and mainly limited to differences in theoretical underpinning. Within the traditional camp, financial institutions are populated not by 'error prone and emotional homo sapiens, but by the awesome homo economicus', who makes rational decisions based on specific economic criteria (Bloomfield, 2010, p1). Traditionalists apply positivist theories to support the view that apparent deviations from rationality by competitive financial institutions are unimportant provided the abridging supposition is sufficient to predict how the dependent variables correlate to one another. Traditionalists therefore hold the view that investors are influenced neither by the way information is presented nor by their emotions. In contrast, behavioural finance is concerned with explaining why market participants make irrational systematic errors. It principally draws upon the research and methodologies of psychology in order to explain why market anomalies occur, and its proponents argue that, unlike the traditional approach, this can account for market inefficiencies. Behaviourists defend their position with Maslow's hierarchy of needs or Kuhn's *The Structure of Scientific Revolutions* (1962), the latter being not concerned with social science, but rather a treatise on the philosophy of the natural sciences.

From the above discussion we can see that, in contrast to natural science disciplines, which are concerned with natural phenomena, research in accounting and finance falls into the domain of the social sciences, being generally concerned with economic and social issues. Like the neighbouring discipline of management, accounting and finance have not developed the unique research methodologies or theoretical positions seen in other social sciences (e.g. economics, sociology or psychology), but have instead adapted instruments from other social and natural science disciplines (Smith, 2004). This array of possibilities can make choosing a methodology somewhat bewildering; you will find help with this in Chapter 4.

We have discussed the nature of the research process and traditions in accountancy and finance, but not the areas or fields of activity that are available as potential subjects of research. We will now highlight some main areas of research activity and key debates to which your project might contribute.

Topical areas in accounting and finance research

Any cursory inspection of accounting and finance research will reveal that there is great scope in terms of researchable areas: the broad functions of financial accounting, management accounting, auditing, taxation, corporate finance and financial markets offer a host of opportunities. This, however, is far from a comprehensive list; recent decades have seen research development in areas such as the accounting profession, social and environmental accounting, gender issues, accounting in developing economies, accounting in the public sector, the history of accounting, governance, and the impact of technology.

It is not uncommon to find crossover in these areas; the following paragraphs seek to illustrate some ways in which research informs our current thinking and are linked to some exemplar studies, to which you may wish to refer.

We will begin with financial accounting research, which tends mainly to focus on regulation and disclosure. The process by which standards are created is undoubtedly fascinating in its highly politicised nature, but perhaps does not easily lend itself to the scale of research in a research project. We therefore tend to find that many students favour working on the process outputs, whether in terms of exploring the adoption of particular standards within industries or geographic locations, or studying organisations' financial statements to see the extent and impact of mandated or voluntary disclosures (e.g. Abraham and Shrives, 2014).

Auditing provides another wide source of topical research. The classic auditing debates concern such issues as auditors' responsibilities, particularly with respect to fraud and how this has opened up the audit expectations gap. Auditor independence is always high on the agenda and strongly linked to the audit fees debate (e.g. Fraser and Pong, 2009). The advent of the Audit Practices Board in 1991 formalised audit regulation and generated another researchable field; audit practice lends itself well to investigation, especially as the effects of technology are increasingly felt. The work of Ndiweni (2011) offers alterative insight as it explores the role of forensic accounting and the impotence of auditing practices in a corrupt environment. Significant work has gone into trying to understand auditor decision making, and ethics and governance are hotly debated, as are the effects of auditing on the financial reporting process. Non-standard forms of audit are also increasingly subject to research, offering scope for development as increasing effort goes into the examination of environmental and social audit.

In contrast to the regulatory focus of financial accounting research, the efforts of managerial accounting researchers appear relatively diverse. In recent years, substantial work has gone into understanding the impact of change on the role of management accounting practitioners and its place as a practice exposed to technological developments in shifting organisational, cultural and increasingly globalised contexts. Some of these issues feature in the work of Ndiweni, (2010) who explored the role of management accounting information in a volatile environment and found a trail of unintended consequences resulting from the use and abuse of management accounting information in a large African company. The emergence of a range of new techniques and their implementation and application has also drawn the attention of researchers to practices such as strategic management accounting, the balanced scorecard, activity based costing/management and increasingly sophisticated approaches to performance management and control. The work of Roslender and Hart (2003), for example, provides useful theoretical and fieldwork perspectives in the search for strategic management accounting. Environmental management accounting and sustainability have also become popular areas of research (e.g. Thomson and Bebbington, 2013). These few examples serve only to show that the scope of managerial accounting research cannot be fully encompassed in the space available here. As a practice, or set of practices, that has been shown to transcend the organisational context, the diversity of topics in management accounting research has continued to grow in recent years and offers great potential to researchers.

In other directions, there have been studies of the underlying accounting information systems (AIS) which collect, store and generate data for a range of purposes, including reporting, performance management and audit. AIS have historically been, and continue to be, subject to constant change, most recently from computerisation and the advent of enterprise resource planning (ERP) systems, which has necessitated research to understand the resultant impacts. For example, the work of Kobelsky *et al.* (2014) demonstrated the considerable impact of information technology on organisational performance in the not-for-profit sector. Other research strands in AIS explore issues such as design science, decision aides, support systems, processing assurance, security systems and controls.

Tax research tends to be practically focused. For example, Simon and Alley's (2008) work on successful tax reform compared the experience of value added tax in the United Kingdom to the goods and services tax in New Zealand. Others have considered taxpayer decision-making, the process of determining tax allocations, tax computations, incentives, market reactions to tax levels and disclosures, systems to meet tax goals, and explorations of how new tax laws impact on both clients and employees. These are just a few examples of tax research, but it should be noted that not all tax research is constrained to practical issues in the corporate setting. Opportunities also exist to investigate more controversial, politically influenced issues (e.g. Frecknall-Hughes *et al.*, 2014).

Specific areas of research interest within finance include capital markets and derivatives, stock prices or returns, mergers and acquisitions, capital structure and sources of financing, and corporate governance. Concerning research into stock prices, the work of Hyde and Sherif (2010) provides insight into consumption asset pricing and the term structure, while the work of Ibrahim and Brzeszczynski (2014) questions the usefulness of international stock market information for domestic stock market trading. In the analysis of performance,

1

Mousavia *et al.* (2015) apply an orientation-free, super-efficiency, DEA-based framework to the performance evaluation of bankruptcy prediction models in order to evaluate bankruptcy modelling frameworks. Carbon futures have also become an important area of finance research in recent years (e.g. Kalaitzogloua and Ibrahim, 2013). In another direction, Caglayan *et al.* (2012) examined the effects of exchange rate uncertainty and sources of finance on firm productivity, while Kabir *et al.* (2013) examined the relationship between executive pay and the cost of debt. Corporate governance and capital structure in developing countries have also opened up research opportunities. For instance, Haque *et al.* (2009) applied agency theory to investigate the influence of firm-level corporate governance on the capital structure pattern of non-financial listed firms in Bangladesh. The above examples demonstrate that we have only scratched the surface of finance research, and offer a flavou r of the diversity of work that exists in this area.

A similar array of research opportunities lies in the area of public sector management and administration. Research in this area tends to focus on topical issues and problems, such as the success or failure of public projects, improving government efficiency and the effects of new public management (NPM) on performance, crisis management and sustainability. For example, Grubnic *et al.* (2015) argue that managing and accounting for sustainable development across generations in public services warrants greater investigation. The impact of public sector reforms on the managerial processes and the effectiveness of accounting and finance practices provide further avenues of research. For example, the work by Jackson and Lapsley (2003) on the diffusion of accounting practices in the new 'Managerial' public sector and the transformation of the public sector provided important insights into the public sector's adoption of accounting technologies. Likewise, Jackson *et al.* (2014), utilising the theory of professions, investigated the impact of imposing cash limits to prescribing in NHS Scotland, thus crossing the boundary between accounting and public policy. Such studies not only provide insights, but also make clear the potential for further work in a sector that consumes a large percentage of GDP but does not attract proportionate attention from academics.

Being located within the social science domain, accounting and finance research transcends many boundaries and offers enormous scope for researchers from various disciplines, creating areas of research that do not fit into predefined categories (Ryan *et al.*, 2009). The subject matter and methodologies employed vary widely and cover areas such as education, health and well-being, law and regulation, the accounting profession and the impacts of the practices of accounting and finance right across their social setting (e.g. Jackson *et al.*, 2013; Paisey *et al.*, 2007; Gallhofer *et al.*, 2013). Historical approaches have done much to recalibrate the functions and meaning of accounting, and the work of Jackson (2012) questioned the perception of unidirectional accountability with respect to annual reports in hospitals, while Paisey and Paisey (2011) revised notions of visibility and governance in the context of financial management in the Pre-Reformation Scottish Church. The concepts of governance and accountability are further explored in the work of Khair *et al.* (2015), who investigated the personalisation of power, neoliberalism and the production of corruption, and in the work of Sheridan *et al.* (2006) on the effects of corporate governance codes and the supply of corporate information in the UK. Finally, the work of Jackson *et al.* (2012) provides an example of the influence of accounting practice in the realm of popular culture through the rise and fall of the Scotch whisky industry at the turn of the 20th century.

The above discussion reflects the great diversity of accounting and finance research as it spans a multitude of areas and plays an essential role in knowledge creation concerning the effects that financial and economic events, institutions and structures have on business, society and the environment. The next section will explore some of the ways in which the outputs of accounting and finance research are important to real-world issues.

How accounting and finance research can make a difference in the world

As outlined in previous sections, accounting research encompasses a broad range of research areas and issues. It is conducted by both academic researchers and practicing accountants, although the nature of the work done by each is substantively different. Within academia, accounting research serves an important role in the continual assessment of current practice with a view to ensuring its fitness for purpose in the changing business, economic and financial environment (Paisey *et al.*, 2007). In addition, accounting research also takes into consideration societal and environmental needs and the development of new practices to address these issues (Kamla *et al.*, 2009). Research also facilitates greater understanding of the needs of society, stakeholders and other users with respect to the information produced by accountants and finance experts (Gallhofer *et al.*, 2015). It is through such research that developments in areas like fraud risk assessment, environmental accounting, international accounting standards and the future direction of the profession have been facilitated. It also helps to inform the teaching curriculum in universities, thereby enabling courses and programmes to maintain currency in issues of key importance to business, the accounting profession, governments, future generations, etc.

Furthermore, it facilitates the production of educational texts that apply sound philosophical approaches to financial reporting, accounting for economic reality, and rule-governed accounting, thereby providing opportunities to engage students in activities that require critical thinking with respect to real-world problems (Hatherly *et al.*, 2013).

The scope of the issues addressed in the previous paragraph differs greatly from the research conducted by practicing accountants. Practitioners are generally tasked with solving immediate problems for a client or a group of clients. Such work may involve the development and implementation of a new accounting practice, critiquing drafts of financial accounting and auditing standards, or the provision of information on the impact of new tax laws on their clients. This type of research is typically conducted by those working in the technical departments of large accounting firms and is usually informed by the specific interests of clients. This work, while valuable, generally does not engage with accounting issues that impact more widely on society. As a result, practitioner research tends to have a narrower, more technical focus, and arguably lags substantially behind the issues raised in cutting-edge academic work. It is reasonable to observe, for example, that the current focus of practitioners on environmental issues is many years behind academia. This gap can create tension between academics and practitioners, as the latter often fail to see the relevance or practical value of the work of the former. Indeed, it may be the case that much work done by academics will not materialise into practical applications in the foreseeable future. However, that does not reduce its value, because the prime objective of academic research is to increase the stock of human knowledge, not simply to conduct a search for immediate applications. There can be little doubt that, as in most academic disciplines, most of the seminal pieces of accounting research are theoretical in character, and it is this theorisation that leads to new understandings from which real-world applications will eventually emerge.

The situation is similar for finance researchers. Despite a perception that finance researchers have remained closer to practitioners in their work, there are numerous examples of theoretically driven studies that have altered understandings of how finance functions in the real world. For instance, the work of Caglayan *et al.* (2012) on inventories, sales uncertainty, and financial strength illuminates the central role of finance in managing risk; Myers and Majluf's (1984) research on curbing agency problems and Jensen and Meckling's (1976) research on alleviating informational asymmetries enable a deeper understanding of global issues in finance. Furthermore, there is copious evidence to support the view that finance fosters growth (Levine, 2005), promotes entrepreneurship (Zingales, 2013), supports education (Flug *et al.*, 2008), helps to alleviate poverty and reduces inequality (Beck *et al.*, 2007).

Fundamental to its activities are sophisticated methods for measuring risk, as well as return, within the financial sector. Such research is also useful to those working in financial services, such as banking. Indeed, risk management is central to the services banks provide and a legitimately value-added activity within finance. Financial innovation has been important in promoting growth and is essential for a well-functioning economy. Furthermore, advances in academic research in the area of forensic finance contributed to the identification of many improprieties in the financial industry, exposing market distortions and uncovering financial scandals. From an education perspective, such revelations create opportunities to enhance the current content of the curriculum in areas such as financial ethics and governance. Furthermore, the active interaction between academic researchers and finance practitioners enables finance educators to identify specific educational and training aspects that are required in practice (Chen *et al.*, 2003), and thus stimulates the production of pedagogically innovative and interactive corporate finance textbooks and courses that more adequately prepare graduates for the workplace (Marney & Tarbet, 2011).

Summary

In this chapter we have introduced topical areas of research within the accounting and finance disciplines and explored ways of thinking about the nature of research. This should help you to see the difference between traditional, theory-led approaches to research and more contemporary, problem-centred and multidisciplinary approaches. We have also demonstrated that the disciplines of accounting and finance offer rich areas of investigation for researchers from a range of disciplines and are open to interdisciplinary research projects.

We have emphasised that research essentially concerns the production of knowledge, which comes from mastering a set of skills that empower the researcher to engage in activities that will advance existing knowledge and stimulate new avenues of academic enquiry. While there are some distinct traditions within accounting and finance research, there is no single 'right' way to conduct research. Indeed, we must not lose sight of the fact that research is a social activity made up of 'communities' that exhibit specific social norms, methodological principles, ontological and epistemological assumptions and theoretical positions which are closely guarded and thus can be a source of conflict between researchers, who may have differing assumptions and views regarding the nature of reality, the importance of empirical investigation, and theoretical propositions (Harre, 1986). Furthermore, the notion that research can be value-neutral and objective is barely credible within the natural sciences, let alone within the social sciences, and is an aspect which cannot be ignored.

Good research is conducted in a focused and systematic way, seeking to expand knowledge by acquiring specialised and detailed information, while providing a basis for analysis and illuminating observations on the subject of investigation (White, 2000). Before embarking on any research project, it is important to understand what 'research' constitutes within the disciplines of accounting and finance and to develop the appropriate skill set that will enable you to complete your research project. Be aware that ideas do not exist on their own; they have a past and a potential future, stakeholders and context. As such, it is vital that you spend time formulating and clarifying your research focus. This should be articulated in the form of one or more specific research questions that constitute the main focus of your research and should be accompanied by specific aims and objectives (Gordon and Porter, 2009). Consideration also needs to be given to how you will contextualise your research ideas within the existing literature. Chapter 2 will steer you towards understanding your ideas in the context of academia so that, even if your idea came to you as a 'eureka!' moment, you will be able to give it roots in extant and firmly founded scholarship.

References and further reading

Abraham, S., and Shrives, P. J., (2014), Improving the relevance of risk factor disclosure in corporate annual reports, *The British Accounting Review,* **46**(1), 91–107.

Black, F., and Scholes, M., (1973), The Pricing of Options and Corporate Liabilities, *Journal of Political Economy,* **81**(3), 637-654.

Bloomfield, R.J., (2010), *Traditional vs. Behavioral Finance,* Cornell University - Samuel Curtis Johnson Graduate School of Management Johnson School Research Paper Series No. 22-2010.

Caglayan, M., Mateut, S. and Maioli, S., (2012), Inventories, Sales Uncertainty, and Financial Strength, *Journal of Banking and Finance,* **36**(9), 2512-2521.

Chen, L.W., Adams, A., and Taffler R., (2003), What style-timing skills do mutual fund 'stars' possess? *Journal of Empirical Finance,* **21**(1), 156-173.

Coyne, J.G., Summers, S.L., Williams, B., and Wood, D.A., (2010), Accounting Program Research Rankings by Topical Area and Methodology, *Issues in Accounting Education.* **25**(4), 631–654.

Fama, E., (1970), Efficient Capital Markets: A Review of Theory and Empirical Work, *Journal of Finance,* **25**(2), 383–417.

Flug, K., Spilimbergo, A., and Wachtenheim, E., (1998), Investment in education: do economic volatility and credit constraints matter? *Journal of Development Economics*, **55**(2), 465–481.

Fraser, I. & Pong, C. (2009), The future of the external audit function, *Managerial Auditing Journal*, **24**(2) 104-113.

Frecknall-Hughes, J., James, S., and McIlwhan, R., (2014), *The tax implications of Scottish independence or further devolution*, Institute of Chartered Accountants Scotland Report, Edinburgh.

Gallhofer, S., Haslam, J. & Yonekura, A., (2013), Further critical reflections on a contribution to the methodological issues debate in accounting, *Critical Perspectives on Accounting*, **24**(3), 191-206.

Gallhofer, S., Haslam, J. & Yonekura, A. (2015), Accounting as differentiated universal for emancipatory praxis: Accounting delineation and mobilisation for emancipation(s) recognising democracy and difference, *Accounting, Auditing and Accountability*, **28**(5), 846-874.

Gibbons, M., Limoges, C., Nowotny, H., Schwartzman, S. (1994). *The New Production of Knowledge: The Dynamics of Science and Research in Contemporary Societies*, Sage, London

Gordon, T.P., and Porter, J.C., (2009), Reading and Understanding Academic Research in Accounting: A Guide for Students, *Global Perspectives on Accounting Education*, **6**, 25-45.

Grubnic, S., Thomson, I. H. & Georgakopoulos, G., (2015), New development: Managing and accounting for sustainable development across generations in public services – and call for papers, *Public Money and Management*, **35**(3), 245-250.

Haque, F., Kirkpatrick, C., and Arun, T., (2009), Corporate governance and capital structure in developing countries: a case study of Bangladesh, *Applied Economics*, **43**, 673-681.

Hatherly, D., Leung, D. and MacKenzie, D., (2013), The Finitist Accountant in *Living in a Material World: Economic Sociology Meets Science and Technology Studies*, Edited by Trevor Pinch and Richard Swedberg, MIT Press Scholarship.

Harre, R. (1986), *Varieties of Realism*. Basil. Blackwell. Oxford.

Hyde, S. & Sherif, M. (2010), Consumption asset pricing and the term structure, *Quarterly Review of Economics and Finance*, **50**(1), 99-109.

Ibrahim, B. M. and Brzeszczyński, J., (2014), How beneficial Is international stock market information in domestic stock market trading?, *European Journal of Finance*, **20**(3) 201-231.

Jackson, A.S., (now Paterson) & Lapsley, I., (2003), *The Diffusion of Accounting Techniques in Public Sector Organisations, in Transforming the Public Sector*, ICAS Monograph.

Jackson, A.S., (now Paterson) & Lapsley, I., (2003), The diffusion of accounting practices in the new 'managerial' public sector, *The International Journal of Public Sector Management*, **16**(5), 359 – 372.

Jackson WJ, Paterson AS, Pong CKM & Scarparo S, (2014) Cash Limits, Hospital Prescribing and Shrinking Medical Jurisdiction, *Financial Accountability and Management*, **30**(4), 403-429.

Jackson WJ, Paterson AS, Pong CKM & Scarparo S, (2013) Doctors under the microscope: the birth of clinical audit, *Accounting History Review*, **23**(1), 23-47.

Jensen, M.C., and Meckling, W.H., (1976), Theory of the firm: Managerial behavior, agency costs and ownership structure, *Journal of Financial Economics*, **3**(4), 305–360.

Jones E.A.E., Danbolt J. and Hirst I.R.C., (2004), Company investment announcements and the market value of the firm, *European Journal of Finance*, **10**(5), 437-452.

Kabir, R., Li, H., and Veld-Merkoulova, Y.V., (2013), Executive compensation and the cost of debt, *Journal of Banking & Finance*, **37**, 2893–2907.

Ahmad Khair, A. H., Haniffa, R., Hudaib, M. and Mohamad, M. N., (2015), Personalisation of power, neoliberalism and the production of corruption, *Accounting Forum*, **39**(3), 225-235.

Kalaitzogloua, I. & Ibrahim, B.M., (2013), Does order flow in the European Carbon Futures Market reveal information? *Journal of Financial Markets*, **16**(3), 604–635.

Kamla, R., Gallhofer, S. & Haslam, J., (2009), Educating and training accountants in Syria in a transition context: Perceptions of accounting academics and professional accountants, *Accounting Education: An International Journal*, **18**(4 -5), 345-368.

Kobelsky, K., Larosiliere, G., and Plummer, E., (2014), The impact of information technology on performance in the not-for-profit sector, *International Journal of Accounting Information Systems*, **15**(1), 47–65.

Kuhn, T., (1962), *The Structure of Scientific Revolutions*, Chicago: University of Chicago Press.

Levine R., (2005), Finance and growth: Theory and evidence, in Philippe Aghion and Steven N. Durlauf, eds., *Handbook of Economic Growth 1A*, 865-934, (North-Holland Elsevier, Amsterdam).

MacKinlay, A. C., (1997), Event studies in economics and finance, *Journal of Economic Literature*, **35**(1), 13-39. Available at: http://www.jstor.org/stable/2729691

Maddala, G. S., (2001). *Introduction to Econometrics* (Third edition). New York: Wiley.

Markowitz, H., (1952), Portfolio selection, *The Journal of Finance*, **7**(1), 77-91.

Available at: http://www.jstor.org/stable/2975974

Marney, J.P., and Tarbet, H., (2011), *Corporate Finance for Business*, Oxford University Press, London.

Mattessich, R., (1989), Accounting and the Input-Output Principle in the Prehistoric and Ancient World, *Abacus*, **25**(2), 74-84.

Modigliani, F. and Miller, M.H., (1958), The cost of capital, corporation finance and the theory of investment, *The American Economic Review*, **48**(3), 261-297.

Mousavia, M.M., Ouennichea, J. and Xu, B., (2015), Performance evaluation of bankruptcy prediction models: An orientation-free super-efficiency DEA-based framework, *International Review of Financial Analysis*, In Press, Available online 21 January 2015.

Myers, S.C., and Majluf, N.S., (1984), Corporate financing and investment decisions when firms have information that investors do not have, *Journal of Financial Economics*, **13**(2), 187–221.

Ndiweni, E., (2010), A trail of unintended consequences: Management Accounting Information in a volatile environment, *Research in Accounting in Emerging Economies*, **10**, pp.1-28.

Ndiweni, E. (2011), The impotence of auditing practices in a corrupt environment: Some evidence from Zimbabwe, *International Journal of Critical Accounting*, **3**, 204-219.

Oldroyd, D., (1995), The role of accounting in public expenditure and monetary policy in the first century AD Roman Empire, *Accounting Historians Journal*, **22**(2), 124.

Oldroyd, D., and Dobie, A., (2008), *Themes in the History of Bookkeeping, The Routledge Companion to Accounting History*, Routledge, London,

Oler, Derek K., Mitchell J. Oler, and Christopher J. Skousen. 2010. Characterizing accounting research, *Accounting Horizons* **24** 4), 635–670

Paisey C., Paisey N. J., and Tarbert H., (2007), Continuing Professional Development Activities of UK Accountants in Public Practice, *Accounting Education: An international journal.* **16**(4), 379-404.

Paisey, C. & Paisey, N. J., (2011), Visibility, governance and social context: Financial management in the Pre-Reformation Scottish Church, *Accounting, Auditing and Accountability Journal*, **24**(5), 587-621.

Pfeffer, J. (1993). Barriers to the advance of organizational science: Paradigm development as a dependent variable. *The Academy of Management Review*, **18**(4), 599-620

Robson, K., (1992), Accounting numbers as 'inscription': Action at a distance and the development of accounting, *Accounting, Organizations and Society* **17**(7), 685–708.

Roslender, R., and Hart, S.J., (2003), In search of strategic management accounting: theoretical and field study perspectives, *Management Accounting Research*, **14**, 255–279.

Ryan, B., Scapens, R.W. and Theobald, M., (1992), *Research Method and Methodology in Finance and Accounting*, Academic Press, London.

Ryan, B., Scapens, R.W. and Theobald, M., (2009), *Research Method and Methodology in Finance and Accounting*, Academic Press, London.

Sangster, A., Stoner, G. and McCarthy, P., (2007), The market for Luca Pacioli's Summa Arithmetica, *Accounting, Business & Financial History Conference*, Cardiff, September p.1–2, Cardiff.ac.uk.

Sharpe, W.F., (1964), Capital Asset Prices: A Theory of Market Equilibrium under Conditions of Risk, *The Journal of Finance*, **19**(3), 425-442.

Sheridan L., Jones E.A.E. and Marston C.L., (2006), Corporate governance codes and the supply of corporate information in the UK, *Corporate Governance: An International Review*, **14**(5), 497-503.

Simon, J., and Clinton Alley, (2008), Successful tax reform: The experience of Value Added Tax in the United Kingdom and Goods and Services Tax in New Zealand *Journal of Finance and Management in Public Services*, **8**(1), 35 -47.

Smith, M, (2004), *Research Methods in Accounting*, Sage, London.

Saunders, M., Lewis, P. and Thornhill, A., (2003), *Research Methods for Business*, Pearson Education, London.

Thomson, I. H. & Bebbington, J., (2013), Sustainable development, management and accounting: Boundary crossing, *Management Accounting Research*, **24**, 277-283.

Walliman, N., (2001), *Your Research Project: A Step-by-Step Guide for the First-Time Researcher*, Sage, London.

Watts, R. L. and Zimmerman, J. L. (1986), *Positive Accounting Theory*, Prentice Hall, New Jersey.

White, B., (2000), *Dissertation Skills for Business and Management Students*, Cassell, London.

Zingales, L., (2013), Preventing economists' capture, in *Preventing Regulatory Capture: Special Interest Influence and How to Limit it*, Edited by Daniel Carpenter and David Moss, The Tobin Project, Cambridge University Press.

2 Formulating a Research Project

Mercy Denedo, Andrew MacLaren and Emma Hill

Much of the research conducted within accounting and finance is concerned with seeking answers to broader questions such as "What are we for?", "What problem do we aim to address?" and "How can we address these problems through researchable and pedantic procedures?" It enables the researcher to understand how his/her research ideas, choices and experiences have arguably affected his/her knowledge and livelihood. Consequently, in this chapter, we begin by considering where you could generate your research ideas to answer those basic questions, followed by how to understand and contextualise your research ideas within prior literatures in order to create a space for them. Furthermore, we help address how your research should contribute to the partially or already established conversation of your discipline, as well as illustrate how this is done in the accounting and finance discipline. Finally, we highlight how you could make your research ideas fit together through a well-structured research proposal. This would enable you to understand what you are required to do for your dissertation as well as enable you to plan and work yourself through the rigorous research process without much stress. Therefore, we will start by identifying where we can generate our research ideas.

Where might ideas come from?

In accounting and finance studies, ideas are distinctly valued for their contribution to accounting or finance principles and their relevance to the development of the society, managerial and financial practices for organisations and stakeholders (Ronen, 2012; Srinidhi, 2013). Accounting and finance studies are essential economic growth tools in fostering innovations and entrepreneurial activities (Chua, 2011; Ronen, 2012). They permeate through numerous disciplines in order to provide relevant and effective decisions making frameworks for users of accounting and finance information.

Accounting and finance research[1] could result in the postulation of a normative and descriptive framework through which decision-making and performance could be benchmarked. For instance, in finance the Markowitz (1952) model is often used to select a portfolio of diversified shares to mitigate risk and maximise investors' returns. The fundamental objective of contributing in the development of a set of 'good accounting and finance principles' which could subsequently contribute to 'good accounting and finance practice' should drive any research ideas in this discipline. Consequently, the conceptualization of your research ideas, which could contribute in the development of 'good accounting and finance principles' should receive a relatively high attention.

Conceptualising accounting and finance research and scholarship problems could provide answers to broader issues such as "What are we for?[2]", "What problem do we aim to address?" and "How can we address these problems through researchable procedures?" Ability to answer these questions, which often influence decisions made by institutions, is what gives meaning to accounting and finance research. It enables researchers to understand how their research ideas, choices and experiences have arguably affected their knowledge and livelihood. Finally, it enables the users of accounting and finance information to understand why such research ideas and choices help define the nature of knowledge (De Loo and Lowe, 2012; Gray and Milne, 2015).

The starting point for any research project therefore is grounding your ideas in the literature. In research, your idea should be developed relative to the existing literature on the subject as, whether you like it or not, it is that same literature-base that led you to come up with the idea in the first place. For some students research ideas may be formulated or clearly refined from preconceived ideas of what they want from the literature. Regardless of whether or not you have preconceived ideas, a conscientious effort should be placed on consulting the relevant literatures when identifying or refining research ideas in accounting and finance because they are not static. The research ideas could be adapted during the research design cycle (see Figure 2.1). The adaptation of research ideas could be while reviewing the literature, incorporating theory (ies), formulating the conceptual framework or when identifying the fieldwork approach or negotiating access with your research participants (Hennink *et al.*, 2011).

---

1   'Accounting and finance' is generically used in this text. It is not restricted to financial accounting research but covers a broader spectrum of the accounting and finance research, e.g. research into historical accounting, management accounting, financial reporting, corporate governance, auditing and corporate finance, social and environmental accounting, public sector accounting, accounting education etc. The focus of this chapter is not so much on the many researchable accounting and finance subject areas but on how research ideas could be explored regardless of the subject area.

2   Research problems in accounting and finance could be social, economic and in relation to the environment. It would be erroneous to claim that research in these fields is restricted to these broad fields of study but often it tends to address problems that influence decisions, processes or practices within an organisation or within the society.

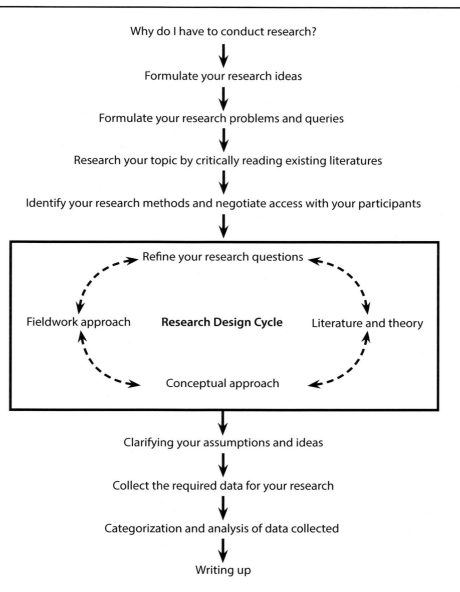

Why do I have to conduct research?

Formulate your research ideas

Formulate your research problems and queries

Research your topic by critically reading existing literatures

Identify your research methods and negotiate access with your participants

Refine your research questions

Fieldwork approach   **Research Design Cycle**   Literature and theory

Conceptual approach

Clarifying your assumptions and ideas

Collect the required data for your research

Categorization and analysis of data collected

Writing up

Figure 2.1: The research process. Adapted from *Qualitative Research Methods* by Hennink, Hutter and Bailey (2011)

Whether you have preconceived ideas, which you will want to explore or your ideas are formulated from the literature, at some point you should be able to identify if your proposed subject will solve a research problem relevant to the users of accounting information or contribute to knowledge building within a specific area. Furthermore, you should be able to identify whether you have the skills, financial resources and the time needed to research the topic.

Research v. re-search: Where might ideas come from?

Identifying and selecting a research idea can be a daunting task but your research ideas should emanate from what interests you strongly, because your research could be influenced by your level of commitment and enthusiasm. A good starting point therefore is listing the ideas that fascinate or puzzle you, which could be further explored. Learn to thoroughly understand and think about your research ideas by keeping a note of them and brainstorming them on a flow chart. Brainstorming would enable you to narrow your ideas into something manageable within the time allotted for the research. This activity would enable you convey your research ideas to your audience or reader, and subsequently enable them to explicitly evaluate and understand your research ideas without confusing them. For instance, your discipline could be in accounting and your research ideas could be narrowed down to a specific area of research in accounting that fascinates or puzzles you. For example:

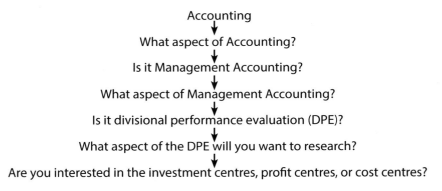

Accounting
↓
What aspect of Accounting?
↓
Is it Management Accounting?
↓
What aspect of Management Accounting?
↓
Is it divisional performance evaluation (DPE)?
↓
What aspect of the DPE will you want to research?
↓
Are you interested in the investment centres, profit centres, or cost centres?

Whatever your research ideas are, you should learn to explicitly articulate and convey them to your audience. Where you are unable to explicitly articulate your research ideas to your audience, it might limit the feedback you receive from them and the value of your research.

Never be scared of venturing into a subject area that fascinates or puzzles you despite not knowing what to expect, because some of the outstanding research comes from those that ventured into ideas out of curiosity. However, having clear ideas of what you might research enables you to plan how you are going to research the subject area. Whatever you decide to research, you should realise you need enthusiasm and commitment to conduct this research. You need lucid ideas to plan your way through the research process. The process of generating your research ideas is not complete until you have been able to explicitly state what you would like to research without mumbling. Consequently, your research ideas should be SMART (Wilson, 2010).

- **S** - Specific: Are my research ideas clearly stated?

- **M** - Measurable: Can my research ideas measure what I have proposed to evaluate?

- **A** - Achievable: Are my research ideas achievable?

- **R** - Relevant: What is my contribution to knowledge?

- **T** - Timed: Can I conduct my research ideas within the time allotted by the university?

Another good source of research ideas in accounting and finance could be from current societal or organisational problems. These ideas could be found in blogs, documentaries, research papers, practitioners' articles or policy papers that discuss contentious social, historical, economic, managerial and financial problems. Use your search engine freely to refine the research ideas generated from the aforementioned media (Booth, *et al.*, 2008).

Another source of research ideas in accounting and finance could be from evaluating previous course assignments where you had an excellent grade and you have confidence that pursuing research in that subject area would produce a high quality and robust project. Critically evaluating your areas of strength could produce research ideas that you could diligently and confidently explore.

Research ideas could also be generated from reviewing previous research projects or peer reviewed articles. Simply browse the research project or peer reviewed articles to understand "what is good or bad about it?" and subsequently evaluate "the suggestions for future research". This is a useful mechanism for generating research ideas in accounting and finance. This should be done by browsing the university's project or journal repository for research topics, which align with your ideas. After identifying a list of projects or articles, that fascinate you, gradually study these and provide answers to Table 2.1.

Additionally, discussion with your colleagues, family, friends, lecturers or supervisor can help generate and refine your research ideas. Remember that your supervisor will be someone with a wider knowledge of the research process and with an extant knowledge of your unrefined research ideas or subject area. It is advisable that you respectfully seek their opinion on the viability of your proposed research ideas within the time allotted for the research project by your institution. Always remember that the research process could be the loneliest phase of your life; never be reluctant to seek for help or feedback to refine your research ideas. You can never be an island of knowledge!

Finally, it is essential or sensible to consider your career goals when formulating your research ideas, because your research project could develop the expertise you need for a particular segment of the economy. For instance, if your career goal is situated within the financial service sector, it is advisable that your research ideas should also be distinctly situated within it. This would help improve your knowledge of the sector as well as enhance your prospect of being employed within it.

■ Everything comes back to the literature

The key is in the reading; there are two reasons for this. First, your conclusions and the contribution of your dissertation would be measured relative to the literature it discusses, thus for academic research, individual ideas mean little without being contextualised in a particular literature. Your idea would likely fall into one of two categories: either it would target a perceived research black hole about which little has been written, or perhaps it would attempt to correct, advance or redirect existing concepts. Either way, your ideas gain a scholarly past, present, and future that represents a valuable connection to a wider literature.

Second, ideas that are not developed at least in part through consultation with the literature tend to be broader in scope and lacking nuance and complexity. Nuance and complexity are essential to an academic contribution. Where you fail to understand this subtlety from reading the existing literature, your ideas might struggle to do full justice to your research question from the beginning. Consequently, one approach to understanding the breadth and depth of your research ideas would be through a diversified and open reading process into the world of literatures, theoretical perspectives and methodological approaches within your chosen discipline. Indeed, Chua (2011) argues that a diversified and open reading process, to identify and refine research ideas and interest, create the foundation and sparks required for the successful completion of a research project.

■ What does the literature tell us?

The body of literature to which you will be referring consists of a range of different types of study: qualitative/quantitative; inductive/deductive; conceptual/empirical. Your aim is to understand the features of prior contributions to the literature, with which you are engaging, in order to determine exactly what they are telling you, and how they are taking you closer towards an idea. A piece of published research that you consult in the pursuit of ideas will have core characteristics. It will most often have:

■ A contextual literature that it references in the generation of its own particular idea.

■ A broader body of theory that underpins that literature.

■ A form of contextual literature relating to, commonly in accounting and finance, a specific market, industry or segment of the economy.

■ An articulated methodological approach.

There is some detective work to be done here. Look for the clues that tell you what area of literature this study belongs to, and in which field it is looking to contribute. The clues are in the language and terminology used within the writing but you will also find clues that support your detective work elsewhere in a peer-reviewed journal articles. The title of the journal in which the article is published will give you clues as to the sort of literature to which the study will be contributing. For example, the *Journal of Corporate Finance* informs you that this journal publish articles relating to corporate financial structure, pay-out policies, financial budgeting and financial management necessary for organisational decision-making. This is one clue we can get as to the sort of literature you might see being referenced in an individual article. The other considerable source of clues about an article is its reference list. This will present the field of enquiry that an article is hoping to make a contribution to, as it must use the existing literature in the field to form its ideas, just the same as you are having to do in the formation of your own ideas.

■ ## Creating a space for your idea

It is important to be clear about the space in which you locate your idea and your research because, whether you aspire to conduct qualitative or quantitative research, it could be a challenging task to squarely define the space in which you wish to locate your study. That space is likely to be complex and require a degree of understanding of the literature in order to fully appreciate it. For example, there may be little empirical enquiry into an area, in which case there is a space in which your ideas may contribute to the prevailing discourse. Alternatively, there might be an apparent assumption within the literature that has not been explored for its validity, for example, a body of literature may imply that "institutions are rational investors". In this case, your idea might be to explore the potential for "the irrationality of institutions when making investment decisions". The clearer you can make your idea, the more you can defend it as a space representing an opportunity for contributing to the literature.

Of course, if you are reading widely, then you may identify different research spaces, which clash with each other. It is best to keep a record of your reading so that you remain on top of your literature. It is surprising how quickly one article or paper blends into another when you are reading a large volume of material, and you will need to be able to justify why you have decided to investigate your chosen research path at the expense of others. Table 1 suggests how you might systematically approach each article, such that you can both manage and analyse the content and record any ideas that arise from your analysis.

Table 1: Identifying your research gap

	Existing scholarship	Research space	Moving forward...
Prompt questions	What does the article say? What is good or bad about it? What assumptions has it made to say these things? What methods has it used to research its conclusions? What should have been done differently that was not included in this article?	Where is the gap in this article? Which assumptions or methods has it excluded to reach its conclusions? Which of these excluded elements might be used productively in context?	Of the excluded elements you have identified, which are relevant to your research? What might you do with these elements? How do the excluded elements fit into the broader structure of accounting and finance research? How could the excluded elements be explored/explained/fit into a theoretical or methodological perspective? How will you access the necessary data to address the excluded elements? What might come after the excluded elements have been critically addressed?
Exercise	1. 2. 3. 4.	1. 2. 3.	1. 2. 3. 4. 5.

In text exercise

Ideas for research should have theory, context and data. Can you name yours? Choose an article you have read recently and create your own version of the table above. Identify a possible research gap and suggest what you might do with it next.

Who cares? How to make your ideas 'interesting'

Accounting and finance research students are encumbered with the responsibility to facilitate dialogue that could permeate through positivist and interpretivism paradigms (see Chapters 1 and 4) without underestimating the objectives of the discipline. Consequently, if the aim of the discipline is to facilitate dialogue that would improve our socioeconomic and political environments, your research ideas should be situated within this discourse. Your research ideas should be confined within one of these paradigms to establish your voice within the dialogical framework of the discipline (Chua, 1986; Lukka, 2010).

It is pertinent to note that your chosen paradigm's ontology and epistemology will define your conversation within the dialogical framework of the accounting and finance research. Your chosen paradigm will not be uniquely restricted to your research topic but traverse several aspects of it. Your paradigm will define your research ideas and what you want to study (Gray and Milne, 2015). It defines how your research questions will be formulated, your research methods, how the results would be interpreted and communicated to the users of accounting information (Lukka, 2010; Richardson, 2015). It is imperative that you understand that your research paradigm (see Chapters 1 and 4) does not only inform your research ideas, but also influences your literature review (see Chapter 3), data collection and analysis method (see Chapters 5-10). Additionally, you should understand that you are venturing into a conversation that is already fully or partially established. Finding your research voice and interest within the accounting and finance discipline provides the context within which your research choices would be critically evaluated through conducting a positivist, action, interpretivist or critical realism research project (Chua, 1986; Richardson, 2015).

■ Developing a value proposition for your idea

The key to generating and holding your community's or audience's interest in your idea is your ability to state it as a value proposition. If you are able to demonstrate that your idea is of value, and that on delivery this value would be experienced, then your audience would be persuaded to invest (at least their time and attention) in your research. Of course, the willingness of your audience to invest depends on good value management. You should be able to persuade your audience and demonstrate why your chosen methods would bring the best returns. What this means for your research is that you need to be on top of your idea so that you can clearly answer the questions:

1 What will your research ideas contribute?

2 How will your research ideas contextually contribute?

3 Why should your audience or community of interest listen to your research ideas? Why is it important? Why does it matter?

The identification of your research space would help you develop your answers to these three questions. You can then break your idea down into the first two questions: *what* would it contribute? And *how* does it contribute? These two questions can then be divided into five subsets:

- *What* does your idea contribute to the **field**? *How* does it contribute **contextually?**

- *What* does your idea contribute to the **academy** in its widest sense? *How* does it contribute **theoretically?**

- Does it contribute **methodologically?** How does it contribute to **practice?**

- *What* does your idea contribute to the **wider society**? *How* does it contribute **publicly?**

- What are the ethical implications associated with your research ideas? How would you address these ethical challenges?

Your knowledge of the literature will give you a good understanding of the scholarly context to judge what elements your audience might find interesting, or might be persuaded to find interesting. Once you have settled on *what* your idea would contribute and *how* it would make this contribution, you can begin to consider *why* this contribution is important. This final step will consolidate your idea's value, as it will enable you to state if you intend to make a contextual, theoretical or methodological contribution – or a combination of two or all three.

■ Who cares? 'Selling' your idea

Having established why your idea matters, you now need to consider to whom your idea might matter. Your research space will provide you with clues to your audience – if, for instance, you have chosen to pursue a theoretical research gap, your audience is likely to be scholars; whereas if you have chosen a contextual, socially-oriented research gap, your research might matter to policy-makers or industry. Although your research project is intrinsically academic, your writing should take into account your target audience, for this will determine the assumptions you make about your readership's knowledge base, the direction in which you angle your research question and your rhetoric, tone and style.

Accounting and finance research and ideas

In this section, we deconstruct an academic research paper, Apostol (2015), to provide an examples of idea generation and justification in accounting and finance research practice respectively. We will show how the author stated and placed her ideas in a scholarly context and framed her ideas in theoretical terms. We will also discuss the ways in which the author justifys or 'sells' her ideas – both in terms of content and contribution, and in terms of language and rhetoric. We intend that our discussion of this paper acts as a guide to our arguments as we progress through this chapter.

■ ## Responding to a call

This section deconstructs elements of an exemplar journal article (from accounting, but which could be applied to any finance articles) which clearly articulated its research space and contribution. As revealed by Apostol (2015, p.211), it is highly essential to deconstruct your research ideas by distinctively identifying the research space you are situating your research project. This should be stated when explaining the rationales of your study. This would enable your supervisor and readership to understand and follow through each chapter of your project by clearly projecting what you aim to achieve at the end of the research process. For example, from Apostol (2015, p.211) we can see that the study aims and idea are distinctively identified with the researcher stating:

"This paper aims to understand the role of civil society's counter-accounts in enabling the development of emancipatory and radical accounting."

Thus by articulating the study aims within a research space at the beginning of the paper it is easy to understand the subject matter without wondering what the research idea was. This good practice enables readers to understand the research ideas, the author's choice of paradigms and methodology.

In addition, the nuance of this research space is developed further as the literature review commences, citing multiple established authors in their field and plainly laying out where there is a current gap in knowledge. For instance, Apostol (2015, p.212) identified her contribution to knowledge by stating where the research gap was observed as:

"This study contributes to the scarcely researched area of counter-accounting [...]. Despite the increasing production of counter-accounts by civil society organisations in recent years, especially due to the widespread use of the internet (Gallhofer et al. 2006), academic research has yet to catch up."

It is good practice to highlight your research space at the beginning of your project whether you have a research idea, which you want to explore, or you have discovered a gap in the literature, which you intend to fill with your research. When identifying this research space, it is important that you support your assertions with prior literatures' evidence. Reflecting back to the exemplar article, Apostol (2015) was able to carve her research space by clearly identifying the research gaps. It is worth noting that she was able to situate her research ideas within a dialogical network using prior literatures. This gives validity

2

to her study and could influence the feedback she receives from her readers. Therefore, identifying your research ideas using prior literatures enables you to situate your research ideas within a research space in order to contribute meaningfully to the body of knowledge. Furthermore, identifying your research ideas within a research gap through prior literatures would enable you to clearly set boundaries and benchmarks for your research ideas. In addition, setting boundaries and benchmarks would enable you to compare your findings against prior literatures. This would create a platform through which you can evaluate the validity of your research findings within the dialogical framework at the end of the research process.

■ Explore the contribution

After exploring the articulation of a research space and opportunity for a contribution, it is worthwhile checking to see exactly how that contribution is presented at the end of the paper. Any project needs to present well-supported and justifiable conclusions and comparing the research space stated at the outset of the study with the conclusions at the end will help you understand how well the idea has been developed and defended.

For instance in our exemplar article, we see the idea being framed and justified following the execution of the study. The broad contributions that most closely relates to their initial research space were also clearly articulated in their conclusions. For example, Apostol (2015, p.211) claimed that her *"…paper aims to understand the role of civil society's counter-accounts in enabling the development of emancipatory and radical accounting."* The paper developed the nuance of the original idea by discussing specific contributions to the literature and even more specifically to the theory, which underpins the literature.

For instance, Apostol (2015, p.231) claimed

> *"The vision for emancipatory accounting will imply that counter-accounting is able to meet expectations such as: making business practices visible, exposing and criticising negative aspects of business structures, giving a voice to marginalised and underrepresented groups, facilitating democratic dialogue and being a catalyst for societal change (see Gallhofer and Haslam, 1997). This paper shows that civil society's counter-accounts have the potential to accomplish all these expectations and that it can be considered as a more enabling form of accounting."*

It is essential that you clearly state whether you were able to address your research aims at the concluding section of your research by highlighting how you have been able to contribute to the body of knowledge through your project. Situating your research ideas within a research space will enable you to develop the conceptual and theoretical framework necessary for your project but distinctively stating whether your research was able to contribute meaningfully by filling the research space identified will enable your readership to evaluate the credibility of your nuance within the conversation.

■ Frame the limitations

The next section will discuss assumptions and how to ensure these are informed assumptions that you can frame in the same way you framed your idea in the first place. Thus, the idea space is defined as much by what was not explored as what was. Therefore, an awareness of limitations and assumptions will strengthen your original idea and make your proposed contribution easier to defend. For instance, Apostol (2015, p.231) identified her research limitations as:

> "Counter-accounts are not without limitations. [...] Despite all these arguments, it is here contended that the truthfulness of information contained in counter-accounts is of less significance than their potential to generate social dialogue."

Apostol (2015) was able to articulate her assumptions and limitations of the study. This action did not only give credibility to her study but help strengthened her argument and research idea firmly in prior literatures. Therefore, stating your assumptions, your biases or identities and limitations would enable your readership to understand your ontology and epistemological framework. In the above extract, you could see the value of the research conducted still being defended yet the limitations are clear, which prevent the study from overreaching its intended contribution.

Make your ideas fit: Writing a research proposal

You've got an idea and you've framed it. You've read relevant literature and can locate your idea in a broader tradition (see Chapter 3). You've grasped the theory and your methodology is ready to go (see Chapter 4). Congratulations! You are now ready to write your research proposal.

■ Build the skeleton

Writing a research proposal is about structure. This is a snapshot of your overall project and it allows you to consider how it will be linked together as a whole and what obstacles may stand in your way. This helps you prepare and plan before you become concerned with the fine details of writing and thinking through the inevitable daily challenges that come your way as you progress through the process.

In text exercise

Fill-in the blanks of a research proposal structure

Title	
Background of the study/ Introduction/Research problem	
Research aim	
Research objectives	
Literature Theory Context Research space	
Research question	
Methodology Research philosophy Method Data collection Data analysis Research ethics	
Contribution and limitations	
Research timeline	
References	

Title

The title of your research proposal or project should reflect the nature of your research ideas. This should be distinctively articulated and precise because it is often the mirror through which your research ideas would be evaluated. Remember, your audience or reader would look at your research title before reading your project. It is essential you ensure that your title is simple to understand.

Background of the study/introduction/research problem

This section could be split into 'background of the study/introduction' and 'research problem'. This is a crucial and indispensable section of your research proposal and research project. This should be clearly stated because it often serves as the bedrock upon which you build your research ideas. In this section, you should be able to guide your reader to understand 'why your research matters' by providing a distinct guide into the nature of knowledge/problem you want to address or solve with your research. You should be able to 'capture' the interest of your reader and define key concepts on your research ideas in this section.

Research aim/objective/questions

These are mutually inclusive concepts and consequently, the importance of your research aim, to your research objectives and your research questions cannot be understated. The success of your research proposal and project will be evaluated on whether you have lucid research aims, objectives and questions. Wilson (2010) argued that your research aim constitutes a generic statement of what your research will achieve while your research objectives and research questions are specific statements highlighting what has been articulated in your research aim or stating how you are going to achieve your research aim. There are no right or wrong answers to how your research aim, objectives and questions should be framed. However, you should desist from using complex rhetoric when drafting these sections rather they should be able to capture the research space you want to fill. In some cases, the research questions may not emerge after your research aims and objective. Do not worry if it comes after your literature review. What is important is that it should be SMART!

Literature

As previously discussed, this involves an abridged but critical review of previous research that informs your research ideas. Remember that the significance of your research ideas would depend on your ability to identify relevant literatures that help answer or define your research questions. Chapter 3 provides some guidance on the purpose of the literature review and explains the steps involved in conducting an extensive literature review. It is essential you carefully study Chapter 3.

Methodology

This section should comprehensively explain your research philosophy, method, and data collection, data analysis and research ethics, each of which are discussed in more detail in the following chapters (Chapters 4-10). This section should explain how you planned to achieve your research objectives and research questions. It should explain what you intend doing and the rationale for making the choice to use a particular approach for your project.

Contribution and limitations

Within any research project, it is essential that you explain your contribution to knowledge and your research limitations. Your research contribution section is an important part of your research project because it enables the reader to critically evaluate if you have been able to fill the research gaps you identified in your literature review section and whether your research aim, objectives and research questions had been adequately answered.

Likewise, a statement of your research project limitations is also required. This would enable prospective researchers to generate their research ideas and avoid some pitfalls you have observed while conducting your research. Be kind enough to simplify this section for your reader and prospective researchers.

References or bibliography

Your research proposal and project should end with a list of references. This could be a bibliography or references. *Bibliography* refers to all sources of information consulted whether cited in your project or not. On the other hand, *References* contain sources of documents you cited in your proposal or project. It is imperative that you are aware of the referencing style stipulated by your institution because this varies from one institution to another, though the majority of the institutions in the United Kingdom adopt the Harvard Referencing Style. You should consult your project course handbook for the referencing style stipulated by your institution.

Remember to reference all sources of information as you use them, in order to avoid unnecessary panic at the end of the research process. You can use reference generators such as *Endnotes*, *Refworks*, *Zotero* or *Mendeley* to compile and store your references and bibliography. It is sensible to keep copies of the documents you have consulted, for future review and unforeseen circumstances.

■ Make it hang together as one

As you go through, develop a meta-narrative that introduces each chapter or section and provides continuity when you reach its end. No reader will understand the project as well as you do and so you should act as their guide through the structure of the research as well as communicating the specific content. A way to ensure that every element of your work is communicating the same message is to remind yourself of the answers to the following questions. Try answering them while you develop your idea:

1 What is the research about?

2 Why is it important?

3 What research conversation will your work contribute to?

4 Who are the key voices in that conversation and what are their big ideas?

5 What are my research questions?

6 Is it theory building or theory testing?

   and where appropriate

7 What is the dependent variable?

8 What is the unit of analysis?

2

■   ## Flesh it out

Now for the fun part. Once you have the technical elements complete, you are ready to create that linchpin of *interest* we discussed earlier. No matter how innovative your theory or how technical your methodology, there are two key bits of content that will make your proposal come alive: *examples* and *evidence*. These two elements will not only provide context for your project, but will give a real flavour of the kind of research you intend to do. Before you start writing, consider whether there is an example that could explain the problem you are trying to solve, or whether there is an anecdote that contextually demonstrates the point you wish to make. Once you have these, the *social* aspect of your research will be clear, which, if nothing else, is the foundational *interest* of the Accounting and Finance discipline.

Summary

The purpose of this chapter is to provide some insights to the process of generating research ideas for your dissertation. You should understand that the development of your research project depend on your commitment and enthusiasm. Therefore, at the commencement of your research process, it is imperative that you allocate sufficient time to identify and refine your research ideas. Your research ideas influence your literature review, methodology, research paradigms, data collection, data analysis, and research ethics and how you structure your findings. This chapter is a prerequisite for the other chapters in this text. It is essential you internalise the concepts and recommendations highlighted in this chapter. If your research ideas are not distinctly articulated, the foundations upon which the other elements of the dissertation are framed are unlikely to be solid. Spend valuable time to formulate and clarify your research ideas and the research space you want to fill.

References and further reading

Apostol, O. M., 2015. A project for Romania? The role of the civil society's counter-accounts in facilitating democratic change in society. *Accounting, Auditing and Accountability Journal*, **28**(1), 210-241.

Booth, W. C., Colomb, G. G. and Williams, J. M., 2008. *The Craft of Research*. 3rd ed. Chicago: The University of Chicago Press.

Chua, W. F., 1986. Radical developments in accounting thought. *The Accounting Review*, **61**(4), 601-632.

Chua, W. F., 2011. In search of 'Successful' Accounting research. *European Accounting Review,* **20**(1), 27-39.

De Loo, I. and Lowe, A., 2012. Authoritative interpretation in understanding accounting practice through case research. *Management Accounting Research,* **23**, 3-16.

Ebrahim, A., 2003. Accountability in practice: mechanisms for NGOs. *World Development,* **31**(5), 813-829.

Gallhofer, S. and Haslam, J., 1997. Beyond Accounting: the possibilities of Accounting and Critical Accounting research. *Critical Perspectives on Accounting,* **8**(1-2), 71-95.

Gallhofer, S., Haslam, J. and Monk, E., 2006. The emancipatory potential of online reporting. The case of counter reporting. *Accounting, Auditing and Accountability Journal,* **19**(5), 681-718.

Gray, R. and Milne, M. J., 2015. It's not what you do, it's the way you do it? Of method and madness. *Critical Perspectives on Accounting,* (in press).

Hennink, M., Hutter, I. and Bailey, A., 2011. *Qualitative Research Methods.* London: SAGE Publications Ltd.

Lukka, K., 2010. The roles and effects of paradigms in accounting research. *Management Accounting Research,* **21**, 110–115.

Markowitz, H., 1952. Portfolio Selection. *The Journal of Finance,* **7**(1), 77-91.

O'Dwyer, B. and Unerman, J., 2008. The paradox of greater NGO Accountability: a case study of Amnesty Ireland. *Accounting, Organizations and Society,* **33**(7-8), 810-824.

Richardson, A. J., 2015. Quantitative research and the critical accounting project. *Critical Perspectives on Accounting,* (in press).

Ronen, J., 2012. The state of Accounting Research: objectives and implementation. *Asia –Pacific Journal of Accounting & Economics,* **19**(1), 3-11.

Saunders, M., Lewis, P. and Thornhill, A., 2009. *Research methods for business students.* 5th edition. Essex: Pearson Education Limited.

Srinidhi, B., 2013. An essay on conceptualization of issues in empirical accounting research. *China Journal of Accounting Research,* **6**, 149-166.

Unerman, J. and O'Dwyer, B., 2006. Theorising Accountability for NGO advocacy. *Accounting, Auditing and Accountability Journal,* **19**(3), 349-376.

Wilson, J., 2010. *Essentials of Business Research.* London: SAGE Publications Ltd.

3 Critical Reflections of Academic Literature

Anthony Kyiu, Nana Abena Kwansa,
Audrey Paterson, Norin Arshed and Mike Danson

Having presented an outline of the nature of accounting and finance research and some advice on how to get started on a research project, we now turn our attention to the nature and purpose of the literature review. Any research project, regardless of its scope, necessitates investigation into prior writings on the subject area. As Chapter 2 demonstrated, this is particularly pertinent for identifying gaps in prior studies and where research opportunities might exist, refining the research question and setting the parameters of the study. Equally important is providing a good grounding and demonstration of critical awareness of existing studies within the chosen subject area, identification of its limitations and how the planned project will contribute to knowledge building. Indeed, the originality and intellectual context of a research project is influenced by the critical evaluation of a wide range of extant literature.

Conducting a literature search/review is often considered as a straightforward task. However, in reality it requires understanding of the design issues, methodological traditions and the nature of research. Likewise, the ability to identify the structure, substance and logic of an argument and conceptual issues of what is being reviewed is required in order to evaluate the logic of theories, methodologies, research findings and their contribution to informed scholarship. In addition, it may require understanding of the moral, ethical, political and ideological position of the author.

The research process invariably involves reading and synthesising a large volume of academic literature. As researchers, the aim of the literature review is to elicit and extract appropriate core assumptions, ideas, concepts and methodologies that have been applied to research problems and how these have been applied to empirical studies. Within this chapter we outline the purpose and importance of the literature review as the underpinning of the research project. The various approaches to conducting a literature review, search tools and skills required to produce a literature review that is of good quality, appropriate breadth and depth are also introduced. This is then followed by a discussion of the importance of critically analysing the literature and presentation of logical and coherent arguments that relate to your project. Finally some advice on how to avoid some common pitfalls in analysing the literature and some practical advice on approaching the literature review are put forward.

Purpose of a literature review in research

It is not uncommon to find some novice researchers questioning what a literature review is and its importance in the research process. Indeed, the following question is fairly common, *is it just a cumulative summary of what has already been done in the topic area or it is just one of the formalities of a research work?* Literature simply refers to the published work on a particular subject. The literature review could either be a component of a piece of research work, which usually is the case, or be an entire research project on its own. It usually serves as an introduction and underpinning to the research topic or research questions and involves critically examining facts, evaluating, comparing, and identifying differences or limitations in literature that generally relates to the area of interest; and specifically affects the topic under review. It forms the foundation of the entire research and is a section that should not be ignored. As such, it should be organized with clarity, precision, relevance, depth, logic and the element of fairness in analysis existing literature (Paul and Elder, 2006). Below are three main reasons why a literature review is necessary in research.

1 It develops understanding of existing research related to the topic. This involves examining existing research that has been conducted, theories proposed, history, possible generalisations or contradictions and potential limitations that provide grounds for shaping the proposed topic of interest. Knowledge in a research area can only grow when researchers understand the basics (O'Leary, 2004). This helps in identifying viable research opportunities (Boote and Beile, 2005). The literature review is thus an important starting point for the research.

2 It provides the means to justify the research on the topic. Understanding the background and contributions of existing research helps the researcher to capitalize on the limitations of previous research, thus making a meaningful contribution to existing literature. In some cases, this could lead to an original idea. Knopf (2006) argues that a literature review should provide a summary of the outcomes of previous research on the subject and a decision about how conclusive the information is. This provides the writer with in-depth understanding of the major issues and helps to identify gaps that can shape the research so as to avoid replicating previous research.

3 It demonstrates how the proposed research fits into the existing literature. The literature review process helps in identifying research questions and appropriate research designs which provide good foundation for the research (O'Leary, 2004). This helps in constructively reviewing and making a decision on the theoretical and methodological procedures that will be adopted. Doing the literature review helps to connect the research work to the development in the literature (Creswell, 2009) which validates the research.

The purpose of a literature review can therefore be illustrated by Figure 3.1

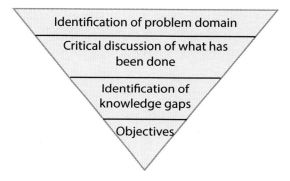

Figure 3.1: The Purpose of the Literature Review. Source: Maier (2013, p. 4)

Approaches to literature reviews

One of the important steps in undertaking a literature review is determining the most appropriate type of literature review method that will be adopted for the research. There are four major approaches: traditional (or narrative), systematic, meta-analysis and meta-synthesis.

■ Traditional or narrative review

The traditional review involves critically assessing the background, theories and methodologies in existing research, evaluating and producing these facts in a logical way to form a basis for the research topic; and not merely a description of existing literature (Jesson *et al.*, 2011). This method provides an extensive analysis of existing literature on the research topic, and by critically examining the existing literature paves the way for the researcher to identify the gaps and how the intended topic fits into the existing literature.

Cronin *et al.* (2008) recommend that the literature review process should involve:

- Selecting the review topic;

- Searching the literature;

- Gathering, reading and analysis the literature;

- Writing the review, and

- Constructing the reference list.

Although this approach provides a good background for the research, it could result in the researcher having an 'impressionistic' view (Neill and Richards, 1998). This method of literature analysis does not follow any predetermined criteria. Hence, it has the potential to be affected by an element of selection bias and subjectivity that could compromise the review.

■ Systematic review

This type of review adopts a systematic and scientific approach which reduces the subjectivity that characterizes the traditional review. Petticrew and Roberts (2006, p.2) define the systematic review as "a method of making sense of large bodies of information, and a means of contributing to the answers to questions about what works and what does not". Uman (2011) asserts that a systematic review involves a thorough and broad research approach to identifying and integrating studies conducted within an area of interest. According to Petticrew and Roberts (2006, p.27), a systemic review will involve the following stages:

1 Clearly define the question that you seek to answer or the hypotheses to be tested in the review

2 Determine the type of studies needed to answer the question

3 Conduct a detailed search for literature to identify those studies

4 Sift through the search to identify the ones appropriate for the review

5 Critically evaluate the included studies

6 Synthesize the studies and assess heterogeneity among the findings

7 Disseminate the findings of the review.

Systematic reviews usually tend to involve some element of meta-analysis through the use of statistical procedures to summarise the data from different studies into a single document (Petticrew and Roberts 2006). This makes it more reliable than the traditional review.

■ Meta-analysis

This is a statistical procedure which cumulates, examines and evaluates outcomes from different studies about a particular topic. It serves as a good alternative to the traditional review (Neill and Richards, 1998), although Polit and Beck (2006) argue that it is similar to a systematic review. It adopts statistical models in its analyses and Randolph (2009) mentions that meta-analysis mainly analyzes the quantitative findings of different studies, and reviews existing research to identify areas that can shape the direction of the current research. According to Stanley (2001), meta-analysis offers a more objective means of reviewing literature because it uses objective procedures – mainly statistical techniques – to analyze empirical literature, and this would have more coverage then the traditional review.

■ Meta-synthesis

Meta-synthesis is another useful tool for the analysis of qualitative research. Meta-synthesis does not only incorporate results from different studies but also uses interrelated qualitative studies (Welsh and Downe, 2005). This makes it a more interpretive method than the meta-analysis approach, which only summarises results. Indeed, Shadish (1996) argues that meta-analysis is centred on descriptive relationships, is less focused on building explanatory concepts and tries to reach a new understanding of the cumulated literature.

The types of literature review described above illustrate the range of approaches available to the researcher. When determining the best choice of literature review approach to adopt for your research, it is important to be clear about what issues you seek to address. The traditional and systematic review tend to be common with accounting and finance research.

Searching and selecting literature

A vast amount of academic material exists in various and can be used for your research. It is therefore important that you familiarize yourself with the various types of academic literature and what information you are likely to obtain from them. Below are the main types of academic literature that you are likely to encounter in the course of your research.

Text books

Text books are generally written to be used for study of a specific subject. They generally are not the product of original research by the author(s). Rather, they provide a summary and synthesis of the key areas and theories within the subject. Hence the information you obtain from text books tends to be generic with the aim of providing you with a comprehensive introduction to the subject usually without too much detail.

Academic journal articles

Academic journal articles are published based on detailed research and are therefore narrower in focus. They have more precise titles compared to books because they are meant to address very specific issues within a subject area. Since your research is expected to add some new knowledge to what already exists from previous research, it is necessary that the bulk of literature you refer to should be articles published in academic journals. Whilst there are other types of articles that you can refer to, more emphasis is placed on academic journal articles because these articles go through a peer review process and therefore provide a guarantee of scholarly quality. It is also important to mention that academic journals by their nature can be quite technical because they are written with the assumption that readers already have background knowledge about the subject. Hence, where necessary, you should refer to textbooks to first get a background understanding of the subject in order to facilitate your comprehension of the articles.

Review articles

Review articles are also types of academic journal articles in that they are subject to a peer review process. Their purpose is to provide a critical commentary on research in a field over a period of time. Reading review articles can give you a useful introduction to research within your subject area in terms of the major publications and key developments.

Dissertations

Dissertations are pieces of research output usually submitted by students as part of the requirements for the award of a degree or some other qualification. Some dissertations are published as books, which are referred to as monographs. Both dissertations and monographs can be useful sources of knowing what prior research is available in your in your chosen topic. Likewise, PhD theses can provide a valuable synopsis of background literature and stimulate research ideas.

Sources for obtaining literature in accounting and finance

There are a number of sources for obtaining literature for your research. For textbooks, the obvious first point of call would be the library. For journal articles, which as earlier indicated might constitute the bulk of your literature, the library is another good source. However, most journal articles can be obtained quicker via online sources. Whilst some of these sources are open, most of them require you to gain access through your university's subscription. Table 3.1 below provides a list of the main sources from which you can obtain published journal articles. As you search through these databases, ensure that you have the parameters of your research well defined with appropriate keywords and search terms that you intend to use (Saunders *et al.*, 2009).

Table 3.1: Examples of databases for obtaining literature

Database	Database information
Business Source Premier	Business Source Premier is the most popular business research database. It provides full text of about 2,300 journals covering such areas as Accounting, Finance, Economics, Management and Marketing.
JSTOR	Primarily provides access articles in the humanities and social sciences.
OmniFile Full Text Select (EBSCO)	Provides access to journals in Arts, Biology, Business, Current Affairs, Education, Humanities, Information Science, Law, Literature and Social Sciences.
ScienceDirect	A full text database proving journal articles and book chapters from about 2,500 journals and 30,000 books respectively
Emerald Fulltext	Provides access to about 217 journals published by the Emerald publishing group covering areas such as Accounting, Finance, Economics, Management and Marketing.
Google Scholar	This is a free web search engine which indexes and provides links to sources where you can obtain published articles and textbooks. It is always a good starting point for many students.
Proquest: Social Sciences	Searches and cross searches sources from different publishers to provide full text articles in social science subjects

Identifying good literature

With a huge amount of literature available at your disposal, it is important that you find a structured and systematic way of identifying good literature for your research (Cronin *et al.*, 2008). Referring to good quality material could positively influence your thoughts, ideas and writing to help you write not only a good literature review, but a good dissertation or other piece of research. For journal articles, you should mostly refer to articles published in top ranked journals in the field or discipline. There are several academic journal guides that can help you determine what the best journals in Accounting and Finance are. One of the popular guides is the *Academic Journal Guide* by the Chartered Association of Business Schools (CABS), commonly referred to as the ABS list. CABS is a representative body of UK Business Schools that directs the path of business education in the UK. The CABS *Academic Journal Guide*, like many other journal quality guides is based on evaluation of many research publications. These evaluations are done by experts, editors and seasoned academics (CABS, 2015). Journals are ranked according to a number of indicators. One of the main indicators is the impact factor, which is the average number of times articles in the journal are cited. Journals with higher impact factors are deemed to be of greater quality. Largely, there is a consensus on which journals are of the best quality among different journal quality guides. Although it is possible that some good journals may not be included on the CABS guide, you should always make it a point to first consider journals that are included.

Another way of obtaining good literature for your research is to look at research publications by the prominent authors in the field. In every topic in accounting and finance or any other discipline for that matter, there are usually well known authors who have gained that status either by virtue of pioneering research in that area or for publishing numerous influential papers. Examples of some key authors within finance, for example, include Andrei Shleifer (Corporate Governance) and Eugene Fama (Asset pricing). Examples of key authors in Accounting are Paul Healy (Firm disclosures) and Stephen Walker (Accounting History). A good starting point will therefore be to look out for publications by such authors. Identifying key authors can be done by looking out for the frequently cited authors in the articles or books you read. Alternatively, you can speak to some academics in your department to assist in identifying them.

Finally, it is important that you refer mostly to recently published articles. Referring only to old publications may suggest that your research is not of contemporary relevance and does not contribute to a current debate. Hence, whilst you could refer to old articles to get an understanding of how the topic might have evolved, reviewing the more recent ones enables you to have a good idea of what the current focus of research in the area is. In line with this, it is also useful to refer to working papers. Working papers are research outputs that are regarded as work in progress because they have not yet been published. These could help you have an idea about what researchers are currently working on at the frontiers of knowledge. Since it might be difficult to determine the quality of journals such working papers will be published in, it is prudent to refer to working papers of the key and prominent authors within the area. Table 3.2 provides you with some useful points to consider when evaluating articles.

Table 3.2: How to evaluate articles

How to evaluate the literature article by article	Yes	No
Content - Is the article easy to understand?		
Does it use good arguments?		
Is evidence given for any claims made?		
Does the article make clear any limitations?		
Is the writing biased?		
Context in discipline - Is this one of the key articles in the discipline?		
Does the writer agree with other writers?		
Does the writer disagree with other writers?		
Methodology - Is the methodology appropriate for the study?		
Is enough information given for another researcher to replicate the study?		
Was the sample size adequate?		
Author - Is this a reputable, academic author?		
Does the writer refer to other literature to support some of their claims?		
Relevance - Is the research recent?		
Is the purpose of the research similar to your own?		
Was the study conducted under similar circumstances to your own subject?		
Can you draw on the research for your own work?		

Source: Adapted from Roberts and Taylor (2002).

■   Selecting relevant literature

Not all good related literature might be relevant for your research topic. Hence, beyond looking at the title of the publication, there are other steps you can take to ensure that the literatures you review are the most relevant under the circumstance. One efficient way of determining whether a piece of literature is relevant to your research is to skim through some sections of the material.

For books, skimming through the table of contents, introduction, first and last few paragraphs of chapters can be helpful. In the case of journal articles, skimming through the abstract, introduction and conclusion is useful. You can also vet literature for relevance by looking at the individual or organization that published the material. Whilst doing all this, you should concentrate on identifying the key words and concepts. After identifying that a piece of literature is relevant to your research, you can then proceed to read it in more detail and synthesize the key ideas.

Critically reviewing literature

As discussed in Chapter 1, a good deal of accounting and finance research takes an interdisciplinary approach, so if your project has an interdisciplinary focus your literature review will need to contain literature from both your discipline's specific sources and literature from the other discipline. As such, it is important that you have a strong awareness of the literature open to you and how to conduct a critical review of this literature before you start the review process.

As outlined in Chapter 2, the base of your research project is gathered from your knowledge and understanding of prior studies and identification of research gaps. Further investigation into a more extensive range of literature will provide solid foundations on which your project will be constructed. The nature and purpose of the literature chosen will be dependent on the approach you adopt for the study as a whole. For example, the deductive approach will use literature to identify appropriate theories and to formulate hypotheses that can be observed/tested from a data set, to confirm, or not, your original theories. In contrast, the induction approach does not start with preconceived theories or ideas but rather develops them by starting with specific observations from which we can detect patterns that can lead to the formulation of testable hypothesis, the results of which can produce general conclusions or theory (Trochim, 2006).

The main purpose of the literature review is to critically evaluate the logic and coherence of theories, methodologies and research findings from the perspective of informed scholarship (Hart, 1998). Thus in order to effectively conduct a critical review of the literature some knowledge and understanding of the design issues, methodological traditions, practicalities and conceptual issues of what you are reviewing is also required. This can only be achieved through reading into the subject area. This does not, however, imply that you must read everything in the area, but the readings should be focussed on your research questions and objectives. From this literature, you need to critically consider the academic theories and ideas that have been produced; assemble the key points, arguments, debates trends etc., identifying any omissions or bias, and present these in a logical and coherent manner. The term 'critical' thus relates to the process of dissecting and analysing key literature in order to extract the important information and identify flaws, to provide a detailed and justifiable commentary on the pros and cons contained within current literature.

A critical review should:

■ Include the work of recognised authors within the subject area;

■ Include work that both supports and opposes your research idea;

■ Provide rational assessment of the value of prior studies to your research;

■ Provide valid support to your arguments; and

■ Differentiate fact and opinion.

In short, your literature review should provide a critical analysis and description of key literature related to your study that, when linked together, forms a logical and coherent argument that provides the context and justification of your research project.

Argumentation

The most effective literature reviews are those where themes and ideas identified in the literature have been exposed to thorough evaluation and critical scrutiny, the results of which are then woven into a logical and coherent argument. The ability to identify the substance and structure an argument is an essential skill for any researcher. An argument has two components: a point and a reason (Hart, 1998). It involves laying out the reason (or logic) of your stance on a particular point and providing evidence to support your view in order to influence or convince another party that what you are positing is true, makes sense and is justifiable. Furthermore, it should also compare and contrast the varying authors' thinking and inform your own opinions and conclusions.

The structure of an argument has three main elements: premises, inference words and conclusions. Premises relate to the assumptions or claims that a particular point is true or fact. Inference words are indicators that the author is drawing a logical interpretation or conclusion from the premises put forward (see Table 3.3). These words and phrases also help you to connect your ideas with evidence in order to make your writing flow coherently and logically. Conclusions demonstrate the value of your developed argument by providing a considered statement of the relationship between the premises or inference of potential consequences given the circumstances and premises (Fisher, 2007).

In order to evaluate the strength or truthfulness of premises, inferences and conclusions presented in the literature, some judgement on the appropriateness and application of the research method utilised within the research project being assessed is required.

Table 3.3: Forming critical sentences using inference words

> As a consequence of x then y
>
> Consequently…
>
> Hence…
>
> Therefore,…
>
> Thus…
>
> In short…
>
> In effect…/It follows that…
>
> This indicates that…
>
> This suggests that…
>
> It should be clear now that…
>
> This points to the conclusion…
>
> This means that…
>
> Finally,…

Source: Browne and Keeley (2004)

Having outlined the purpose of the literature review and the importance of critical analysis and argumentation we now turn our attention to writing up literature review.

Writing the literature review

Once the literature has been read and critically evaluated, the next step is to begin writing the literature review. As noted by Cronin *et al.* (2008), the key to producing a good piece of research is to present the arguments and findings in a clear, consistent and coherent manner. Hence, in writing the literature review, sufficient attention should be paid to how the material is structured. A well-written literature review usually contains the following features:

1 **Introduction.** The introduction of the literature review should present the research problem and describe the scope of the literature review. Lunenburg and Irby (2008) also recommend that the introduction should end with a paragraph that presents the sequence of the literature review using the headings of the sections.

2 **Main body.** The main body presents the issues identified from reading and reviewing the literature. This can be done in a number of ways:

- **Using a set of themes or categories.** With this, distinct and relevant themes from the literature are discussed under separate headings. This helps to avoid writing a literature review that is simply a description of the content of one article after another, as this is bad practice. Rather, different articles that speak to a common theme or issue are discussed in one or more paragraphs. This is arguably the most popular approach to writing a literature review, as it allows for a combination of both theoretical and empirical literature to be included in the project literature review (Carnwell and Daly, 2001). It is important to ensure that there is a logical flow from one theme to another in order to maintain coherence.

- **Writing chronologically.** With this approach, the literature is divided into time periods. Although not a very popular approach, it can be useful if the purpose and focus of the literature review is to examine the evolution of a topic over a period of time.

- **Examining theoretical and empirical literature under separate sections.** Both the theoretical literature and empirical literature are discussed separately. A separate section is used to discuss the theoretical underpinnings of the study by reviewing prior theoretical research papers. Another section is used to discuss the studies that have been undertaken to test the underlining theories your study. However each of these sections will be discussed under themes and sub themes.

3 **Summary.** The literature review should conclude with a summary of the major issues identified and discussed. Research gaps should also be identified as a way of motivating the current study. On this basis, where appropriate, a testable hypothesis can be formulated. In some cases, the discussed themes from the literature can be used to develop a conceptual framework that will guide the study.

■ Tone and tense

It is important to note that the literature review should be written in reasonably formal language (as should the entirety of your research output) and should possess some academic rigour. Hence the use of slang, clichés and colloquialisms must be avoided. Also, show respect for the work of others by using appropriate words when you engage in criticism of their argument or position.

On the issue of tense, it is generally more appropriate to write in the present tense. This is especially the case when you are discussing the assertions made by other authors. For example:

"In his seminal paper, Campbell (2014) argues that…"

When presenting your own observations on the literature, the present tense is equally used. For example:

"On the need for stronger banking regulation, the arguments of Smith (2011) are inconsistent with those of Hull (2009)"

According to Webster and Watson (2002), the present tense is preferred to the past tense for a two key reasons. First, the present tense provides the reader with a greater sense of immediacy. Second, the present tense is more quickly processed by the reader. The past tense can, however, be used when reporting events. For example:

"Richards and Brown (2008) undertook a cross country study on the adoption of International Financial Reporting Standards in Europe and found that …"

■ Updating and revising

Writing a literature review is an iterative process as it involves making changes in order to improve it (see Figure 3.2 below). As you progress with the rest of your research, you might come across additional literature which has just been published or articles that you did not find during your initial search. If these are relevant, it is necessary that you update your literature review to make it more comprehensive. With a good structure of your literature review in place, it should not be difficult to insert additional information to existing paragraphs or creating new paragraphs or sections. Again, it is important to note that the totality of your research should be one coherent piece of writing. Since the literature review helps to connect your research with prior research, you will have to keep revising it until a desirable level of coherence is achieved. Finally, you should keep editing your literature review to correct mistakes on grammar and spelling.

Figure 3.2: The iterative process of writing. Source: Machi and McEvoy (2009, p. 130).

Plagiarism and paraphrasing

The literature review is the most likely location in any piece of research for the commitment of acts of plagiarism or paraphrasing. This is because the literature review is primarily based on the work of others. Plagiarism means expressing the views of other authors verbatim, without acknowledging them through citation in both the text and reference list. Paraphrasing, on the other hand, is the re-composition of parts of the original authors' work, without quotations being applied or acknowledgement of the source. Both paraphrasing and plagiarism are acts of academic misconduct and as such are not tolerated. Authors who commit such an offence will be subject to discipline by their home institution. Where you have used any ideas, information or arguments from other authors these must be acknowledged and the source cited in the text and reference list.

Note that the idea of a literature review is to write your understanding of the literature, based on diligent reading and critical evaluation, in your own words; even in this circumstance you must fully cite your sources. Where the exact words of the authors are used, these should be put in quotation marks and referenced appropriately, usually by indicating the page or paragraph number in addition to the author and year of publication. For example, *"Smith (2011, p.10) states that '…'."* The style of referencing used should be consistent not only across all sections of the literature review, but across the entire research.

Different academic institutions, schools or departments adopt different referencing styles; it will therefore be necessary to find out which style is recommended by your department, school or university. Additionally, academic institutions have their own specific policies and rules on plagiarism and paraphrasing. It is the researcher's responsibility to know the rules and adhere to them.

Practical questions/advice

The following techniques, as suggested by Lunenburg and Irby (2008), will help in developing the literature review chapter.

- Organize your material like a funnel, starting with the general analysis and narrowing down as you get to the bottom. Be thorough by covering the key areas that relate to the research topic.

- Be selective as to which literature adds to the subject matter of your research project and puts the study into context.

- Make an outline of the major headings that would cover the aspects of the research.

- Write the introduction covering the research problem, the key theories or variables and the structure of the literature review.

- Use headings to divide the literature review into major sections and subsections to help organize the literature. Write with authority, showing the critical perspectives of the field, including key authors that provide researchers in the major issues.

- Critique rather than report on the literature, by undertaking critical analysis of the literature and the arguments they propose. Use transitions between paragraphs to link arguments, and ideas to provide a logical flow of arguments. Avoid excessive use of quotations, only using one when it is required.

- Write a summary of the literature review to highlight the key ideas that have emerged.

- Be careful to avoid plagiarism by giving credit to the authors of the sources used in the analysis.

The literature review process requires detail, analytical skills and logical reasoning and sometimes, researchers make some mistakes in the process. Gall *et al.*, (1996, p. 161-162) claim that the most common mistakes made during literature review are that the researcher:

1 Does not clearly relate the findings of the literature review to the researcher's own study;

2 Does not take sufficient time to define the best descriptors and identify the best sources to use in reviewing literature related to the topic;

3 Relies on secondary sources rather than on primary sources in reviewing the literature;

4 Uncritically accepts another researcher's findings and interpretations as valid, rather than examining critically all aspects of the research design and analysis;

5 Does not report the search procedures that were used in the literature review;

6 Reports isolated statistical results rather than synthesizing them by chi-square or meta-analytic methods; and

7 Does not consider contrary findings and alternative interpretations in synthesizing quantitative literature.

Summary

The literature review is a fundamental element of the research process that provides the essential ingredients from which your research project develops. An essential part of the literature review is the mapping of the main concepts, ideas and arguments that relate to your project. This chapter has provided you with insights on what a literature review entails. It emphasises the point that good academic research involves acknowledging and providing a critical analysis of the findings of prior related studies which then serve as the foundation on which your study will be constructed. Some of the major sources for obtaining academic literature and the processes involved in identifying and selecting literature of the best quality have been outlined. The chapter has also provided some important guidelines on how to make the literature review a product of critical reflection and not just a descriptive summary of prior studies. It further stresses the importance of coherence, conciseness, careful reasoning and clarity of argument. Finally, it is imperative that your analysis and critical reflection of the literature should be written in a clear, consistent and logical manner.

References and further reading

Boote, D. N., & Beile, P. (2005). Scholars before researchers: On the centrality of the dissertation literature review in research preparation. *Educational Researcher,* **34**(6), 3-15.

Browne, M. N. and Keeley, S. M. (2004). *Asking The Right Questions: A guide to critical thinking* (7th ed.). London: Pearson Prentice Hall.

Carnwell, R., & Daly, W. (2001). Strategies for the construction of a critical review of the literature. *Nurse Education in Practice,* **1**(2), 57-63.

Chartered Association of Business Schools (2015). *Academic Journal Guide 2015.* Retrieved from http://www. charteredabs.org

Creswell, J. W. (2009). The selection of a research design. *Research Design: Qualitative, Quantitative and Mixed Methods Approaches.* Thousand Oaks, CA: Sage Publications.

Cronin, P., Ryan, F., & Coughlan, M. (2008). Undertaking a literature review: a step-by-step approach. *British Journal of Nursing,* **17**(1), 38-43.

Fisher, C., (2007). *Researching and Writing a Dissertation: A Guidebook for Business Students.* Essex: Prentice Hall

Gall, M. D., Borg, W. R., & Gall, J. P. (1996). *Educational Research: An Introduction.* London: Longman Publishing.

Jesson, J. K., Matheson, L.& Lacey, F. M. (2011). *Doing Your Literature review: Traditional and Systematic Techniques.* London: Sage.

Knopf, J. W. (2006). Doing a literature review. *PS: Political Science & Politics,* **39**(1), 127-132.

Lunenburg, F. C., & Irby, B. J. (2008). *Writing a Successful Thesis or Dissertation: Tips and strategies for students in the social and behavioural sciences.* Thousand Oaks, CA: Corwin Press.

Machi L. A. and McEvoy, B. T. (2009). *The Literature Review.* Thousand Oaks, CA: Sage.

Mair, H. R. (2013). What constitutes a good literature review and why does good quality matter? *Environment Modelling & Software* **43**, 3-4.

Neill, J. T., & Richards, G. E. (1998). Does outdoor education really work? A summary of recent meta-analyses. *Australian Journal of Outdoor Education,* **3**(1), 1-9

O'Leary, Z. (2004). *The essential guide to doing research.* London: Sage.

Paul, R., & Elder, L. (2001). The miniature guide to critical thinking: Concepts & tools. *Proceedings at the 28ᵗʰ Annual International Conference on Critical Thinking*

Petticrew, M. & Roberts, H. (2006). *Systematic Reviews in the Social Sciences: A practical guide.* Oxford: Blackwell.

Polit, D., & Beck, C. (2006). *Essentials of Nursing Research: Methods, Appraisal and Utilization* (6ᵗʰ ed.). Philadelphia: Lippincott Williams and Wilkins.

Randolph, J. J. (2009). A guide to writing the dissertation literature review. *Practical Assessment, Research & Evaluation,* **14**(13): 2-13

Saunders, M., Lewis, P., &Thornhill, A. (2009). *Research methods for business students* (5ᵗʰ ed.). Italy: FT Prentice Hall.

Shadish, W. (1996). Meta-analysis and the exploration of causal mediating processes: A primer of examples, methods, and issues. *Psychological Methods* **1**(1): 47–65.

Stanley, T. D. (2001). Wheat from chaff: Meta-analysis as quantitative literature review. *Journal of Economic Perspectives,* **15**(3), 131-150.

Trochim, W.M.K., (2006). *Deduction and Induction, Research Methods Knowledge Base.* Available at: http://www.socialresearchmethods.net/kb/dedind.php

Uman, L. S. (2011). Systematic reviews and meta-analyses. *Journal of the Canadian Academy of Child and Adolescent Psychiatry,* **20** (1), 57-59.

Walsh, D., & Downe, S., (2005), Meta-synthesis method for qualitative research: A literature review. *Journal of Advanced Nursing,* **50**(2): 204-211.

Webster, J., & Watson, R. T. (2002), Analysing the past to prepare for the future: Writing a literature review. *Management Information Systems Quarterly,* **26**(2): 13-23.

4 Research Philosophy and Paradigm

Kevin O'Gorman and Robert MacIntosh

For no apparent reason, research philosophy tends to send dissertation students into a mild panic. The befuddlement caused by a range of new terminology relating to the philosophy of knowledge is unnecessary when all that you are trying to achieve is some clarity over the status of any knowledge claims you make in your study. Accounting and Finance sits within the broader context of the social sciences, and this chapter offers a guide to the standard philosophical positions required to specify the particular form of research you plan to undertake. Collectively, these positions will define what we refer to as a research paradigm (see Figure 4.1: Methods Map). For us, a comprehensive artic- ulation of a research design draws together five layers of interlocking choices that you, the researcher, should make when specifying how you plan to execute your research. There is no single 'right' way to undertake research, but there are distinct traditions, each of which tends to operate with its own, internally consistent, set of choices.

The Methods Map offers a clear and structured approach that will ensure that you can identify each of the choices you make in selecting the research design for your project. The process of developing a research design begins with the location of your proposed work within a particular research paradigm. Certain methods of data gathering and analysis tend to follow from certain paradigms, although it is important to notice that these implied pathways are not fixed. What is truly important is your ability to recognise and justify the interlocking choices which represent your own research design. Later chapters will deconstruct and explain the subsequent stages of the Map, namely those choices relating to both data gathering and data analysis. The sections that follow in this chapter relate to the starting point of the Methods Map, labelled 'Research Paradigm.' We shall first consider the reasons for articulating a research philosophy, before explor- ing objective and subjective ontologies, and the epistemological positions known as positivism, critical realism, action research and interpretivism. In passing, we will also look at *rhetoric* (the study of persuasive language) and *axiology* (the study of value) as a means of rounding out your understanding of some key phrases and concepts.

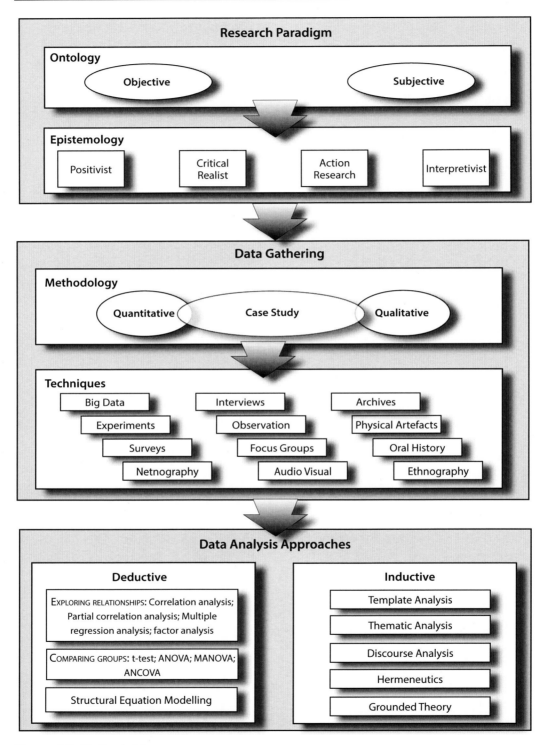

Figure 4.1: Methods Map

Whilst these concepts emanate from philosophy, it is not necessary to have studied philosophy in order to make sense of the terminology. In essence, the purpose of setting out your research philosophy is to help signal to other researchers those claims you might make in your findings, and the basis on which you would make such claims. However, it is highly likely that the same broad research question or objective could have been approached using a very different style of research. All that you are required to do is demonstrate that you engaged in a conscientious selection and defence of what you deemed to be the most suitable approach, given your chosen topic. Historically, certain paradigms may have been used for certain topics and methods, yet it would be foolhardy to dismiss the potential for innovation to be found in combining ideas and mixing methods.

Some of the ideas that follow may at first seem challenging and difficult to work with. As a health warning, we would acknowledge that we have made some simplifying assumptions in the approach that we have set out. Those well versed in the philosophy of knowledge may take issue with some aspects of our presentation here. However, we are confident that the structured approach we are proposing will suffice for the vast majority of individuals tasked with articulating a methods statement. Let's first look at why this is important.

4

Articulating a research philosophy

When undertaking any research project it is considered good practice to clearly outline the basis for claiming to know what we know. Kuhn (1971) set in place the tradition that once a paradigm is chosen it is advisable for the researcher to remain within that paradigm. For the purposes of this discussion, as defined by Harré (1987, p. 3) a paradigm is considered to be "a combination of a metaphysical theory about the nature of the objects in a certain field of interest and a consequential method which is tailor-made to acquire knowledge of those objects." At the philosophical level it could be perceived as dualistic if the researcher were to argue simultaneously that they believe that social reality is separate and external, whilst maintaining that reality is merely a construction of the mind. Hussey and Hussey (1997) emphasise the importance of researchers recognising and understanding their philosophical orientations within the paradigm adopted for their project.

In 1781 Immanuel Kant published his *Critique of Pure Reason* (1780/1998) and caused a revolution in philosophy. Kant argued that there are ways of knowing about the world other than through direct observation, and that people use these all the time. This proposition provided the platform for the launch of many of the ideas associated with research philosophy. Kant's view proposes considering not how our representations may necessarily conform to objects as such, but rather how objects may necessarily conform to our representations.

Prior to this, objects were considered in isolation, separate, and unchangeable. Kant theorised that things could be considered as objects of experience: *phenomena*, rather than things in themselves (specified negatively as unknown beyond our experience)*: noumena*. Therefore, if human faculties of representation are used to study these phenomena, *a priori* conceptualisations can be envisaged. An 'a priori' judgement is based on theory and argument rather than verified by experiment. For example, if we had only ever had the experience of sitting in chairs before and we saw a stool for the first time, rather than categorise it as unknown, we could conceptualise *a priori* that it would be possible to sit on a stool just like we do on a chair. Kant also showed how flawless logic can prove the existence of God and at the same time prove that there is no God at all; illustrating that opposing philosophies can be equally logical and at the same time contradictory and incomplete: a salient warning to any emergent researcher defending their philosophical stance.

The roots of research method

Gorgias, a fifth century Sophist, is remembered for his provocative aphorisms. The most notable is his treatise *On What is Not*:

> *"Firstly ... nothing exists;*
>
> *secondly ... even if anything exists, it is incomprehensible by man;*
>
> *thirdly .., even if anything is comprehensible, it is guaranteed to be inexpressible and incommunicable to one's neighbour"*

(Gorgias 500 BC, quoted in Arist. De Melisso Xenophane Gorgia *980a: 19–20)*

Gorgias' treatise *On What is Not* is just a rhetorical parody of philological and rhetorical philosophical doctrines. The aphorism deals with ontology, epistemology and introduces the problem of rhetoric and language in a world where communication was shifting from the spoken to the written word. Plato (Phaedrus) in 320 BC argued that writing would deteriorate memory, wreak havoc on logical constructions, and create an artificial reality. Yet despite being written 2500 years ago, Gorgias' writing neatly summarises the central concepts of this chapter. Before exploring some philosophical concepts (first relating to ontology), Table 4.1 gives the meaning of some commonly used terms:

Table 4.1: Some commonly used terms. Adapted from O'Gorman (2008)

Term	Meaning
Axiology	The branch of philosophy dealing with values, as those of ethics, aesthetics, or religion.
Deduction	*a priori* argument: deriving a proof or using evidence to test a hypotheses.
Epistemology	The branch of metaphysics that deals with the nature of knowledge, its presuppositions and foundations, and its extent and validity. • The study of knowledge • Theories of what constitutes knowledge and understanding of phenomena • How we explain ourselves as knowers, how we arrive at our beliefs
Induction	*a posteriori* argument, deriving knowledge from empirical investigation.
Metaphysics	The branch of philosophy concerned with the ultimate nature of existence.
Ontology	The branch of metaphysics that deals with the nature of being and of reality.
Methodology	The study and application of methods.
Paradigm	Theoretical framework, within which research is conducted.
Philosophy	The academic discipline concerned with making explicit the nature and significance of ordinary and scientific beliefs, and with investigating the intelligibility of concepts by means of rational argument concerning their presuppositions, implications, and interrelationships; in particular, the rational investigation of the nature and structure of reality (metaphysics), the resources and limits of knowledge (epistemology), the principles and import of moral judgment (ethics), and the relationship between language and reality (semantics).
Reflexivity	Critical self-awareness and examination of beliefs and knowledge-claims. • Need for conscious, reflexive thinking about our own thinking, and critique our pre-understandings, and their effect on our research
Rhetoric	The art or study of using language effectively and persuasively. • In particular the style of speaking or writing, especially the language of a particular subject as used in the dissertation process

Onto logy

As the Methods Map shows, the first stage in formulating your research design is to articulate your ontology. In the most basic sense this means that you must articulate whether you see the world as objective or subjective. We'll define both terms in a moment but first let's look at ontology. The term ontology is rarely used beyond academic institutions and it can be difficult to know how to use it confidently. As with much specialist terminology, a brief look at the linguistic components that form the word can help to unlock a more practical meaning. If you can understand and use the word 'biology' (where 'bios' means life) then you can do the same with ontology and epistemology. Biology is the study of life since the suffix ('-logy') is derived from 'logos', which in this context can be taken to mean the 'study of.' The word 'ontos,' which provides the root 'onto-', at its most basic means 'being' or 'reality'. Therefore ontology is the study of being or reality. In lay terms it may be considered as how we view reality.

Outside of science fiction and fantasy novels, we might think of there being only one reality, in which we live, breathe, and die. Yet the aforementioned fictions are often inspired by the thought experiments through which philosophers and theorists question our understanding of reality. The most well-known of these is the brain-in-a-vat scenario, whereby a scientist stimulates a disembodied brain with such precision as to simulate an entirely realistic participation in what we call reality. Does the brain experience reality, or is the experience of the scientist somehow more real? In more contemporary terms, popular stories such as the *Narnia* novels or the *Matrix* film series are based on the premise of stepping into a different reality. In ontological terms, the philosophical notion of solipsism asserts that since we cannot know other minds, the world and those other minds do not exist. Similarly, a nihilist ontology contends that knowledge is impossible, and that there is no such thing as reality. A rather more mundane example of an altered reality relates to illness or pain: do we experience the world in the same way when we are suffering? For example, if you were asked to remove a hot dish from an oven, you would instinctively look to put a protective glove on your hand to perform this task. You would do this because you would expect to feel pain in your hand if you attempted to remove the dish without protection. The pain would be caused by your nervous system reacting to the heat of the dish so as to protect the skin from being burned. If you were to remove the hot dish with an unprotected hand the pain you would suffer as your skin burned would subconsciously be associated with the dish itself: the dish is painful. However ontologically we can understand that the dish itself is simply hot and the body's reaction to the heat is to suffer pain. Therefore, the interaction between the two things (hand and dish) has 'created' or precipitated pain to be felt, but we can ask ourselves: is the pain real? Can it be objectively measured? If it is just our body trying to send a message to our conscious brain that lifting the hot dish with unprotected hands is a bad idea, then surely we can override this message and lift the dish anyway? Pain is possibly the most visceral sensation we experience as human beings but the important word to remember here, as with Husserl's work on phenomenology, is *experience*. The theoretical reality of pain, as simply a sensory message to our brains to protect us from harm, versus our experiential reality of pain, as something that is unpleasant and negative, presents the different ways in which ontology can be considered. Despite knowing that viruses don't *intend* to cause their hosts any pain, don't we sometimes feel a grudge against the natural world when we get ill? Can suffering even exist without being experienced?

As shown by the Methods Map, ontological assumptions can be broadly divided into two fundamental configurations: objective and subjective. Although these terms are far more commonly used, it may be helpful to develop clear distinctions relating to their use in the context of research. An **objective** perspective might be thought of as looking at reality as made up of solid **objects** that can be measured and tested, and which exist even when we are not directly perceiving or experiencing them. In particular, an objective perspective would allow that something as simple as measuring your height would result in the same answer, regardless of who does the measuring. In more complex settings, we might aspire that our objectivity allows us to make the judgements necessary to decide upon the guilt of a defendant in a court of law. In contrast, a **subjective** perspective looks at reality as made up of the perceptions and interactions of living **subjects**. For instance, our response to a particular piece of music varies such that we might find something delightful whilst our friends find the same piece entirely unlistenable.

Having established these basic definitions, we can return to the process of researching organizational settings. For instance, take the claim that happier workers are more productive. We might hold the belief that the lives of others continue independently of our perceptions, and so we can measure and test their actions and reactions whilst maintaining our role as detached observers. This belief, typical of enquiries into the physical sciences, would be described as an **objective** ontology. An objective ontology thus assumes that reality exists independently of our comprehension of it, and that it is possible to establish and explain universal principles and facts through robust, replicable methods. At this point, you may find yourself agreeing that this seems rather obvious and sensible. Alternatively, you may feel a sense of discomfort at what you perceive to be an oversimplification of the myriad factors that might influence happiness, productivity, motivation, duty or fear, each of which may be influencing how productive an individual worker is in a given circumstance on a given day.

In contrast to an objective stance, a **subjective** ontology assumes that our perceptions are what shape reality, and this is a belief expressed in large sections (though not all) of the social sciences. A subjective ontology sees facts as culturally and historically located, and therefore subject to the variable behaviours, attitudes, experiences, and interpretations – what we call the subjectivity – of both the observer and the observed. This is sometimes known as a relativist ontology, although this is arguably misleading, as one can appreciate the power of subjectivity without necessarily being a moral or cultural relativist. Subjective ontology approaches reality as multiple in the sense that each individual experiences their place and time in the world in a different way. For example, the subjectivity of an African-American woman in 1960s Mississippi is likely to be entirely different from that of a Native American Indian male in the same time and place (although both are likely to have their experiences shaped by severe oppression). You may already notice a problem with the subjective approach, namely that it seems to require a certain objectivity to make a universal claim for a subjective ontology. This is not a problem that we shall attempt to solve here. A simpler criticism of an entirely subjective ontology would be to say that there *are* things in the world with observable characteristics, without which they would be something else. For instance, zinc, or ethanol. A subjective approach might counter this by saying that these characteristics are only observable relative to a particular vocabulary, set of assumptions, and people who subscribe to them; that scientific knowledge is widely accepted as true does not mean that it is universally accepted.

Questions of objective and subjective ontologies continue to fuel philosophical debate, perhaps because they are largely irresolvable. Our perceptions of ourselves and of others *are* mutually influential. Like it or not, when interacting with other people we are constantly making subconscious comparisons and judgements, to ascertain our position within that interaction. We may change the way in which we act if we know that we are investigating something, or indeed our actions are being investigated. At the same time, it seems there *is* an observable reality that exists outside of human interactions, the properties of which can be measured and predicted. As such, it should be understood that objective and subjective ontologies are not mutually exclusive, and many researchers delineate their positions in relation to these poles, somewhere between the two.

If this leaves you uncertain as to which way of studying reality is the most appropriate for your research, then take some comfort from the fact that this is a healthy sign that you are engaging with an exploration of the underlying philosophy of your research. At the beginning of any project (and often towards the end!) this uncertainty is entirely warranted, and very much desirable. Ontological questions require careful and continuous answering, and there will always be a valid argument against any position you select. The one certainty is that considerations of how the researcher and the act of researching might unwittingly impact upon that being researched must be expressed, in order for the study to demonstrate an appropriate depth of investigation. In academic research (particularly within the social sciences) asserting our ontological position is crucial, since this sets out the basis on which we view reality. All that we can really hope for is a general consensus within the parameters deemed acceptable by a given community, and it is therefore important to recognise that the somewhat manufactured and exaggerated opposition between objective and subjective ontologies acts as a catalyst for critical thinking.

Following the Methods Map from our considerations of ontology, we now encounter and must make decisions about our epistemology.

Epistemology

Epistemology concerns the way in which we obtain valid knowledge. The Methods Map illustrates four epistemological positions: positivist, critical realist, action research, and interpretivist. Although there are others, articulating your epistemological position in relation to these four allows you to define your own ideas about the way in which we decide what constitutes reliable knowledge. For instance, if you are asked for the time, and guess it correctly without a watch, is this reliable knowledge? Or should this guess be verified somehow? Would hearing a time announcement on the radio represent confirmation, or would you be unsettled to know that digital transmission of radio signals introduces a small delay? The importance placed on the verified accuracy of the time would depend upon the context in which you need confirmation, e.g. you may want to catch a connecting flight, announce the turning of a new calendar year on live television or you may want to measure the heartbeat of a newborn baby.

The term epistemology can be deconstructed in a similar way to ontology. '*Episteme*' means knowledge and therefore, epistemology is the study of knowledge. By being clear about the way in which we might obtain valid knowledge we are in turn being clear about the nature of any knowledge claim that we might make. For instance, the observation that happier workers tend to be more productive is a form of knowledge claim. In everyday life we might engage in a debate as to the validity of such a claim, citing other factors that might influence happiness, productivity, or the relationship between the two. However, as researchers, we are required to draw connections between the assumptions we hold about reality (ontology) and the ways in which we might develop valid knowledge (epistemology).

Again referring to the Methods Map we can see a 'positivist' epistemology on one side, opposed to an 'interpretivist' epistemology on the other. These are placed in similar opposition to objective and subjective ontologies, as representing two different ways of thinking about knowledge. As implied by the vertical flow of the Map, an objective ontology is typically aligned with what is called a positivist (sometimes 'foundationalist') epistemological approach to knowledge, while subjectivity tends to be driven by an interpretivist (sometimes 'constructivist', although there are differences) epistemology. Again, these are specialist terms that can seem difficult to grasp, but a useful shorthand is to think of **positivists positing** and explaining principles, and **interpretivists interpreting** and understanding relationships. As we progress, it will be become clear that a research study expressing an objective ontology with a positivist epistemological approach might naturally be aligned with a quantitative methodology, whilst a study expressing a subjective ontology with an interpretivist approach tends to be aligned with a qualitative methodology.

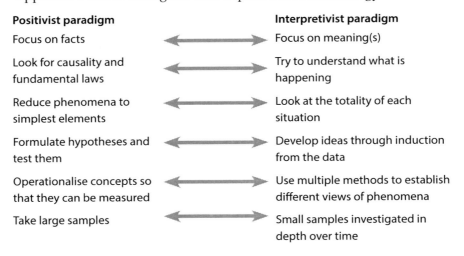

Positivist paradigm	Interpretivist paradigm
Focus on facts	Focus on meaning(s)
Look for causality and fundamental laws	Try to understand what is happening
Reduce phenomena to simplest elements	Look at the totality of each situation
Formulate hypotheses and test them	Develop ideas through induction from the data
Operationalise concepts so that they can be measured	Use multiple methods to establish different views of phenomena
Take large samples	Small samples investigated in depth over time

Figure 4.2: Epistemologies with positive and interpretivist influence

There now follows a presentation of four different epistemologies in social science research: *Positivism, Critical Realism, Action Research* and *Interpretivism*. There are many others being applied within social sciences research, however, particularly when it comes to undergraduate and postgraduate research, a solid understanding of these epistemologies is necessary to make an informed decision about the approach you will take.

■ Positivism

Positivism is most commonly associated with the natural sciences, but there are advocates who suggest that social science would benefit from adopting the same basic assumptions (see Donaldson, 1996). Three assertions are associated with positivism:

- ■ Methodological procedures of natural science may be directly adapted to the study of human social actions;

- ■ The outcomes of research in the social sciences will take the form of causal laws; and

- ■ The results of social research are value-free.

Comte (1830/1853) first used the term positivism; he had envisaged that sociology was to be the apex of positivism. This view is summarised in Giddens (1974, p. 1) as "the science of man completed the historical evolution of the hierarchy of the scientific disciplines, and for the first time made possible an adequate understanding of that evolution". Durkheim (1895/1964) was to defend Comte's (1830/1853) traditional version of positivism, which accentuated the supremacy of logic and scientific knowledge as the paradigm of all valid knowledge; the solution to the major practical problems facing mankind. Durkheim (1895/1964) understood sociology to be the objective study of 'social facts'; and that social facts were to be considered as things. However positivism was used in a derogatory sense by the Frankfurt School (typical examples can be seen in Horkheimer and Adorno (1944/1988), Marcuse (1967), Adorno (1969)), in the 1960s, to describe the assertions of Popper (1957) that science offers the best method in the pursuit of objective knowledge. Popper (1957) describes the scientific method as the "method of bold conjectures (hypotheses) and ingenious and severe attempts to refute them (falsification)" (cited in Checkland 1999, p. 57). Popper (1957) argues that sociologists must adopt the procedural rules, standards and intellectual conventions of science and embrace the point that there are no such things as 'truth' other than conjectural, relative truth.

The popularity of positivism in business research is probably because the data used is highly specific and precise. Babbie (1998) argues the place for positivism in social research and points out the interacting links between positivism and phenomenology by noting that "every observation is qualitative at the outset" (Babbie, 1998, p. 36), whilst observing the reason "qualitative data seem richer in meaning is partly a function of ambiguity" (Babbie, 1998, p. 37). In social science, unlike physical sciences, paradigms cannot be true or false, as ways of looking; they can only be more or less useful.

■ Critical realism

Critical realism is a relatively recently articulated epistemological position, derived from both objective and subjective ontologies, and chiefly espoused by Roy Bhaskar (1978; 1989; 1993). Critical realists assume that there *is* a reality that exists independently of human perceptions, but that our access to this reality is always limited and skewed *by* those perceptions. Our perceptions are both physically limited (e.g. we can't see into the past or future) and ideologically limited (e.g. we are biased by personal experiences). Although the critical realist makes assumptions about the world in order to produce knowledge from observations grounded in reality, it is accepted that these assumptions only create a temporary reality, which may well take on a different appearance from another perspective. Put simply, this position is 'realist' in believing in an external reality, but 'critical' of our ability to access and measure it.

Building on this, critical realists hold that although it is not possible to objectively verify universal characteristics of reality, humans nevertheless behave as if this were possible. We interpret and act upon situations as though causal relationships (e.g. **if** I drop this **then** it will fall) exist independently of our perceptions and actions. This view assumes that the power of perceptions can and does shape the world, but at the same time sees the effect of that shaping as the construction of often reliable and measurable circumstances. For example, when I strike a match, I assume that the flame will not be so large as to engulf and ignite the rest of the box. Furthermore, even when performing the same action with the unshakeable belief that the striking of a single match *would* ignite the box, this wouldn't happen unless an unusual set of physical conditions were met to make it so. Our perceptions inform and guide our decision-making, yet many scientific theories have physical consequences independent of human experience.

This layering of reality is expressed by critical realists as **stratification**, which is a principal feature of this perspective, although there is arguably some ambiguity in the application of the term. Briefly, stratified reality consists of a hierarchy of overlapping layers, with lower (or deeper, invisible) levels causing effects at higher (more easily perceived) levels. We might consider this as the distinction between what we can see happening, the events leading up to this, and the various forces that may or may not come into play at a given moment. This uniquely structured interaction of layers produces a particular outcome that cannot be reduced to its constituent parts, but nevertheless can be observed at the higher levels of stratification.

This becomes more complicated when we start to think about social reality, such as the case of happy workers. Phenomena such as happiness are subject to similarly layered distinctions based on what we assume to be reality, and again tempered by our limited ability to perceive what is occurring. Critical realists are particularly interested in the differences and interactions between the individual and society, and between individual actions and social structures. Although this is not the space to fully explore the stratification of reality, nor the 'emergent' powers stemming from its layers, it might be helpful to consider the stratification of this small section of the chapter. We (the author and imagined reader) acknowledge that there *is* something called 'critical realism' in the real world, but we can only gain access to this through language. We can read the words on these pages without having access to the process of writing, the chemical properties of ink, the historical chance and measurement that led to the printed word, or to the discussions that preceded the decision to write. The way in which we read these words is likely to be altered if, for instance, we have had an unfortunate prior experience with a spontaneously combusting box of matches. Such idiosyncratic elements of human experience and biography come together to create a perspective on critical realism that is completely individual, yet refers to something that certainly seems to exist.

Even if this all seems quite remarkably *un*realistic in its apprehension of what we understand as reality, it is hoped that this brief summation of critical realism will both prompt further investigation and generate searching questions about the nature of one's philosophical inquiries.

■ Action research

Far from being a single approach, **action research** is an umbrella term used to cover a wide range of styles of research unified by a shared emphasis on effecting change to the situation being studied. One of the most commonly used definitions of action research is that it involves working with organizational members on matters of genuine concern to them and over which they have a genuine need to take action (Eden and Huxham, 2001). It is therefore a highly applied and engaged form of research which sees managers and researchers collaborate to foster change.

Kurt Lewin introduced the term in 1946 to denote a new approach to social research that combined generation of theory with changing a social system through the researcher acting on or in the social system. He suggested that action research was concerned with two rather different questions "the study of general laws and the diagnosis of a specific situation" (Lewin, 1946: 36). Lewin's early action research projects concerned critical social problems, like racism and anti-Semitism, since he believed traditional science was failing to make an adequate response to such problems. Sadly, Lewin only wrote 22 pages on the topic of action research (Peters and Robinson, 1984), and died suddenly in 1947, aged 57 years old. Nevertheless, action research evolved in two related but distinct traditions. In the US, with the help of Douglas McGregor, Lewin set up the Center for Group Dynamics at MIT and then at the University of Michigan. Working with Lewin's guidance Cook, Chein and Harding outlined four varieties of action research – diagnostic, participant, empirical and experimental. (see Cunningham, 1993:15). In the UK, a group of war-time researchers who later formed the Tavistock Institute of Human Relations in London, developed their own variant of action research using a steering committee to develop a strategy for carrying out the research and implementing the findings in a particular context. Researchers would gather background data, perform analysis and implement changes, often in the first instance using a test area of the organization.

Today there are a number of variants of action research in use (see Reason and Bradbury, 2001 for a comprehensive overview). Some approaches to action research use "survey feedback" where systematic feedback of data from, for example, a company-wide employee attitude survey would be used to bring about change through group discussion and involvement. However, action research is more commonly associated with qualitative data. Indeed, MacIntosh and Bonnet (2007 p. 321) note:

> *"Qualitative research is sometimes styled as the poor cousin of 'real science'…*
> *if this is the case, action research is the poor cousin's downtrodden neighbour".*

The validity of action research is often challenged precisely because it places heavy emphasis on developing a deep understanding of one specific setting, thus critics claim it has a limited capacity to develop generalizable knowledge. Despite its popularity as a method, only a handful of empirical publications in the most prestigious journals feature action research in their method statements. Researchers considering Action research therefore face two challenges. First, they must find a host organization willing to (a) participate in the research and (b) committed to taking action on the basis of the research conducted. Second, they may face greater difficulty in publishing their findings in mainstream peer-reviewed journals.

■ Interpretivism

Interpretivism is often considered the generic paradigm of the social sciences and was developed in reaction to the dominance of positivism in the 19th and 20th centuries. Interpretivism identifies that there are fundamental differences between the natural and human sciences and these distinctions stemmed from the different aims – explanation versus understanding. Weber (1924), a key proponent of this paradigm, argued that the social sciences seek to 'understand' social phenomena in terms of 'meaningful' categories of human experience and therefore the 'causal-functional' approach of the natural sciences is not applicable in social inquiry. Weber (1924) recognised the nature of 'subjectivity' in studying humans, and noted that whilst physical systems cannot react to predictions made about them, social systems can. He pointed out that the 'self-consciousness' of human beings and the 'freedom of choice', which that consciousness entails, implies that an observer can never obtain an up-to-date account of the subject's state of mind, which would be correct for the agent to accept. Hence in the interpretivist tradition, the social scientist can only reveal 'trends' rather than 'laws'.

Weber's interpretive social science, based on the 'attribution of meaning', is closely related to Husserl's (1950/1964) work on phenomenology. The basic premise of the interpretivist paradigm is that unlike the physical sciences, which deal with objects external to the researcher, the social sciences deal with action and behaviour generated from within the human mind. There is a clear interrelationship between investigators and the investigated, researcher and the researched. Verification of what actually exists in the social and human world depends on the researcher's interpretation; the researchers' beliefs regarding the metaphysical realm could influence their interpretation of the physical realm.

In essence, the interpretive paradigm takes into account the multiple realities which are inevitably revealed by the perspectives of different individual(s), the context of the phenomenon under investigation, the contextual understanding and interpretation of the collected data and the nature and depth of the researcher's involvement. Broadly speaking, *interpretivism* allows the focus to be fixed on *understanding* what is happening in a given context rather than just *measuring* it (Patton, 1990; Klein & Myers, 1999).

A note on (research) paradigms

St Anselm, the 11th century philosopher and Archbishop of Canterbury, wrote, "I do not seek to understand so that I may believe, but I believe so that I may understand" (Anselm *Proslogion* 154-5). St Anselm asserts that nothing is achieved or ascertained by merely speculating from the sidelines; a certain level of committed involvement is necessary. Indeed, different research vantage points would yield different types of understanding, whilst accentuating these diverse perspectives does not negate the existence of an external reality. Hammersley (1992) referred to 'subtle realism'; the acceptance that the social world does exist independently of individual subjective understanding, although highlighting that the social world is regulated by normative expectations and shared understandings. The theory of the independent existence of the social world was established by Aristotle (circa 350BC) when he argued that something exists apart from the concrete thing:

> *"If, on the one hand, there is nothing apart from individual beings, and the individuals are infinite in number, how is it possible to get knowledge of the infinite individuals? For all things that we know, we know in so far as they have some unity and identity, and in so far as some attribute belongs to them universally. But if this is necessary, and there must be something apart from the individuals, it will be necessary that something exists apart from the concrete thing" (Aristotle Metaphysics 999a 25 – 28).*

At the ontological level, the scientific method has been questioned with observations that there are many more social processes at play than are usually acknowledged in the development of new scientific 'facts' (Latour and Woolgar, 1986). Also, developments in chaos theory and quantum physics have led to an increasing number of studies questioning whether the natural world is as stable and law-like as had been previously supposed (see for example Prigogine and Stengers, 1984). Businesses, events, organisations, and even individuals do not, in themselves, possess meaning; meaning is conferred on them by and via interaction. Interpretivism seeks to observe the general trends and perceptions of a social phenomenon. Fundamentally, qualitative methods are useful for unravelling and understanding what lies behind any phenomenon about which little is known. Management is a practice rather than a science and even proponents of the unity of science (such as Popper (1957) who assumes that facts can be gathered in the social sciences in much the same way as in natural sciences) have unfortunately devoted little attention to the particular problems of social science.

Recognition also needs to be given to the importance of being as objective and neutral as possible in the interpretation and presentation of the research. Current thinking would consider it essential for a research project to be framed within one philosophical paradigm, and to remain within it: the philosophical paradigm and the basic research assumptions must be compatible and clearly understood. Whilst mixed methods are increasingly popular, we would contend that mixed philosophies are likely to be a recipe for confusion. In summary, the research assumptions which relate to the philosophical paradigm are:

- Ontological issue (nature of reality);
- Epistemological issue (relationship of the researcher to that being researched);
- Rhetorical issue (language selection in research); and
- Axiological issue (role of values in a study).

We shall now turn to the effective use of language, before considering the role of values in your research.

Rhetoric or the use of language in a dissertation

Rhetoric is the art or study of using language effectively and persuasively, and within the context of the research process it normally applies to the particular style of speaking or writing, especially the language of a particular subject. This section briefly explores two aspects of rhetoric which are central to the dissertation and underpinned by your research philosophy: metadiscourse and authorial voice. You are more familiar with this subject than you think. For a start we all use rhetoric every day to serve our agendas in conversation with friends and family, at university or at work. A *rhetorical question* is a question used in a context where the question in itself drives a particular agenda without needing answered, for example if someone asked you if you liked ice cream, your likely response would be *yes* but instead of simply saying yes, you might choose to drive a persuasive rhetorical agenda by responding with the rhetorical question, "Do fish live in water!?!". By responding in the form of a rhetorical question you are enforcing the idea that someone shouldn't have to ask if you like ice cream because *everyone* likes ice cream.

Metadiscourse is a term for words used by an author to mark the direction and purpose of a text. It refers to all those devices which you use to organise the text for the reader and can include textual as well as interpersonal functions. It includes use of language, first person pronouns, and evaluative expressions. When you are writing your dissertation you should consider the reader looking over your shoulder. You write to meet the reader's needs at the time, and you must always consider your hypothetical reader when writing. In the case of this book the reader is multifaceted: students who are taught by the authors and other students; colleagues who also engage their own students; the wider academic community who have an interest in the subject; and there is always the possibility of other readers looking at the content as an example of how to write a text book. In writing a dissertation you must address your reader who is probably your marker too, whilst proving you are making a contribution and demonstrating yourself as a competent member of the academic discipline.

How you use aspects of metadiscourse will also help shape your authorial voice – the way in which you write to differentiate yourself from other authors. This does not mean that as an author you have to write the same way all the time, just as different social occasions require different dress codes, different texts require different writing styles. A reflective essay would require a strong personal voice whereas a report or an exam would require a more formal tone. This view of authorial voice also has close parallels with a major tenet of post-structuralist thought. According to Foucault (1981) people have, by their very nature, multiple instead of unitary personalities or subjectivities. The Russian literary and linguistics scholar Bakhtin (1986) proposed the notion of *heteroglossia*, (from the Greek meaning many tongues). All language is made up of words, phrases, and ideas in effect borrowed from other authors and infused with their intentions; an author's voice is inevitably multiple, intertextual, and appropriate to the situation. Most academic writers develop an autobiographical self, the identity they bring with them to their writing.

The underpinning philosophy that informs the research design that you adopt for your study will shape how you write your dissertation. If you adopt an interpretivist stance then you might be more inclined to write in a personal voice, using personal pronouns (if considered appropriate by your supervisor) and the tone could highlight the evolving decision making which took place during the research process. Whereas if you were positivist in your approach, your writing might more naturally take a more formal tone, based on set definitions and with a rather impersonal voice. As has been implicitly mentioned in this chapter, language itself is a construction that we use to communicate our work and our ideas. Within the area you are studying there will be prevailing assumptions relating to the meaning of words and phrases and their appropriate uses. With the same precision that you would seek to spell and arrange words appropriately, you must endeavour to be aware of the *meaning* of the language you use to the particular literature space to which your dissertation will belong. For example, you may intend to interview for your dissertation business owners who could legitimately be described interchangeably as *entrepreneurs, leaders and managers*. However, each of these three terms has a vast area of literature that inform their meanings, and thus by using all three your metadiscourse would be weakened, thereby jeopardising the strength and validity of your conclusions. Your writing style and language choices will influence your marker, and should be appropriate to your academic community. Finally, and most importantly, it should be readable. This might seem like an obvious thing to say but how often have we read academic papers that are full of incomprehensible words and groaning under a writing style so impenetrable that the text is rendered unreadable. Writing should use language that is accessible to as many people as possible.

Axiological considerations

Axiology is the philosophical study of value, often seen as the collective term for ethics and aesthetics; the two branches of philosophy that depend on notions of value. This is distinct from Research Ethics which should inform your data collection. Values here inform the bias, which you as an individual bring to the research project. We all have biases; it is how we deal with them or at the very least acknowledge them that is important.

One of the defining features of contemporary industrial society is postmodernity and the development of reflexivity or self-consciousness. Simply put, reflexivity is that stage beyond reflection: reflecting back on oneself. Reflexive modernity or postmodernity, and the vagaries of the post-modern condition are virtually unavoidable in contemporary research within the social sciences, which include business management. Personal subjective experiences are often central to the choice of research path, and should not go unacknowledged.

In social science research we deal with human interaction and feelings, not the cold hard facts normally studied in the natural sciences and engineering. This can present individuals in sensitive and demanding situations, such as the complex dynamics studied in Alexander *et al.* (2012), where the subjective interpretation of the concept of bullying is dealt with among organisational teams. In his address to the universities, Pope John Paul II (2000, p.3) states that it is the duty of academics and researchers to make *"universities 'cultural laboratories' in which theology, philosophy, human sciences and natural sciences may engage in constructive dialogue"* and observes that in universities "there is an increased tendency to reduce the horizon of knowledge to what can be measured and to ignore any question touching on the ultimate meaning of reality."

In the research process a positivist axiological approach would be a value-free and unbiased process, whereas interpretivism could be more value-laden and biased. That said we might also keep in mind the words of Benedict XVI (2005, p.2) when he observes that today *"we are building a dictatorship of relativism that does not recognize anything as definitive and whose ultimate goal consists solely of one's own ego and desires."* Now, it seems likely that Benedict had his own bias when he said that, after all he was a cardinal at the time, and he made that speech to the other cardinals the day before he was elected Pope. Most texts are value-laden and have inherent bias.

Assumption	Question	Positivism	Critical Realism	Action Research	Interpretivist
Ontological	What is the nature of reality?	Reality is singular, set apart from the researcher	Reality is stratified and engaged with by the researcher	Reality is knowable through interaction with the specifics of a given situation	Reality is multiple and interpreted by the researcher
Epistemological	How do we obtain knowledge of that reality?	Researcher is independent from that being researched	Interdependent but analytically distinct nature of society, culture (structure) and individual (agency)	Researcher interacts with what is being researched with the express intention of changing the situation	Researcher interacts with that being researched
Rhetorical	How is language used in the research?	Formal based on set definitions; impersonal voice	Formal as well as considers first and third person voice	Tends toward the first person voice	Informal evolving decisions; personal voice
Axiological	What is the role of values?	Value-free and unbiased	Considers the influence of values as experience	The values of the researcher are imposed through the overt attempt to effect a particular kind of change	Value-laden and biased

Figure 4.3: Research assumptions and positivistic and interpretivist paradigms. Adapted from O'Gorman (2008)

Research assumptions

Once you have formed your research paradigm, a further set of choices can be made relating to the approach that you take to gathering your data. As illustrated by the Methods Map, this involves the selection of a general methodology, and specific techniques. Chapter 5 looks at case studies, and Chapter 6 explores different sources of data. Chapter 7 offers a discussion of qualitative data gathering techniques, while Chapter 8 looks at quantitative data gathering techniques. Again, following the Map, you will then come to select an appropriate approach to data analysis. These approaches are broadly categorised as **deductive**, which typically works to analyse quantitative data, and **inductive**, which tends to be used to analyse qualitative data. Chapters 8 and 10 provide the accompanying discussions on analysing qualitative and quantitative data respectively.

Only since the era of the Enlightenment, and the rise of rationalism—with its rigid view of a nature governed by intractable rules—has the written word been straitjacketed by very clear ideas of just what is and is not physically possible. Imagination and a refusal to take things at face value play a big part in scientific understanding, research and discovery. For instance the King James Bible, first published in 1611, refers several times to the unicorn, while dragons were often hunted in the Dark Ages. The ability to take an imaginative leap beyond accepted scientific dogma and the entrenched views of academic colleagues, disciplinary boundaries or even apparent common sense has been at the heart of a significant number of scientific or technological advances in the last few hundred years. For example, throughout most of the 20th century, the conventional wisdom was that peptic ulcers were caused by gastric juice. Only by a pioneering doctor infecting himself with a bacterium (*Helicobacter pylori*) could he prove that conventional wisdom was incorrect and win the Nobel Prize for medicine. This is true even for advances that seem to be based on objective fact or cold hard logic, as the physicist Max Planck said: "*New ideas are not generated by deduction, but by an artistically creative imagination ... Science, like the humanities, like literature, is an affair of the imagination*" (McFague 1982:75). After all, as Shakespeare's Hamlet tells Horatio "*There are more things in heaven and earth, than are dreamt of in your philosophy*" (Hamlet Act 1 Scene v).

References and further reading

Classical sources

Anselm, St., *Proslogion , with, A reply on behalf of the fool by Gaunilo; and The author's reply to Gaunilo translated, with an introduction and philosophical commentary*, by M. J. Charlesworth. Clarendon Press Oxford (1965).

Aristotle, *Metaphysics, Oeconomica, and Magna Moralia*. Loeb Classical Library, Volume 17. Heinemann 1968.

Modern sources

Adorno, T. W. (1969). *Der Positivismusstreit in der deutschen Soziologie*. Berlin: Luchterhand.

Alexander, M., MacLaren, A., O'Gorman, K., & Taheri, B. (2012). "He just didn't seem to understand the banter": Bullying or simply establishing social cohesion? *Tourism Management*, **33**(5), 1245-1255.

Babbie, E. (1998). *The Practice of Social Research*. Belmont, CA.: Wadsworth.

Checkland, P. (1999). *Systems Thinking, Systems Practice*. New York: Wiley.

Comte, A. (1830/1853). *Cours De Philosophie Positive*. London: John Chapman.

Cunningham, J.B. (1993) *Action Research and Organizational Development*, Praeger, Westport, CT.

Donaldson, L. (1996) *For Positivist Organization Theory: proving the hard* core SAGE: London

Durkheim, E. (1895/1964). *Les Règles de la Méthode Sociologique*. New York: The Free Press of Glenco.

Eden, C. and Huxham, C. (2001) The Negotiation of Purpose in Multi-Organizational Collaborative Groups, *Journal of Management Studies*, **38**(3), 373-391

Foucault, M. (1981). The Order of Discourse. In R. Young (Ed.), *Untying the Text: a post-structuralist reader* (pp. 47-78). London: Routledge & Kegan Paul,.

Giddens, A. (Ed.). (1974). *Positivism and Sociology*. London: Heinemann.

Hammersley, M. (1992). *What's Wrong with Ethnography?* London: Routledge.

Harré, R. (1987). *Enlarging the Paradigm. New Ideas in Psychology*, **5**(1), 3-12.

Horkheimer, M., & Adorno, T. W. (1944/1988). *Dialektik der Aufklärung: philosophische Fragmente*. Frankfurt am Main: Fischer Taschenbuch.

Husserl, E. (1950/1964). *Die Idee der Phänomenologie. The Idea of Phenomenology*. The Hague: Nijhoff.

4

Hussey, J., & Hussey, R. (1997). *Business Research, A Practical Guide for Undergraduate and Postgraduate Students*. London: Macmillan Business.

Kant, I. (1780/1998). *Kritik der Reinen Vernunft. Critique of Pure Reason* (P. Guyer & A. W. Wood, Trans.). Cambridge: Cambridge University Press.

Kuhn, T. S. (1971). *The Structure of Scientific Revolutions*. Chicago: University of Chicago Press.

Latour, B. and Woolgar, S. (1986*) Laboratory Life: the construction of scientific facts*, Princeton University Press: New Jersey

Lewin, K. (1946) Action research and minority problems, *Journal of Social Issues*, **2**, 34-46.

MacIntosh, R. and Bonnet, M. (2007) "International Perspectives on Action Research: introduction to the special issue," Management Research News, **30**(5), 321-324

Marcuse, H. (1967). *Der Eindimensionale Mensch: Studien zur Ideologie der fortgeschrittenen Industriegesellschaft*. Berlin: Luchterhand.

McFague, S. (1982) *Metaphorical Theology: Models of God in Religious Language* SCM Press, London.

O'Gorman, K. D. (2008). *The Essence of Hospitality from the Texts of Classical Antiquity: The development of a hermeneutical helix to identify the philosophy of the phenomenon of hospitality*. University of Strathclyde, Glasgow.

Popper, K. R. (1957). The Unity of Method. In J. Bynner & M. Stribley (Eds.), *Social Research: Principles and Procedures* (pp. 17-24). Essex: Longman and The Open University Press.

Prigogine, I. and I. Stengers (1984) Order out of chaos: man's new dialogue with nature. New York: Bantram

Reason, P. and Bradbury, H. (eds) (2001) *Handbook of action research: participative inquiry and practice*, Sage Publications, London.

Weber, M. (1924*). Gesammelte Aufsätze zur Soziologie und Sozialpolitik*. Tübingen: J.C.B. Mohr.

5 Data and Case Study Research in Accounting and Finance

Roza Sagitova, Darren Jubb, Anees Farrukh, Angeliki Papachroni and Sean Lochrie

By this stage in your research you will have identified your research focus and defined your research questions. Attention should next be turned to how you plan to gather the necessary data to meet the requirements of your research project. Before collecting any data, however, it is important to carefully consider the issues related to the data collection process. Without careful consideration and adequate planning, it is easy to become somewhat overwhelmed by the amount of information that can be collected and end up 'drowning in data' (Berg and Lune, 2013, p.53) or to find yourself in the opposite situation of being unable to collect a sufficient amount of data because of a lack of appropriate sources. The first step in thinking about data, then, is to identify appropriate sources and plan how you are going to capture the required data from these sources. Different areas of accounting and finance research have different traditions for conducting research, which will have a direct impact on the researcher's choice of data collection method. One method of collecting data, the case study approach, is a methodological process that utilises a wide range of data sources and techniques. The strengths, difficulties and practicalities of using this approach in a research project are discussed below in order to give you an opportunity to assess the applicability of this approach to your particular research focus and questions.

Data and different research traditions

Within accounting and finance research there are a diverse range of approaches that can be employed when carrying out research and, as a result, there is a plethora of collection techniques that are applicable to this type of research. The selection of a particular method of data collection is motivated by several factors. At the centre of this decision is your view of what constitutes knowledge and your consideration of the nature of social reality. Space restrictions prohibit us from embarking on a full discussion of these issues; however, in previous chapters, consideration has been given to the various viewpoints that may underpin accounting and finance research and which result in the myriad approaches that are employed in that research. It is important to note at this stage how these viewpoints influence your choice of research focus and questions, and thus have a direct impact on your choice of research method. To demonstrate this point we will take one example, alluded to in Chapter 1, of financial accounting research, which can be split into the two traditions of realist research and relativist research. The methodologies applied across these approaches will vary widely; those approaching financial accounting research from the realist tradition will be more likely to take a viewpoint that lies towards the positivist side of the Methods Map (displayed in Chapter 4) and will favour methods that seek to verify hypotheses using statistical generalisations (Guba and Lincoln, 1994), thus making them more likely to adopt quantitative research methods. On the other hand, the views of researchers whose outlook is born of relativism lie closer to the interpretivist approach to conducting research; these researchers would likely be aiming to understand the underlying processes of a phenomenon as experienced by the social actors themselves and will favour qualitative methods of inquiry. In short, the approach you take in carrying out your research and the data sources that you select will depend upon the wider methodology and philosophical orientation that you adopt as a researcher, as well as the purpose and nature of the research projects you are conducting.

Sources of data

Moving on from your ontological and epistemological beliefs, there is a further important decision at the inception of your research project that you must address; this concerns the data sources that you intend to draw on in the course of your investigation. There are two main types of data that are used in accounting and finance research: primary and secondary. These can each be used singularly or, in certain situations, there may be greater benefit to be had in combining both types of data. This is discussed further in the sections below.

■ Primary data sources

We will first consider primary data sources, as these constitute the most common type of data used in accounting and finance research. Primary data sources are materials that provide first-hand evidence concerning the topic under investigation. As a researcher, they allow you to get as close as possible to the source of the event or phenomenon under study. As such, primary data sources cover a wide range of materials and methods. These materials can be in written or non-written form. The following table contains some, but not all, types of primary source that have been utilised in accounting and finance research, many of which are captured within the methods discussed in later chapters of this book.

Table 5.1: Sources of primary data

Written primary sources	Non-written primary sources
Annual reports	Audio recordings
Interview transcripts	Video recordings
Field notes from focus groups	Oral histories
Diaries, journals and memoirs	
Newspapers (written at the time of the event)	
Photographs	

Your choice of data sources will depend upon the wider methodological and philosophical orientation that you adopt as a researcher, as well as the purpose and nature of the research projects you are conducting, as described earlier. These issues will impact on the relevant unit of analysis; that is, the identification of who the correct person(s) or organisation(s) are for your current research project (Ghauri & Grønhaug, 2005). Naturally the number of variables present here means there are a wide variety of potential topics and viewpoints to be considered; there is a plethora of primary data collection sources applicable to accounting and finance research, which results in the uptake of a number of different methodological approaches. These range from qualitative methods, such as case study methods (see below), interviews, focus groups and ethnography (Chapter 7) and archival and oral history sources (Chapter 6), to quantitative data gathering methods (Chapter 9).

Once you have identified a primary data source, it is important to carefully consider the implications of your choice before embarking on data collection. Problems during the data collection process may halt progress in your research project and should be accounted for in advance so that they can be mitigated when they arise. With that in mind, Table 5.2 includes a summary of some of the strengths and difficulties associated with primary data sources.

Table5.2: Strengths and difficulties of primary sources

Strengths	Difficulties
Collecting primary data gives you greater control and allows you to focus on the specific issues that you identified when formulating your research questions. Getting as close as possible to the original source allows for a more targeted research project. This is particularly the case where utilising qualitative techniques such as research interviews	The time and resources required to successfully gather primary data can be substantial. Careful planning is required before conducting primary data collection, especially for those techniques that require you to enter the field to collect data. The individual requirements of collecting such data are discussed later both in this and in subsequent chapters
Primary data are somewhat free from the bias of other researchers, as they comprise information generated directly by the desired source	Caution should be exercised, however, with regard to the bias that the source data bring to the phenomena. Depending on the nature of the source, it should be remembered that the subjective viewpoint of the creator has certainly been implicated in the creation of the data
Depending on the data collection method used, large volumes of data can be gathered. Web-based surveys, for example, can yield a large quantity relatively easily	Gaining the access to the appropriate research site and being granted that access for the appropriate time period required by your project can be problematic

■ Secondary data sources

Secondary data are useful to your research project in two ways; they can not only help you solve your research problem, but they can also aid in understanding and explaining that research problem (Ghauri & Grønhaug, 2005). The collection of secondary data consists of using data that have already been collected for another purpose by another party. These data can be repurposed for use and analysis in your own research project. The use of secondary data alone may successfully answer your research question, in which case no further data collection is required. Should the secondary data collected not be sufficient, it may be used in conjunction with primary sources, a process which is elaborated on below.

It is important to bear in mind that secondary data have been most likely collected for a purpose different to that of your project and will therefore be incongruent with your research focus and questions. When considering the type of data source that you plan to utilise in your research project there are again a few issues that warrant careful consideration. Much like primary sources, secondary data come in a number of forms and can consist of written or non-written sources. Table 5.3 lists some of the most common types of written and non-written secondary sources of data. Again, this table is not to be considered exhaustive, but rather gives an indication of some of the sources that may be useful for your research project. As a general rule, secondary sources are usually written or produced at time removed from the phenomenon that is at the centre of the source.

Table 5.3: Sources of secondary data

Written secondary sources	Non-written secondary sources
Books	Audio commentaries of past events
Journal articles	Video commentaries of past events
Biographies	
Censuses	
Surveys	
Newspapers (written after the event)	

Secondary data sources have been utilised in a number of ways in accounting and finance research, both in qualitative research (see Chapters 6, 7 and 8), and in quantitative research (Chapter 9). Historical research, in particular, uses secondary sources, both in addition to primary sources and as the main focus of the research. As an example, consider the study of budgets and budgetary control in British businesses until around 1945 conducted by Boyns (1998), in which he uses the published literature on the subject to challenge the prevailing generalisations surrounding the development of accounting techniques. Historical data collection is considered further in Chapter 6.

Similarly to primary data sources, while there are characteristics that make secondary data sources useful for your research project, there are also a number of areas of weakness of which you should be aware. Table 5.4 highlights some of the strengths and difficulties of using secondary data sources that you should consider before commencing your research project.

In addition to the strengths and weaknesses detailed in Table 5.4, particular care should be employed when using certain sources, such as newspaper articles. As shown in Tables 5.1 and 5.3, a distinction must be made between newspaper articles that are written contemporaneously with the event (primary source) and articles that are written after the event (secondary sources). The key point to remember is that the classification of a source as primary or secondary differs, based on the when the data was generated and gathered. If it was captured at the time of the event then it is a primary source.

Table 5.4: Strengths and weaknesses of secondary sources

Strengths	Difficulties
By going through the process of collecting the data by secondary means, you make a saving on both time and resources. As ever, caution should be exercised and the source of the data appropriately assessed and verified.	When not collecting data first-hand, there is always the chance that, as the data has been collected for a different purpose, it might be inappropriate for your current research project; for example, it may be out of date. It is therefore important that you make allowances for the possibility that not all of the information contained in secondary data may be useful to your project
Where access to primary data is difficult to obtain, secondary sources may provide alternative insights that it would not otherwise have been possible to access	Access to secondary data may also be problematic. Some access to secondary data, particularly in that case of quantitative data, may be costly to obtain
Applying a new perspective to data that has previously been collected can result in new and previously unforeseen discoveries being made.	By looking at data that has already been collected, you have no control over the quality of the data. Care must be taken to establish and evaluate the quality of such data
Using secondary data sources may make it easier to conduct research across geographical boundaries, as you can compare similar data from different countries. For example, annual reports from companies in different countries can be easily compared	Related to the above difficulty is the issue of bias. Published secondary sources, such as books and newspapers, are often produced with a particular agenda in mind. It is important to remain of this when selecting and using a particular data source

■ Triangulation and time horizons

Finally, there are two further aspects that will impact on your research project and your data: triangulation and time horizons. The application of more than one method or source in research is called triangulation. This can be useful where you wish to confirm the accuracy of data collected from one source with data collected from another, or where you want to add an additional element of completeness to your research project in order to provide a more substantial picture of the phenomena under study.

It is important to also consider the time horizon of your project. There are two main options to consider here in terms of the style of project you wish to undertake: you must decide whether your project will be either cross-sectional or longitudinal. A cross-sectional study investigates particular phenomena at a particular point in time. A longitudinal study, on the other hand, considers events occurring over a period of time and relies on methods and sources which offer the opportunities to track these particular phenomena over time.

■ Section summary

The above sections have discussed the numerous issues that you should contemplate before beginning your research project. A number of elements will influence your choice of data collection technique, including your philosophical beliefs, the sources of your data and the desired time horizon for your project. The following sections consider a common method for conducting qualitative research, the case study approach, which is an approach that usefully demonstrates the use of a range of different sources of data.

Case studies

■ What is case study research?

Case study research is a form of social science research involving in-depth investigation of a phenomenon. This method is popular in accounting research, especially in managerial and organisational accounting studies, yet traditionally it has not often been applied in the discipline of finance. More recently, however, several finance studies have adopted the case study approach (Holland and Doran, 1998; Esty 2001; Duffie *et al.* 2003; Mills 2005).

According to Yin, a case study is "...an empirical inquiry that investigates a contemporary phenomenon in depth and within its real-life context, especially when...the boundaries between phenomenon and context are not clearly evident" (Yin 2009, p.18). The objective of this research strategy is to develop an analysis of the context and processes to enlighten the issue being researched (Gillham, 2001). Therefore, as opposed to research in a laboratory, as is usual in the study of natural sciences, in case study research the scenario is not divorced from its context but rather aims to understand how behaviour and processes affect, as well as are affected by, their context.

■ When to use case study research

The case study approach should be used when:

- the main research questions are 'how' and 'why'
- the observer has limited or no control over behavioural scenarios
- the study is focused on contemporary situations rather than historical events.

Case study research is employed when the phenomenon under investigation is too complex and when there is a need to explore the relationship between events and context, especially if the situation is unique. This approach can also be applied when seeking to discover meaningful differences between organisations, practices, etc., rather than common characteristics (Cooper and Morgan, 2008).

In accounting research, case studies can help to understand the nature of accounting practice in terms of the systems, procedures or techniques applied. Ryan *et al.* (2002) suggest when case studies, which are outlined in *Table 5.5*.

Table 5.5: Types of case study

Type	Description	Example
Descriptive	Describes accounting systems, techniques and procedures in practice; provides information about the nature and form of contemporary accounting practices	Smith (1994)
Exploratory	Explores the reasons for particular accounting practices. It is a preliminary investigation that enables the researcher to generate a hypothesis, which then can be tested on larger scale studies.	Scapens and Roberts (1993); Spence and Rinaldi (2014)
Explanatory	Provides convincing explanations about why particular practices were adopted. This type of case study does not attempt to make generalisations but instead attempts to explain causal relationships and to develop theory.	Larrinaga-González and Bebbington (2001); O'Dwyer (2005)
Illustrative	Explores the implementation and outcomes of new accounting practice developed by particular companies.	Kaplan and Norton (1992); Walker and Robinson (1994)
Experimental	Used to conduct an experiment by implementing a procedure or a technique developed from a theoretical perspective. This research method is not often applied.	Kunz (2015)

There are different traditions in case study literature that can influence the methodological choices of the researcher. Table 5.6 illustrates the differences in these traditions and how they relate to case study research.

Table 5.6: Traditions in case study research

Approach	Aim	Example
Positivist	To enhance theory through testable assumptions and arrive at conclusions by applying an induction process. Applicable when there is limited knowledge about a phenomenon or when existing knowledge is contradictory or unclear	Kunz (2015)
Interpretivist and constructionist	To understand the social world and social nature of accounting practices. Focus is on perception and discovering the meaning of those being studied and their understanding of events	Jackson et al. (2014)

■ Advantages and disadvantages of the case study approach

When considering the use of case studies for a research project you should evaluate the benefits and weaknesses of the approach; these are highlighted in Table 5.7. Although there are some limitations, case study research can provide valuable insights that open new areas for accounting and finance research.

Table5.7: Advantages/disadvantages of case studies

Advantages	Disadvantages
Useful for exploring novel practices, behaviours or under-researched phenomena. Ideal for testing or building theory	Subjective in nature and because of that have been accused of lacking rigour
Holistic and offer an all-encompassing description of real-life situations, which is often not captured by other approaches	Limited ability to generate generalisable conclusions, particularly in single cases. A frequently posed question is: 'How can you generalise from a single case?' Yin (2009, p.15)
Allows to show the details of social life and to explore alternative interpretations and meanings within the evidence	Can be time-consuming and costly. Access to the focus of study may be problematic if continual contact is required
Takes advantage of multiple techniques to gather data	The quantity of data can be overwhelming

■ Research design

Research design refers to the steps required to relate the study's questions to the data collection and analysis stages in a coherent way. Research design encompasses how data is collected, w1hat instruments will be used and what methods will be adopted for analysing the evidence. According to Yin (1989), good case study research starts with a careful research design, in which the researcher identifies the questions of the study (how and why), the study's propositions (if there are any), the unit(s) of analysis (which cases will be analysed), the logic that communicates the data to the propositions and any assumptions for interpreting the findings (see Cooper and Morgan, 2008; Yin, 2009). Taking each of these in turn:

Research questions

When beginning case study research it is important to identify as clearly as possible your **research question(s)**, as these will inform your research design. You should choose the questions carefully, making sure that they can realistically be answered within the limited time available for conducting your research. As discussed earlier, case studies can be used in research with different objectives: explanatory, exploratory, descriptive or generating theory and initiating change (Blaikie, 2000). Depending on the research question(s), you should consider these objectives, establish a preference and choose which type of case study research you will employ.

Moreover, for any type of research, the development of research question(s) is a very important phase, as it will allow you to test or build the theory. Thus, according to Eisenhardt (1989, p.536) "an initial definition of the research question, in at least broad terms, is important in building theory from case studies". Indeed, cases studies are likely to assist in the generation of theoretical statements and creative insights (Otley and Berry, 1998; Cooper and Morgan, 2008). You should therefore devote some time to thinking about the research question. Your literature review can be very useful in this regard; Chapter 3 looks in greater detail at how to conduct a thorough literature review.

Study propositions

Yin (2009) explains that sometimes it is not enough to simply establish 'why' and 'how' questions in order to determine the boundaries of the case study; it is also necessary to establish propositions of what can happen in particular situations, which can guide the researcher to determine what exactly should be analysed. Propositions can be derived from existing theories. Using analytical techniques of explanatory case studies, collected evidence can be linked to your defined propositions.

Units of analysis

It is essential to define the 'case' because it specifically outlines the boundaries of where the case begins and where it accomplishes both its spatial and temporal terms (Stake, 1995). This allows you to be more certain that the research, the questions examined and the data collected are within the boundaries of the area of research interest.

A case is the 'object' of the study or the unit of analysis. In case studies, researchers seek to understand the unit as a whole. According to Stake (2000), these might be an event, phenomenon, time-period, organisation, person, nation, policy or even a social interaction (see Cooper and Morgan, 2008). For example, Jackson *et al.* (2014) analyses the effect of policy and managerial initiatives that promote cost and budgeting upon medical jurisdiction and prescription practice within the context of the NHS. Here, the authors used Scottish acute hospitals as the units of analysis.

Connecting data to propositions

Yin (2009) lists examples of how data can be linked to propositions: pattern matching, time-series analysis, cross-case synthesis, logic models or building explanations. These are discussed in more detail in the data analysis section of this chapter.

Criteria for interpreting the findings

For studies applying quantitative statistical analysis, the criteria for interpreting the findings are relatively straightforward. If the p-values are <0.05, the variables in the model are statistically significant. This is less straightforward for other types of data analysis, an issue which we will explore later in this chapter.

We have discussed the importance of including these five components in your process at the research design stage. From the discussion in this section, you can see that it is necessary to clearly state in your research design the data that you intend to collect and what will be done with these data once they have been collected.

■ Single or multiple case designs

As mentioned above, it is critical for a case study to define its unit of analysis. It is also important to specify how many cases will be explored. Case study research can consist of a single case study that concentrates on one or more specific entities, for example the study of an organisation, departments, groups and processes. It can also consist of multiple case studies, in which each case can be used to test a theory from a different perspective (de Vaus, 2001). It is worth mentioning that, for both types of case study design, the selection of cases is very important. Good case studies usually start with a concern about an issue that has been poorly comprehended and inadequately explained. Hence, the aim is to analyse an existing issue and to use the insights acquired to develop a new theoretical understanding.

A single case study

As stated, case study design might consist of a single case study focusing, for example, on an organisation, department, individual or even a specific procedure. An example of a single case study being employed in accounting literature can be seen in the study by Larrinaga-González and Bebbington (2001), which considered a Spanish electric utility company in order to analyse the competing themes of 'organizational change' and 'institutional approach'. Another good example of the application of a single case study design is the study by O'Dwyer (2005). In this study, the author examines how and why the social accounting process evolved within one organisation – an Irish overseas aid agency.

Before deciding to use the single case study approach in your research project, it is important to consider the appropriateness of this particular method. Yin (2009, p.47) lists different rationales for determining when a single case study is most appropriate for your research.

- First, if the study represents a **critical case** for testing a well-formulated theory with a distinct set of propositions, the single case study approach is appropriate. This allows the researcher to verify, challenge or extend the theory.

- Second, single case studies are applicable when the research focuses on a **unique** or **extreme case**; when a rare event (case) occurs, it is worth analysing.

- On the other hand, a third situation in which a single case study might be appropriate concerns the **representative** or **typical case**, in which the aim is to capture conditions and circumstances of a typical situation.

- Fourth, a *revelatory case* can be appropriately used singly when a researcher has access to a rare and usually restricted research context.

- Finally, the fifth rationale for a single case study is a **longitudinal investigation**, which involves the study of the same case over a specific period. In this approach, the theory employed would allow the researcher to explain how specific conditions change over time.

However, it is worth noting that when you consider employing a single case study approach you should conduct a very careful investigation of the potential case in order to reduce the risk of misrepresentation. This means that you should be sure that the particular case is subject to the rationales justifying single case study research, as outlined by Yin (2009) (see above). You also have to be sure that they will be able to access enough evidence to support their argument (we will talk about negotiating access to an organisation later in this chapter).

Multiple case studies

Multiple case study research involves the investigation of several cases, allowing exploration of the theory being tested from different perspectives. According to de Vaus (2001), investigation of multiple case studies can help to identify the particular terms under which the theory may or may not hold true. Within the accounting literature, Jackson *et al.* (2014) adopt a multiple case study design and analyse the prescribing work of clinicians, drawing from three acute hospitals within Scotland. Multiple case studies are more advantageous than single case studies because of the belief that the derived findings are more robust and generalisable, and thus the multiple case study approach could be extremely useful for your research project.

Once you have decided that multiple case study is your preferred approach (in cases where none of the rationales for choosing a single case is applicable), be aware that potential cases for study should be carefully considered. At the stage of choosing cases, you should apply a 'replication' design rather than the logic of quantitative sampling. De Vaus (2001) suggests that theory is not accepted or rejected on the basis of only one experiment; instead experiments are replicated and conducted in different conditions. If similar results are found in repeated case studies we can then have a greater confidence in the obtained results (de Vaus, 2001). This approach is provides a more in-depth understanding of specific research question(s).

Replication logic suggests that the results of one single case, similarly to one experiment, should be supported by the findings in other cases. The central reasoning of replication logic is that, according to a theory, one would anticipate that the same phenomenon transpires under the exact or comparable circumstances or that the phenomenon diverges if the conditions are modified. Cases should therefore be carefully selected in order to predict:

- similar results for anticipated reasons (a literal replication)
- contradictory results for predictable reasons (a theoretical replication).

It is the responsibility of the researcher to determine the number of cases employed in the study. Eisenhardt (1989, p.545) argues that this should be "a number between four and ten" as "[w]ith fewer than four cases, it is often difficult to generate theory with much complexity; and its empirical grounding is likely to be unconvincing". However, if the results in these cases are contradictory, assumptions should be examined.

De Vaus (2001) advises that, when the researcher is applying a multiple case study design, it is of value to aim to handle each single case as separate, thus allowing a picture to be drawn of individual cases before the cross-case comparison is carried out.

■   ## Collecting data

Case studies usually collect evidence from multiple sources. For example, they can include all or some of such sources as evidence from documentation, direct observations, interviews, participant observation, archival records and physical artefacts. This method of combining data collected from different sources is known as data triangulation, and was discussed in more detail above. With this in mind, the collection of data for research using case studies is a challenging process. When you start your research, consider the three following questions:

- What would be the most suitable context in which to investigate your research question(s)?

- How feasible is to gain access to this setting?

- What type of data would be best suited to answering the research question(s)?

Gaining access to a company requires you to make preliminary contacts with key decision-makers within that organisation, for example the HR director or the head of a department. These individuals or groups might be able to introduce you to further members of the organization. Known as the 'snowball effect' – where you are introduced to potential participants of the study by someone you already know – this approach might be very useful for students. Researchers sometimes use this method when collecting primary data.

Researchers are also encouraged to familiarise themselves with the research setting through background research about a specific company or a number of companies. Information about the company's history, its financial position, its organisational structure and any other questions relevant to your research would be beneficial. This kind of information is usually publicly available, and can be found on companies' official websites or in company reports (annual reports, sustainability reports; newspaper articles, etc.). Such preparation is not only beneficial in terms of gaining access to the firm but is also crucial when making a decision about the appropriateness of a particular case for your project. It is important to be able to discuss and explain the aim of the study and the type of data you need to collect (interviews, questionnaires, documentation, etc.) when you are negotiating access with potential organisations and managers. It is also important that you are able to answer such questions as how many employees you would need to contact, how much time is required, whether you need access to internal documents and other practical issues of your research design. These questions will be important not only for you but also for the host organisation, as they will have to know what exactly is required of them. Although these questions might be difficult to answer, they will significantly influence the time and effort required to complete the data collection stage and will help you to stay focused.

Sources of evidence

Case studies can use multiple sources of evidence, the application of which provides a more comprehensive examination of the research question(s). Moreover, this allows the researcher to enhance the validity of the research; for example, evidence gathered from interviews can be supported by evidence obtained from written documents. Table 5.8 presents some sources of evidence commonly used in case studies.

Table 5.8: Sources of evidence

Source of evidence	Examples
Documentation	Letters, memoranda, e-mail correspondence, diaries, agenda, announcements, minutes of meetings, annual reports, other reports, administrative documents, etc.
Archival records	'Public use files', for example statistical data made available by the state; service records; organisational records (budget, personnel records); maps, charts, previously collected survey data, etc.
Interviews	Open-ended in-depth interviews (can be over an extended period of time) or focused interviews (person interviewed over a short period of time), formal survey (produce quantitative data), group interviews
Direct observations	Used to provide additional information. Can be formal (observation of meetings, sidewalk activities, factory work) or casual (field visits)
Participant observations	Actively participate in the events being studied. Can be staff in an organisational setting and be involved in making decisions or carrying out accounting procedures.
Physical or cultural artefacts	A technological device, a work of art, photographs, historical ruins, promotional material (adverts or posters)

If the study adopts multiple sources of evidence, each of them must be developed and acquired independently in order for each of them to be properly used (Yin, 2009).

Assessing evidence

Quantitative studies are concerned with such notions as reliability and validity. Reliability establishes consistency with research methods; in other words, when the same instrument is used to analyse the same subject, the same results should be received (Smith, 2015). Validity suggests that the findings of the study are not false: the data has been properly collected and interpreted and conclusions accurately reflect the real world (Yin, 2011). Thus, the definition of reliability requires that the evidence received in the study is independent of the investigator (objective world), while validity represents the extent to which the data is a 'true' reflection of the real world (Ryan *et al.* 2002).

Case study research is concerned with **procedural reliability**: that appropriate and reliable research methods and procedures have been adopted by the researcher. Yin (2009) explains that the objective of the reliability test is to ensure that, if another investigator conducted the same case study using the same procedures, he/she would get the same results. This means that there should be a robust research design with a comprehensive plan, all evidence should be coherently recorded and analysis of all cases should be documented. This would allow the researcher to demonstrate that all the evidence and findings are reliable (Ryan *et al.* 2002). Yin (2009) also suggests that the researcher should maintain a chain of evidence. This approach, according to the author, will allow an external observer to follow the formation of any evidence from the stage of formulating the research question(s) to the conclusions reached.

The concept of validity can be split into two components: internal and external validity. External validity concerns the extent to which findings are generalisable. Unlike quantitative studies, which often rely on statistical generalisations, case studies rely on analytical or theoretical generalisation, which is closely related to the **transferability** of the research results (Ryan *et al.*, 2002). Instead of internal validity, which seeks to prove a causal relationship between variables, the notion of **contextual validity** is more applicable within case study research. Contextual validity is used to demonstrate the credibility of the evidence and the conclusions reached.

In short, as large amounts of data may be required to be analysed, it is important that you make sure that the data collected is not only interesting but is also relevant to your research question(s). This approach will help you to stay focused on the research problem and ensure that you have a manageable amount of data to analyse. In case study design, you should also consider procedural reliability, contextual validity and transferability.

■ Data analysis

Case study data analysis is a relatively complex procedure. According to Miles and Huberman (1994), published studies often do not discuss the process of analysis in great depth, making it challenging to understand how the authors reached their conclusions from the data collected. Generally, after data has been collected, it has to be reduced and then analysed. The methods of data analysis depend on the type of research question, objectives or hypotheses being investigated. The choice of data analysis methods should be straightforward if other design decisions have been made carefully and consistently. Yin (2009) proposes one strategy for choosing your approach to data analysis:

- Build on theoretical assumptions. Assumptions shape your data collection design and so enable you to prioritise the relevant analytical strategies. Your assumptions help to focus attention on particular data and ignore other data.

- Develop a descriptive framework for organising a case study.

- Use both qualitative and quantitative data. Quantitative data facilitates explanation of outcomes in an evaluative study, while qualitative data will be critical in explaining your key assumptions.

- Examine rival explanations. This strategy attempts to define and test different explanations within your research.

Analysis in descriptive case studies

When analysing data in descriptive studies, De Vaus (2001) suggests that case descriptions should be structured around theoretical ideas because every researcher, whether or not they are aware of it, is influenced by implicit theories which guide their selection process. In particular, the author proposes three ways of analysing evidence in a descriptive case study, which are presented in Table 5.9.

Table 5.9: Evidence analysis in descriptive case study

Approach	Description
Ideal type	Construction of theoretically based descriptions of cases' types, which should list the elements of a type, for example 'socially responsible company' or 'authoritarian person'. The ideal type is then used as a template to compare how closely your case fits the ideal type. This approach allows not just simply describe everything you happen to discover but it helps to make the description structured, planned and purposeful.
Typologies	Typology consists of a set of types. You can develop different sorts of typologies, such as types of organisational structure. Typology enables the analysis of the case as a whole.
Time-ordered descriptions	Represents a way of describing a case with an emphasis on the sequence of events. Here a unit of analysis could be histories of events, organisations, policies, etc. This approach facilitates the explanation of a course of events and can be designed to support further specific explanations. It may also be used just to provide record of events without interpretation of those events.

Analysis in explanatory case studies

It should be remembered that theory is central in explanatory case studies: theoretical assumptions will either direct the analysis or be the goal of the research. It is important to first analyse each case individually in the context of the research questions and theoretical propositions before proceeding to do a comparison. Depending on the aim of the study – theory testing or theory building – different approaches can be used. Table 5.10 presents approaches used for **theory testing analysis**.

Table 5.10: Evidence analysis in theory testing case study

Approach	Description
Pattern matching	Establishes a detailed set of predictions before the case study is conducted. Case study then reveals whether a particular predicted pattern proves to be true.
Time series analysis	Similar to pattern matching, but predicts a particular trend or sequence of events (trend or chronological analysis).

Analytical induction is central to analysis for theory building. According to Denzin (1978, p.191), analytical induction is "a strategy of analysis that directs the investigator to formulate generalizations that apply to all instances of the problem". In case study research it is a strategy that allows the researcher to move from an individual case towards an understanding of what is common among various cases. This common element would become the foundation for theoretical generalisations (de Vaus, 2001). Denzin (1978, p.192) suggests the following procedure on conducting induction:

■ Define what exactly you want to explain (the dependant variable).

■ Outline provisional explanations (your theory).

■ Conduct a study of a case chosen to test your theory.

■ Review/revise your provisional theory in the light of the case.

■ Conduct other case studies to test your (reviewed/revised) theory and, if necessary, formulate assumptions.

■ Continue with case studies and revise the assumptions until they achieve a causal proposition that accounts for all the cases.

Summary

In this chapter we have explored one of the central parts of the research process – the collection of data. You should now be aware that there are two types of data: primary data and secondary data. The choice of which type to use in your research will depend on the philosophy behind your enquiry, freedom and flexibility in the structure and methodology of data gathering and the depth and freedom given to your research questions. This chapter has introduced you to the case study approach and explored its possible application in accounting and finance research. We also explored possible research designs in the case study approach, ways of collecting evidence for your projects and approaches you can employ to analyse the data collected in the case study. The case study approach represents only one method of collecting data for accounting and finance research, and the following chapters provide in-depth discussion of many more.

References and further reading

Berg, B. L., & Lune, H. (2013) *Qualitative Research Methods for the Social Sciences*, 8th ed., Harlow, Essex, England: Pearson.

Blaikie, N. (2000) *Designing Social Research*, Cambridge: Polity Press.

Boyns, T. (1998). Budgets and budgetary control in British businesses to c.1945. *Accounting, Business & Financial History*, **8**(3), 261–301.

Cooper, D. J. & Morgan, W. (2008). Case Study Research in Accounting. *Accounting Horizons*, **22**(2), 159-178.

Denzin, N. (1978) *The Research Act: a Theoretical Introduction to Research Methods*, New York: McGraw-Hill.

De Vaus, D. (2001), *Research Design in Social Research*, London: Sage Publications Limited.

Duffie, D., Pedersen, L. H. & Singleton, K. J. (2003). Modeling sovereign yield spreads: A case study of Russian debt. *Journal of Finance*, **58** (1), 119-159.

Eisenhardt, K. M. (1989). Building theories from case study research. *Academy of Management Review*, **14**(4), 532-550.

Esty, B. C. (2001). Structuring Loan Syndicates: A case study of the Hong Kong Disneyland Project Loan. *Journal of Applied Corporate Finance*, **14**(3), 80-95.

Ghauri, P. N., & Grønhaug, K. (2005) *Research Methods in Business Studies: A Practical Guide*, London: Pearson Education.

Gillham, B. (2001) *Case Study Research Methods*, London: Continuum.

Guba, E. G. & Lincoln, Y. S. (1994) 'Competing paradigms in qualitative research', in Denzin, N.K. & Lincoln, Y. S., ed., *Handbook of qualitative research*. Thousand Oaks: Sage Publications Limited, 105-117.

Holland, J. B., & Doran, P. (1998). Financial institutions, private acquisitions of corporate information, and fund management. *European Journal of Finance*, **4**(2), 129-155.

Jackson, W. J., Paterson, A. S., Pong, C. M. & Scarparo, S. (2014). Cash limits, hospital prescribing and shrinking medical jurisdiction. *Financial Accountability & Management*, **30**(4), 403-429.

5

Kaplan, R. S. & Norton, D. P. (1992). The Balanced Scorecard – measures that drive performance. *Harvard Business Review,* **69**(1), 71-79.

Kunz, J. (2015). Objectivity and subjectivity in performance evaluation and autonomous motivation: An exploratory study. *Management Accounting Research,* **27**, 27-46.

Larrinaga-González, C. & Bebbington, J. (2001). Accounting change or institutional appropriation? – A case study of the implementation of environmental accounting. *Critical Perspectives on Accounting,* **12**, 269-292.

Miles, M. B., & Huberman, A. M. (1994). *Qualitative Data Analysis: An Expanded Sourcebook.* London: Sage Publications Limited.

Mills, R. W. (2005). Assessing growth rstimates in IPO valuations – A case study. *Journal of Applied Corporate Finance,* **17**(1), 73-78.

O'Dwyer, B. (2005). The construction of a social account: a case study in an overseas aid agency. *Accounting, Organizations and Society,* **30**, 279-296.

Otley, D. T. & Berry, A. J. (1998). Case study research in management accounting and control. *Accounting Education,* **7**, 105-127.

Ryan, B., Scapens, R. W. & Theobald, M. (2002) *Research Method and Methodology in Finance and Accounting,* 2d ed., London: Thomson Learning.

Scapens, R. W. & Roberts, J. (1993). Accounting and control: a case study of resistance to accounting change. *Management Accounting Research,* **4**, 1-32.

Smith, M. (1994). Benchmarking in practice: Some Australian evidence. *Managerial Auditing Journal,* **9**(3), 11-16.

Smith, M. (2015) *Research Methods in Accounting,* 3d ed., London: Sage Publications Limited.

Spence, L. J. & Rinaldi, L. (2014). Governmentality in accounting and accountability: A case study of embedding sustainability in supply chain. *Accounting, Organizations and Society,* **39**, 433-452.

Stake, R. E. (1995) *The Art of Case Study Research,* London: Sage Publications Limited.

Walker, R. G. & Robinson, S. P. (1994). Related Party Transactions: A Case Study of Inter-Organizational Conflict Over the 'Development' of Disclosure Rules. *ABACUS,* **30**(1), 18-43.

Yin, R. K. (2009) *Case Study Research: Design and Methods,* 3d ed., London: Sage Publications Limited.

Yin, R. K. (2011) *Qualitative Research from Start to Finish,* New York: The Guilford Press.

6 Data Sources from Archives to the Internet

Darren Jubb, Lubaina Zakaria, Keith Gori and Rodrigo Perez-Vega

As shown in the Methods Map in Chapter 4, qualitative data presents itself in a variety of forms and offers researchers the opportunity to conduct research in areas where quantitative methods would be unsuitable, as it produces richer descriptions of the qualities and characteristics of complex phenomena. Two broad approaches to the collection of qualitative data are addressed here: historical research and the utilisation of the internet and social media as a social research tool.

Other common social science data collection approaches are presented in the next chapter, while methods for the analysis of qualitative data are presented in Chapter 8.

Historical research in accounting

Historical sources and methods play an important role in the study of accounting, as discussed briefly in Chapter 1. Conducting research into the history of accounting is a well-established tradition that stretches back to the turn of the 20th century. Early accounting history research was dedicated to seeking out the origins of accounting, combined with a focus on compiling biographies of esteemed individuals responsible for the development of the accounting profession. Such 'traditional' approaches to accounting history research utilised archival research, official documents and other information stored in repositories. During the second half of the 20th century, however, a new approach to accounting history emerged. It became an interdisciplinary subject that incorporated elements of history and accounting while utilising the methodological approaches and sources of data of modern social science. Overall, investigations into the history of accounting remain largely document-based and reliant on written records (Carnegie and Napier 1996), yet more novel sources of historical data have recently been considered; these are discussed below.

■ Archival sources

What is an archive?

Historical research gains much of its strength from a strong basis in the archive (Carnegie and Napier 1996). According to the *Oxford English Dictionary* (2002), an archive can be defined either as the historical collection of artefacts themselves or the environment in which they are stored and used, and can come in a wide variety of forms. With respect to accounting research, records of the past can result in a more detailed analysis of how accounting and business practices have been implicated in shaping the behaviour of individuals and how they have impacted on the function of both organisations and society as a whole (Burchell *et al.* 1980). For this reason, archives remain the most widely used source of data for historical research in accounting.

Table 6.1 briefly summarises some of the key types of archival collection, including a description of their main features and some examples of the sources therein.

The type of archive and the choice of materials to be utilised as the source of data for research are dependent on the nature of the project being undertaken. For example, a project looking at the establishment of professional accountancy bodies (e.g. Walker 2004) will be more interested in the archives of professional organisations, whereas a study concerned with the history of accounting within a particular company will be interested in the business archives for that company (e.g. Carmona *et al.* 1997). Careful consideration of the archival sources that are most relevant to your research project is an important aspect to consider before conducting archival research in order to maximum the use of both time and resources.

The value of archival research

Using archival sources can add significant value to your research project. Table 6.2 displays some of the strengths and difficulties associated with using archives in accounting history research. This table contains only a few of the distinct factors to consider when thinking about archival research and it should not be considered exhaustive. The importance of the points listed below will be impacted by a number of project-specific factors, such as the type of archive used, the material underpinning the research and both the theoretical and contextual elements of the study.

Table 6.1: Types of archive

Archive type	Description	Examples
Government/ state archives	Largely hold material relating to administrative affairs of the state. They often hold information relating to private companies and listings of business/corporate archives (see below)	The National Archives (UK), The National Archives of Scotland, National Archives and Record Administration (USA)
Business/ corporate archives	Hold information detailing the running of a business/corporation	Most large companies maintain an archive. The best way to check for UK company archives is by searching the National Register of Archives database (http://www.nationalarchives. gov.uk/nra/default.asp)
Professional archives	Hold the administrative information of the professional body, such as board and committee minutes	London Metropolitan Records of the Institute of Chartered Accountants in England and Wales and its predecessor bodies
Special collections	Usually organised thematically to hold materials from a wide range of sources relating to a similar subject, e.g. a particularly industry, social movement, political party, etc. Often these archives are located within, or attached to, a university archive (see below)	Scottish Business Archive (University of Glasgow)
University archives	Hold the administrative information of the university, can be very useful for collecting biographical material relating to former students. They also often have affiliated special collections (above)	Heriot-Watt University Archive, Harvard Business School Archive
Religious archives	Hold material relating to a major faith, denomination or physical place of worship	Scottish Catholic Archives, St. Paul's Cathedral Archives, Vatican Secret Archives

6

Table 6.2: Strengths and difficulties of archival research

Strengths	Difficulties
Detailed description of events: evidence from a variety of sources is available, often in vast quantities	**Time consuming:** as archives can hold large amounts of information, navigating through the material can take up a large amount of time
Richness of information: the archive operates as the collective memory of the creators, providing a large amount of useful information that it would be otherwise impossible to gather. It is also possible that additional information held in the records might touch on areas you had not previously considered	**Interpreting sources from the past requires sensitivity:** we cannot think like people did X-hundred years ago; the significance of semantic terms changes over time (and may have been disputed at the time, e.g. the term 'liberty' considered in the American Revolution compared to twenty-first century USA)
Organisation of data: in the majority of cases the basic organisation and preparation of data will have already been completed, saving you time and resources	**There is often a low survival rate of business records**, resulting in the information required often being absent from the archival collection. Further, the material that has survived is often difficult to read and, as such, great care should be taken to ensure accuracy
Chronology: trends can often be traced across time as you proceed through the archival record. Be careful of assuming a causal relationship between events; i.e. just because something happened after something else does not mean it happened because of it…	**Preservation bias:** archives are imbued with the social and political decisions made to maintain some material at the expense of others. This survivorship bias can distort historical findings (Cobbin et al. 2013). Always question archives and their contents

Using an archive

Though archival research can sometimes seem daunting, and can be a long, time-consuming process, there are a number of measures you can take to ensure the process goes as smoothly as possible:

1   Know what to look for and where, starting with the literature on your subject. Which archives have been used to look at the subject matter of your research in previous studies? You can utilise archival databases to try and locate a convenient archive for your project. Further, locator guides for archives written by professional archivists should be utilised where possible (Fleischman and Tyson 2003).

2   Research the archives you identify from a distance, as most archives have comprehensive material available online, and make use of any online cataloguing and indexing that are available. You can contact the archivist directly

to ask for more information. It is also good practice to contact the archive in advance and let them know you wish to use the facilities. When doing this, explain your project and your requirements and ask any questions you may have.

3   If time allows, make a preliminary visit to the archive. In doing so you will be able to get a feel for the collection, understand the requirements of the archive, learn how the archive functions, how it is organised and how to locate and request items. This will also give you an opportunity to assess how appropriate the material contained within the archive is for your project.

4   Reconsider your project, specifically the aim and objectives, and think about what sources are going to be most applicable. Make a list of the items you wish to view at the archive. Be realistic about how much you can get done in one visit and consider how much time you will have to focus in on the most important sources.

5   When visiting archives, be methodical and thorough when making notes on sources and, if permitted, take pictures for subsequent use. You need to ensure that good records are kept so that you can make best use of them in your data analysis (Chapter 8) and the subsequent writing-up of the project.

By considering all of the information above you will be able to approach archival material in a way that will add significant value to your research project.

■ Oral history sources

Although accounting history research relies mainly on the written record, there has been a recent growth in interest in seeking alternative sources of historical data. One such method that has received attention in the accounting literature is the oral history approach to data gathering. This section introduces the oral history method of data collection before going on to consider the methodological value and challenges of using this approach. Consideration is then given to the practicalities of carrying out oral history interviews.

What is oral history?

Oral history is distinct from other, more traditional, historical sources. The following quote neatly defines the approach:

> *"Oral history is a practice, a method of research. It is the act of recording the speech of people with something interesting to say and then analysing their memories of the past" (Abrams 2010, p.1)*

Oral history therefore involves collecting people's stories. The narration of stories as a means of communicating information about the past is not a modern phenomenon. The practice of passing on stories from an individual of one generation to a member of the next is one of the most ancient traditions of human society. Indeed, the cultural history of many groups in societies was previously established through the act of the oral historian of the group transferring knowledge to an apprentice historian (Berg and Lune 2013). Oral history is thus a fruitful means for the collection of historical data. Despite this many historians continue to regard oral history as unscientific and unreliable (Hammond and Sikka 1996) and as such it was only relatively recently that there has been an increase in the use of oral history methods for conducting historical research, despite its obvious value to researchers.

The value of oral history

Oral history can be used as a method for supplementing and clarifying the written record, or it can be useful in situations where no written record is in existence (Collins and Bloom 1991). Either way, oral historical evidence offers something that other methods of historical research cannot provide, namely direct contact with individuals involved in the subject of the study. By offering authentic accounts of historical events from participants, oral history allows the voices of those people normally excluded from written histories to be heard. In challenging some of the traditionally accepted judgements and assumptions used in historical research, oral history opens up new areas of inquiry, bringing an awareness of the fact that those individuals who are usually excluded from historical accounts have stories to tell that are worth hearing (Thompson 2000). In permitting participants to tell their own stories in their own words, oral history sets out to record experiences rather than merely seek out answers, allowing historians to collect information in subject areas where little information has survived from other sources (Lummis 1988). Thus, different kinds of data can be collected as alternatives to the traditional reliance of historical research on the written document, thereby adding value to your research project.

Challenges of oral history

There have been a number of criticisms levied at the use of oral history. The main criticism relates to the subjectivity of the information, as there is a reliance and trust placed on the memories of those speaking. Oral history asks people to recall not only what happened during a particular event but also how they felt about it (Abrams 2010). As such, many claim that oral historical evidence questions the maintenance of memory over time and the extent to which these memories have been infected by the influence of subsequent events. Oral historians recognise that memory is an active, ever-changing process and this should be taken into account when gathering data using this approach.

There are also a number of practical issues that must be considered when gathering oral histories. It is important to consider the ethical implications (see Chapter 11) and the potential impact that the oral history interview will have on the participant. Oral history interviews often encourage people to talk about emotional and personal topics and you should be prepared to deal with this. Lastly, it can be costly and time-consuming to conduct this type of research, with common problems ranging from difficulties associated with interviewees being spread across diverse locations, to the time it takes to transcribe interviews (Collins and Bloom 1991). Although oral history offers a unique and useful source of historical data, the challenges of the approach should be taken into account before utilising the main tool in the oral historians' repertoire: the interview.

Conducting oral history: the interview

There are two main methods used when undertaking a project using oral history: conducting interviews yourself or using a collection of existing oral histories to add depth to your research project. Carrying out the interviews yourself is a time-consuming process. It requires access to participants relevant to your project and access to the resources required to collect and record the interviews. On the other hand, using oral histories that have been recorded by somebody else and are contained in a publicly available library is a faster approach. However, as you are able neither to ask questions specifically designed for your research nor to follow up on points of interest which arise during the interview, the disadvantages of collecting the information via this method must be carefully considered.

First-hand oral history encompasses several forms of interview, with a common thread being that the interviewee tells their own narrative with an initial focus on the events, followed by a greater emphasis on the perception of events from their point of view along with the meanings they attach to such events (Collins and Bloom 1991; Haynes 2010). The oral history process allows the researcher and reader to understand events over a period of time rather than receiving a static interpretation of a situation, as with other historical sources (Yow 2005). This is an additional advantage to conducting oral history interviews first-hand; it allows you to ask questions that are directly related to your research project.

The majority of oral history interviews are characterised by their open-ended nature (Ritchie 2002; Abrams 2010). In order to fully explore the memories of the individual participant, the interview should leave scope for exploring issues as they arise. That being said, oral historians still prepare a list of questions and areas that they wish to cover. In this regard it is important to be well prepared for the interview. You should familiarise yourself with information that is available about the general subject matter and the participants that you are planning to interview. Being well acquainted with the lives of participants will allow you to be sympathetic and help inform follow-up questions to add further value to the oral history interview process.

■   Other historical sources

Though archival and oral history approaches are the most likely sources to inform historical research in accounting, a number of other, more novel, approaches have been adopted. Almost anything left by the past can be used as an historical source for analysis, a few common examples of which are briefly discussed below.

Visual sources

The modern world has become increasingly visually oriented, as visual media have penetrated a wide variety of communication sources and social media outlets (Parker 2009). Several fields of study have begun to utilise visual sources in the conduct of research. Paintings, photographs, posters and advertising material are among some of the most commonly used and such visual sources have recently begun to be more widely discussed in accounting history research (Parker 2009; Walker 2015). The power of images can add value to your research project by complementing the research methods discussed above.

Cultural sources

There is a strong link between aspects of both 'popular' and 'high' culture and wider society. Cultural artefacts offer unique insights into the social perceptions of society, of which accounting is a constituent part. As such, historical sources have been utilised in accounting history research from literary fiction (West 2001), fine art (Gallhofer and Haslam 1996) and even popular music lyrics (Smith and Jacobs 2011). Such sources are useful as they can highlight how different aspects of society are viewed and represented in cultural outputs.

Ancient sources

A number of recent studies in accounting have looked at the role of accounting in ancient societies. In doing so, they have considered archaeological evidence in order to analyse the development of accounting in ancient Egypt (Carmona and Ezzamel 2007), Persia (Vollmers, 2009) and Rome (Oldroyd 1995), to name but a few examples of this research approach. Historical sources are therefore not restricted to the information found in archives, as answers to interesting questions in accounting history research can be found elsewhere.

Online archives

Before moving on to discuss the use of the internet as a social research tool, we will briefly consider the use of the internet for archiving historical material. Digital technology and the internet have created the potential for increased access to archived resources. Archives are beginning to embrace the internet as a medium through which their content is made more widely available, with some offering partial contents and others digitising entire collections, opening up archives to more researchers than ever before. This removes the time and cost associated with travelling to many archives and allows continual access rather than a rush to cram in as much archival work as possible in a short trip.

Although easy access of this kind is extremely beneficial, it should also be approached critically. If only a portion of an archive's material is available online, the researcher has to consider the selection decisions that went into this process and the bias that this creates in the archive (Cobbin *et al.* 2013). It may not always be practical or possible to digitise all parts of a collection. In cases where only partial collections are available by this medium, a further visit to investigate the original material stored in the collection is advisable.

Online archives remove the element of serendipity that accompanies an archival visit, which often leads to important and unexpected discoveries. These can come as a result of a conversation with archival staff or other researchers at the archive, or because you chance upon something while looking at something else held in the same box or file. Online archival research also tends to take place in the same location as the rest of your work, whereas a trip to the physical archive removes you from your regular routine, often takes you away from distractions, such as emails or peers and colleagues with queries, and allows you to fully immerse yourself in archival work in a manner that online access may not.

Summary

The above sections briefly outlined some of the considerations surrounding the use of historical sources in your research project. By using historical data, you open your research project to a large field of research that may not otherwise have been accessible and thus you can add extra depth and meaning to your research. Having considered the use of archival data and the oral history method of data collection, as well as briefly looking at accessing historical sources via the internet, this chapter will now proceed to look more widely at the internet as a research tool in its own right.

Online research – the internet and social media

This section focused on how the internet and social media can be used to gather both primary and secondary data to answer many (if not all) of your research questions.

■ The internet

The internet is a medium of communication that is not new for the majority of the readers of this book, most of whom will have grown up surrounded by it. Figure 6.1 outlines the relatively short and recent history of the internet. With over a quarter of the population now having a directly available internet connection, a higher proportion of users than ever before, we can see how quickly the internet has become an important part of our daily lives. This makes the internet a very powerful and relatively accessible way to conduct both primary and secondary research. To understand the potential of this medium, we will discuss the advantages and disadvantages of using this communication tool when conducting research.

Advantages of using the internet

The internet has made empirical research easier. In general terms, the recruitment of participants, the carrying out of observational research, the application of self-reported surveys and carrying out interviews are all accelerated when using the internet. However, the advantages of the internet are not limited to making empirical research faster; internet research allows for the implementation of more complex studies and an understanding of communities that would be otherwise inaccessible.

The internet as a research tool

The internet makes longitudinal studies more practically feasible, as its duality between synchronous and asynchronous interactions allows for the collection of information that would otherwise require substantial resources and effort. For instance, interactions occurring on Facebook or Twitter can be relatively easily captured for further analysis. Organisational information can also be gathered via its website or any other online platform. Much of this information is both free and easily retrievable. The internet also allows you to reach geographically distant participants and organisations more easily and in a more accessible way.

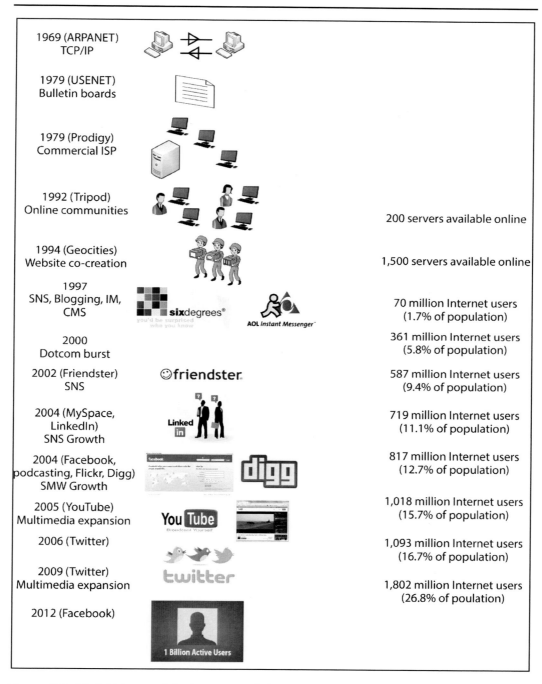

1969 (ARPANET)
TCP/IP

1979 (USENET)
Bulletin boards

1979 (Prodigy)
Commercial ISP

1992 (Tripod)
Online communities

200 servers available online

1994 (Geocities)
Website co-creation

1,500 servers available online

1997
SNS, Blogging, IM,
CMS

sixdegrees®
you'd be surprised
who you know

AOL *Instant Messenger*

70 million Internet users
(1.7% of population)

2000
Dotcom burst

361 million Internet users
(5.8% of population)

2002 (Friendster)
SNS

☺friendster.

587 million Internet users
(9.4% of population)

2004 (MySpace,
LinkedIn)
SNS Growth

Linked
in

719 million Internet users
(11.1% of population)

2004 (Facebook,
podcasting, Flickr, Digg)
SMW Growth

facebook

digg

817 million Internet users
(12.7% of population)

2005 (YouTube)
Multimedia expansion

You Tube
Broadcast Yourself

1,018 million Internet users
(15.7% of population)

2006 (Twitter)

1,093 million Internet users
(16.7% of population)

2009 (Twitter)
Multimedia expansion

twitter

1,802 million Internet users
(26.8% of poulation)

2012 (Facebook)

1 Billion Active Users

Figure 6.1: A brief history of the internet and the emergence of social networking sites

Challenges of using the internet

Despite the increasing penetration of the medium, internet-mediated research has been criticised by many researchers because of the skewed nature of the samples that can be reached through it. For example, if you conduct a study on the impact of social media comments on the financial stock market in the early years of internet adoption, you may exclude representative users who do not have access to an internet platform, which may skew and obscure your research results and findings. As a result, the type of platform you use to conduct your research is likely to influence your sample selection and should be considered when designing and writing up your research.

■   Online qualitative methods

There are three main types of online research methods:

1   Active ones, where the researcher takes a participative role within the online environment

2   Passive ones that are mostly informed by observation of information patterns on websites, as well as the interactions that occur in this environment

3   Ones where the researcher is using the channel uniquely as a recruiting channel in order to gather information online (e.g. online interviews, internet-based surveys) or to invite participants to take part in offline research (Eysenbach and Till 2001).

These are illustrated alongside other methods in the 'Techniques' section of the Method Maps in Chapter 4.

Active research methods

Online focus groups

Internet-mediated communication allows researchers to conduct focus groups via the internet. Similar to an offline focus group, this method allows for interaction between participants and a moderator in a semi-structured manner. The key advantage of doing focus groups is that group interaction can generate insights which are missing in one-to-one interview and remove many geographical barriers, increasing the potential pool of participants. There are also a number of limitations of online focus groups, such as a lack of moderator control and the inability to observe the level of attention of participants.

Online interviews

Interviews in online environments can be conducted both synchronically and asynchronically. They have an advantage in that participants do not have to move in order to attend the interview; this is particularly valuable if you are gathering information from participants across varied locations. However, there are some potential limitations of online interviews, particularly when targeting participants who are not technologically savvy. For example, if your target interview groups are from an older generation or someone from a rural area, they may not have access to an internet connection or computers, and this may pose a problem for you when you conduct online interviews. Instead you may have to conduct face-to-face interviews. Other issues associated with this type of interview include technological problems that may unexpectedly arise during the interview such as a poor internet connection and/or technical errors with your computer applications. In addition, some physical responses (e.g. hand movements, levels of stress) might not come across in online interviews.

Asynchronous interviews are mainly conducted via email. In this format participants have more time to reflect on their answer, allowing them to develop structured ideas about what they want to communicate. Follow-up questions are often sent once answers to the first set of questions have been provided. Examples of research via asynchronous interviews include Illingworth (2001, 2006) and Mann and Stewart (2000). Limitations of this type of interview include loss of spontaneity and issues with time management.

6

Passive research methods

Netnographic research

Similar to ethnographic studies, netnographic studies focus on the understanding of the behaviour and idea systems of a particular culture, organisation, profession or community in an online environment. One of the biggest advantages of doing netnographic research is that finding and joining online communities (e.g. forums, social media sites) can be relatively simple. There are, however, some online communities that are closed or private, and gaining access to these usually requires the researcher to acquire the appropriate credentials or permissions.

Research of forums/blogs

Another type of passive research method is to investigate content that has already been generated in forums and blogs. Research in forums and blogs is advantageous in that the content has been recorded by the participant, which facilitates the collection of data. Another advantage of conducting research in forums and blogs is the abundance of available data and the fact that they are supported by user-generated content in a wide range of topics. Unerman and Bennett (2004) conducted a study that analysed such forums; they examined stakeholder dialogue via a company web forum and addressed an issue associated with stakeholder engagement initiatives, looking at whether it promotes greater corporate accountability or merely serves to reinforce capitalist hegemony.

Online environments as a recruiting channel

The internet can be used as a recruitment channel to seek potential participants before conducting research in a more traditional way. Online communities gather people with similar interests, and can therefore be a productive way to reach people with a certain profile who are scattered geographically. One example would be recruiting people to participate in an online experimental study of stakeholder reactions to organisational events, such as release of company performance or corporate crisis (Beattie and Jones 2002; Cho *et al.* 2009; Schultz *et al.* 2011). If your research context is very specific, online environments could be a better option than traditional recruitment methods as a tool for participant recruitment.

■ Social media

The term *social media* stems from two areas of research: communication science and sociology. In the communication context, a medium is merely a means of storing or delivering information or data. From the perspective of sociology, and in particular social (network) theory and analysis, social networks are social structures comprised of a set of social actors (individuals, groups or organisations) with a complex set of dyadic relationships among them (Wasserman and Faust 1994). In other words, social media are internet platforms that can be used to disseminate information through social interactions with decentralised user-level content and public membership (Abrahams *et al.* 2012; Li and Shiu 2012).

Social media studies are gaining interest among both accounting and finance practitioners and, of particular interest here, academic scholars (Figure 6.2). The interest in this type of site is nested in the impact that these platforms have had as sources of information and as a facility that enables constant interaction with other users. In the field of accounting and finance, the increased use of social media channels is reshaping the way organisations and their stakeholders interact with each other. The following are some examples of social media research that are of particular relevance to accounting and finance:

- the use of social media as public relations tools and to engage with organisational stakeholders (Schultz *et al.* 2011; Waters and Jamal 2011; Lovejoy *et al.* 2012)
- the impact of social media on financial stock market and firm equity value (Blankespoor *et al.* 2014; Sprenger *et al.* 2014; Zhang *et al.* 2011)
- the use of social media to enhance financial performance from an impression management perspective (Schnierderjans *et al.* 2013).

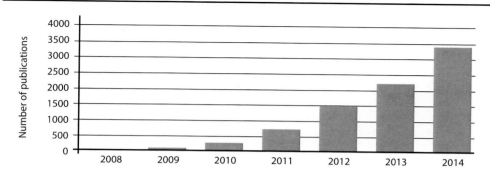

Figure 6.2: Social media in academic research

Classification of social media websites

Given the general definitions above, it is important to further distinguish the various types of social media in order to understand the functionalities of these different platforms. Kaplan and Haenlein (2010) created a classification theme based on two key elements of social media and its corresponding set of theories:

- *Social media research*: social presence theory

- *Social processes*: self-presentation theory.

Social presence theory suggests that visual, acoustic and physical contact can be achieved between two communicating parties (Short *et al*. 1976). The greater the social presence, the greater the social influence that the communicating parties have on each other's attitude. The concept of self-presentation suggests that individuals or organisations have the desire to control the impression others have of them in order to maximise expected rewards and minimise expected punishments (Goffman 1959; Schlenker 1980). Table 6.3 illustrates the classification of social media with regard to both dimensions (self-presentation and social presence).

Blogs, forums and collaborative projects have a low social presence, as the nature of these applications is often text-based and therefore allow for only a relatively simple interaction. Content communities (e.g. YouTube) and social networking sites (e.g. Facebook, Twitter) are on the next level, as they enable the sharing of videos, pictures and other forms of media in addition to text-based communication. The highest level of social presence (virtual social worlds and game worlds) tends to embody all the dimensions of face-to-face communications in an online environment. With respect to self-presentation, blogs, social networking sites and virtual social worlds score more highly, as they are not focused on specific content domain nor governed by such strict user guidelines when compared with collaborative projects, content communities and virtual game worlds.

Table 6.3: Classification of social media by social presence and self-presentation (Kaplan and Haenlein 2010)

		Social presence		
		Low	Medium	High
Self-presentation	Low	Blogs, forums	Social networking sites (e.g. Facebook)	Virtual social worlds (Second Life)
	High	Collaborative projects (e.g. Wikipedia)	Content communities (YouTube)	Virtual game worlds (e.g. World of Warcraft)

■ The practicalities of conducting online research

MacKenzie *et al.* (2013) have developed practical guidelines to help with the design and conduct of online research based on Llewellyn's (2007) framework and insights gained from a case study of innovative virtual business activity conducted in Second Life in 2007. Issues to be considered by researchers include the conduct of online interviews and surveys, recruiting online participants, the copyright implications of taking snapshots and visual activity online, ethical issues and the psychological impact of immersion on the researcher (Minocha *et al.* 2010). These are explored by Mackenzie *et al.* (2013) through Llewellyn's (2007) framework of five virtual dimensions and are summarised in Table 6.4.

■ Ethical considerations in internet research

Online research is not likely to be more harmful than offline research, yet it poses different challenges (Kraut *et al.* 2004). The ethical considerations in online research are based on the harm that participants of the research may be exposed to when being part of an academic study. We will identify three of the most important ethical considerations when conducting research online: the safeguarding of participants, ensuring participants' confidentiality and gaining participants' consent.

Safeguarding of participants

In online research it is harder to assess whether a risk of harm to a participant is likely to occur. This is because of the limitations present in computer-mediated interactions, where the level of distress of a person as a consequence of being part of a certain study cannot be easily assessed. Exit mechanisms and building good rapport with the participant when running research are strategies that can be useful in helping to avoid this happening (Eynon *et al.* 2008).

Table 6.4: Research implications of five virtual dimensions (MacKenzie *et al.* 2013)

Virtual dimension and characteristics	Practical preparations and training for the virtual researcher
Physical	
Visual appearance of a virtual setting and the visible content/objects	Familiarise yourself with a variety of virtual world platforms in order to make an informed choice of a virtual research setting Practice operating in your chosen virtual setting Obtain assistance on the construction of an avatar Become familiar with data collection techniques to reduce the time taken to undertake research
Structural	
Represents the operational processes, roles, rules and systems that inform and govern the development of social understandings and meanings	Study the legal ownership of the chosen virtual setting and understand your legal rights and responsibilities Understand and apply the rules and protocols required in the conduct of research in the virtual setting Ensure ethical approval is obtained from your university/organisation
Agential	
The realm of human endeavour where people act as innovators and agents of change	Determine how to manage your research avatar's identity and behaviour prior to commencing virtual research Joining virtual communities may assist you to access other agents
Cultural	
The inter-subjective realm of a shared cultural experience to understand and create meaning within the virtual setting	Determine the appropriate appearance, skills, competencies, communication protocols and behaviour of your avatar to culturally fit into your chosen virtual setting Be flexible in adapting to new cultural experiences that may challenge your personal and moral values
Mental	
Involves human mental capacity being utilised within a virtual setting, but is complicated with a dual identity through the use of an avatar	Be prepared for a deep psychological experience Focus on the objective tasks at hand, so as not to be overcome by the powerful sensory experience of the virtual setting Keep an open, inquisitive and playful attitude, yet be aware and alert at all times

6

Ensuring confidentiality

Another important element to take into consideration is how the findings in your research are presented, particularly with regard to participant anonymity. In order to ensure the confidentiality of participants the researcher needs to pay special attention as to how data are presented, the type of information that is disclosed in terms of the age, gender or location of the participants and, when quoting from online sources, to ensure that these sources can be easily found using search engines.

Participants' consent

One of the greatest ethical considerations when conducting online research is obtaining the consent of the participant to take part in a study. Depending on the methods and nature of your research, consent will be sought before conducting your study (as in interviews and some types of netnographic studies). It could be the case that you are planning to conduct a covert netnographic study, in which you do not tell the subject community who you are and why you are interested in that community. If you decide to do so, an exhaustive risk assessment of the scope of your research is needed. It is vital to take sufficient preventive measures in order to ensure the confidentiality of your research.

■ Summary

This section has aimed to give an introductory account of the use of the internet in conducting research. Although this is not an exhaustive review of the implications of conducting research online, it is intended to serve as a guide to using the internet in your dissertation.

Chapter summary

Both historical sources and the presence of online resources offer a diverse range of approaches to the collection of data during your research project. However, collecting this material alone does not offer you the opportunity to infer conclusions or answer your research questions. This section should be used in conjunction with those on techniques (in Chapter 7), qualitative data analysis (Chapter 8) and ethical implications (Chapter 11) in order to create the best possible project to answer the problems identified in your research using the preceding chapters.

References and further reading

Abrahams, A.S., Jiao, J., Wang, G.A. & Fan W. (2012), Vehicle defect discovery from social media. *Decision Support Systems*, **54** (1), 87–97.

Abrams, L. (2010). *Oral History Theory*. London; New York: Routledge.

Beattie, V., & Jones, M. J. (2002)France, Germany, the Netherlands, the U.K., and the U.S. In particular, we examine (1. Measurement distortions of graphs in corporate annual reports: an experimental study. *Accounting, Auditing & Accountability Journal*, **15**(4), 546–564.

Berg, B. L., & Lune, H. (2013). *Qualitative Research Methods for the Social Sciences* (8 edition). Harlow, Essex, England: Pearson.

Blankespoor, E., Miller, G. S., & White H. D. (2014). "The Role of Dissemination in Market Liquidity: Evidence from Firms's Use of Twitter," *The Accounting Review*, **89** (1), 79-112.

Burchell, S., Clubb, C., Hopwood, A., Hughes, J., & Nahapiet, J. (1980). The roles of accounting in organizations and society. *Accounting, Organizations and Society*, **5**(1), 5–27.

Carmona, S., & Ezzamel. M. (2007). Accounting and accountability in ancient civilizations: Mesopotamia and ancient Egypt. *Accounting, Auditing & Accountability Journal*, **20**(2), 177–209.

Carmona, S., Ezzamel, M., & Gutiérrez, F. (1997). Control and cost accounting practices in the Spanish Royal Tobacco Factory. *Accounting, Organizations and Society*, **22**(5), 411–446.

Carnegie, G. D., & Napier, C. J. (1996). Critical and interpretive histories: insights into accounting's present and future through its past. *Accounting, Auditing & Accountability Journal*, **9**(3), 7–39.

Cho, C.H., Phillips, J. R., Hageman, A. M., & Patten, D. M. (2009). Media richness, user trust, and perceptions of corporate social responsibility: An experimental investigation of visual web site disclosures. *Accounting, Auditing & Accountability Journal*, **22**(6), 933–952.

Cobbin, P., Dean, G., Esslemont, C., Ferguson, P., Keneley, M., Potter, B., & West, B. (2013). Enhancing the Accessibility of Accounting and Business Archives: The Role of Technology in Informing Research in Accounting and Business. *Abacus*, **49**(3), 396–422.

Collins, M., & Bloom, R. (1991). The Role of Oral History in Accounting. *Accounting, Auditing & Accountability Journal*, **4**(4).

Eynon, R, J Fry, and R Schroeder (2008), The Ethics of Internet Research, in *Sage Internet Research Methods*, ed. P Hughes, London: Sage, 279-304.

Eysenbach, G and JE Till (2001), "Ethical Issues in Qualitative Research on Internet Communities," *BMJ*, 323 (7321), 1103–05.

Fleischman, R. K., & Tyson, T. N. (2003). Archival research methodology. In *Doing Accounting History: Contributions to the Development of Accounting Thought* (Vol. 6, pp. 31–47). Oxford: Elsevier.

Gallhofer, S., & Haslam, J. (1996). Accounting/art and the emancipatory project: some reflections. *Accounting, Auditing & Accountability Journal*, **9**(5), 23–44.

Goffman, E. (1959). The presentation of self in everyday life. Doubleday Anchor Books, New York.

Hammond, T., & Sikka, P. (1996). Radicalizing accounting history: the potential of oral history. *Accounting, Auditing & Accountability Journal*, **9**(3), 79–97.

Illingworth, N (2001), The internet Matters: Exploring the use of the internet as a research tool, *Sociological Research Online*, **6** (2).

Illingworth, N (2006), Content, context, reflexivity and the qualitative research encounter: Telling stories in the virtual realm, *Sociological Research Online*, **11** (1).

Haynes, K. (2010). Other lives in accounting: Critical reflections on oral history methodology in action. *Critical Perspectives on Accounting*, **21**(3), 221–231.

Kaplan, AM and M Haenlein (2010), Users of the World unite! The challenges and opportunities of social media, *Business Horizons*, **53** (1), 59-68.

Kraut, R, J Olson, M Banaji, A Bruckman, J Cohen, and M Couper (2004), Psychological research online: Report of Board of Scientific Affairs' Advisory Group on the conduct of research on the internet, *American Psychologist*, **59**(2), 105-17.

Li, Y.M. & Shiu, Y.L. (2012). A diffusion mechanism for social advertising over micro-blogs. *Decision Support Systems*, **54** (1), 9–22.

Llewellyn, S. (2007), Case studies and differentiated realities. *Qualitative Research in Accounting & Management*, **4** (1), 53-68.

Lovejoy, K., Waters, R. D., & Saxton, G. D. (2012). Engaging stakeholders through Twitter: How nonprofit organizations are getting more out of 140 characters or less. *Public Relations Review*, **38**(2), 313–318.

Lummis, T. (1988). *Listening to History: The Authenticity of Oral Evidence*. Totowa, N.J: Barnes & Noble Books-Imports, Div of Rowman & Littlefield Pubs., Inc.

MacKenzie, K., Buckby, S., & Irvine, H. (2013). Business research in virtual worlds: possibilities and praticalities. *Accounting, Auditing & Accountability Journal*, **26**(3), 352–373.

Mann, C and F Stewart (2000), *Internet Communication and Qualitative Research: A Handbook for Researching Online*, London: Sage.

Minocha, S., Tran, M.Q. and Reeves, A.J. (2010), Conducting empirical research in virtual worlds: experiences from two projects in Second Life. *Journal of Virtual Worlds Research*, **3** (1), 1-21.

Oldroyd, D. (1995) The role of accounting in public expenditure and monetary policy in the first century A.D. Roman Empire, *Accounting Historians Journal*, 22(2): 117–29.

Oxford English Dictionary (2002). *Oxford English Reference Dictionary* (Revised 2nd edition). Oxford, England.

Parker, L.D., (2009). Photo-elicitation: an ethno-historical accounting and management research prospect. *Accounting, Auditing & Accountability Journal*, **22**(7), 1111–1129.

Ritchie, D. A. (2002). *Doing Oral History* (3 edition). Oxford University Press.

Schlenker, B.R. (1980), *Impression Management: The Self-concept, Social Identity, and Interpersonal Relations*, Brooks/Cole Publishing Company, Monterey, CA.

Schnierderjans, D., Cao, E. S., & Schniederjans, M., (2013) Enhancing financial performance with social media: An impression management perspective. *Decision Support Systems*, **55** (4), 87–97.

Schultz, F., Utz, S., & Goritz, A. (2011). "Is the medium the message? Perceptions of and reactions to crisis communication via twitter, blogs and traditional media," *Public Relations Review*, **37** (1), 20-27.

Short, J., Williams, E., & Christie, B. (1976). *The Social Psychology of Telecommunications*. Hoboken, NJ: John Wiley & Sons, Ltd.

Smith, D., & Jacobs, K. (2011). Breaking up the sky: The characterisation of accounting and accountants in popular music. *Accounting, Auditing & Accountability Journal*, **24**(7), 904–931.

Sprenger, T. O., Sandner, P. G., Tumasjan, A., & Welpe, I. M. (2014). "News or Noise? Using Twitter to Identify and Understand Company-specific News Flow, *Journal of Business Finance and Accounting*, **41** (7), 791-830.

Thompson, P. (2000). *Voice of the Past: Oral History* (3 edition). Oxford England ; New York: OUP Oxford.

Unerman, J., & Bennett, M. (2004). "Increased stakeholder dialogue and the internet: Towards greater corporate accountability or reinforcing capitalist hegemony?," *Accounting, Organizations and Society*, **29** (7), 685-707.

Vollmers, G. L. (2009). Accounting and Control in the Persepolis Fortification Tablets. *Accounting Historians Journal*, **36**(2), 93–111.

Walker, S. P. (2004). The genesis of professional organisation in English accountancy. *Accounting, Organizations and Society*, **29**(2), 127–156.

Walker, S. P. (2015). Accounting and Preserving the American Way of Life. *Contemporary Accounting Research*, 32 (4), 1676-1713.

Wasserman, S. & Faust, K. (1994), *Social Network Analysis: Methods and Applications*. Cambridge University Press.

Waters, R. D., & Jamal, J. Y. (2011). Tweet, tweet, tweet: A content analysis

of non-profit organizations' Twitter updates, *Public Relations Review*, **37** (3), 321-324.

West, B. P. (2001). On the social history of accounting: The Bank Audit by Bruce Marshall. *Accounting History*, **6**(1), 11–30.

Yow, V. R. (2005). *Recording Oral History: A Guide for the Humanities and Social Sciences* (3rd Revised edition edition). Lanham: AltaMira Press, U.S.

Zhang, X., Fuehres, H. & Gloor, P. A. (2011). Predicting stock market indicators through Twitter "I hope it is not as bad as I fear", *Social and Behavioral Sciences*, **26**, 55-62.

7 Methods and Techniques for Qualitative Data Gathering

Bridget Ogharanduku, Darren Jubb, Sean Lochrie, Ross Curran and Kevin O'Gorman

Qualitative data gathering techniques are widely used in accounting and finance research. You may recall from Chapter 4, where qualitative techniques are identified in the Methods Map. The use of qualitative techniques could potentially yield valuable, revelatory and rich data. They offer flexibility, and depending on the nature of the research project, can be used alone or in combination with other techniques. This chapter discusses some common approaches to qualitative research methods (see the 'Techniques' section of the Methods Map) and the issues that must be considered with their application.

Interviews

Interviews are one of the most common qualitative data gathering methods in social research. They are also used in accounting and finance research. For example, Kamla (2012) used semi-structured face-to-face interviews to develop an understanding of the attitudes and experiences of Syrian women accountants within a context of globalisation. Interviews involve a deliberate and focused conversation between the researcher and subjects with the aim of developing an understanding of the central themes and questions of the research. This is discussed in three stages: pre-interview, interview and post-interview.

■ Pre-interview considerations: Design and access

It is important to set realistic and achievable objectives when formulating your research ideas (See Chapter 2). This also applies when considering your approach in interviews. Most importantly, you must trust your instincts to guide you. Remember that an interview is simply a conversation between two people, which you should already be familiar with and have the basic skills to ensure a successful outcome.

	Strengths	Weaknesses	Applicability
Unstructured	Provides rich information. Explores previously unknown themes that may arise from the interview. Creates relationships which may lead to more information. Uses informal language.	Time-consuming. Resource intensive. Lacking in generalizability. Can generate a vast, often irrelevant data. Susceptible to interviewer bias.	Exploratory research investigating past events when subjective views and experiences are sought. In conjunction with other research methods.
Semi-Structured	Questions prepared in advance to cover critical points, useful when the researcher is inexperienced. Interviewees still retain freedom and flexibility to express their own views. Increased reliability and scope for comparability. Interviewee is able to respond informally.	Time-consuming. Resource intensive. Needs good interview skills to keep on topic. Interview questions are open to researcher bias. May lack generalizability.	Multiple interviewers. Only one chance to conduct the interview. Researcher has some knowledge of the topic. In conjunction with other research methods.
Structured	Can produce consistent generalizable data. Minimal risk of bias. Large sample size. Less time required. Sophisticated interviewing skills not required.	Little opportunity for feedback. Question responses are limited and restrictive. Little scope to cater for the unforeseen. Real-time changes to the interviews cannot be made.	Clear focus and a question to be answered. High level of knowledge on a topic to allow for appropriate question formulation. A well-developed literature.

Table 7.1: Strengths, weaknesses and applications of interview approaches

There are three different approaches to interviews – unstructured (open-ended), structured and semi-structured. The semi-structured interview lies between the structured and unstructured. Adopting the most appropriate type determines the success of any research project. Your choice depends on the nature of your research project, the characteristics of your participants, and the time and resources available for the research. For example, an unstructured interview may prove ineffective in a resource-constrained and narrowly focused research project. Likewise, in some exploratory studies, structured interviews are unlikely to capture the depth of understanding required for such studies. Moreover, it may be difficult to get approval to conduct unstructured in-depth interviews with auditors who have been involved in investigating or detecting fraud within an organisation. It may also not be the best use of time to ask prescriptive structured questions from the chief executive of a global company if you get the opportunity to speak to one. Table 7.1 illustrates some characteristics of these approaches and suggests suitable applications.

Another challenge is to determine the best approach to conduct the interview. Some approaches include: video, telephone or face-to-face interviews. Unstructured interviews could provoke more information in a face-to-face format, while telephone-based formats may be more suitable for structured interviews when a larger sample is required to strengthen validity, and it is not feasible to meet each respondent face-to-face. Ultimately, the most efficient way should be selected bearing in mind available resources, appropriateness to the context, and the added value of a two-way interaction to the research.

Access to appropriate participants is crucial and must be realistic and achievable within the time frame of any project. Interviewers should brief gatekeepers and participants on the purpose of the project, as the initial exchanges can affect the rest of the interview. The briefing may include:

- What the data will be used for.

- Reassurances of confidentiality.

- How data will be recorded.

- Length of the proposed interviews.

- How many interviews the participant is willing to undertake.

- Reassurance of the researcher's role.

■ The interview

Importantly the interviewer should be able to listen, prompt appropriately, and interact with the interviewee effectively. Good interviewers are friendly, fostering trust and rapport with the interviewee. It is easier to obtain valuable data from an interviewee who is relaxed and enjoying the process than from one who is nervous and suspicious. Table 7.2 illustrates stages of interview techniques that can enhance the quality of the interview.

Activity	Description	Benefits
Pilot study	Ensures the study is designed correctly, but do not contribute towards data. Should resemble the actual study closely.	Improves the robustness of the study. Allows early remediation of project design flaws. Settles the researcher into a routine and process they can execute confidently.
Selecting the setting	Where the interview takes place influences the interview itself.	The interviewee may find hosting the interview more convenient, a neutral setting may prompt more data, some settings may jeopardise interviewee anonymity.
The interview guide	A pre-prepared set of topics/questions, produced with the aim of providing a form of direction for interviews. Lines of enquiry should correspond to the critical themes underpinning the study.	Aides the researcher, helping to ensure coverage of pertinent themes. Briefs the interviewee (but should not lead them).
Recording	Discretely, but with permission, record interviews for later transcribing and analysis, improving accuracy.	Can review the interview innumerable times. Records with minimal intrusion.
Non-verbal communication	Interviews include the verbal conversation, and a range of body language. Hand gestures, eye movements and head movements can all add meaning to an interviewee's words. Note taking can record these.	Interviewee body language is an important part of the data, confirming, contradicting or emphasising what the participant is saying.
Funnelling	When the interviewer begins with open, general questions but gradually, as rapport develops, focuses on more specific points.	Builds rapport. Useful when asking more sensitive questions.
Gaining a follow-up	Arranging follow-up interviews is more likely during an interview. The researcher should grasp this opportunity if it arises.	Can verify findings through further discussion with the interviewee.

Table 7.2: Interview technique

Interviewers should be aware of the implications of cultural factors particularly those undertaking cross-cultural research or those researching unfamiliar cultures. Prior knowledge of participant's culture is vital to minimise the impact of cultural factors on participants, the interview process and the data collected. Further, interviewers should be courteous and appreciative of the time being given to them.

In addition, Alvesson (2003 p. 18) emphasises that an interview is indeed "...a complex social situation". Figure 7.1 presents eight issues interviewers should be aware of.

Interview issues

1   The social problem of coping with an inter-personal relationship and complex interaction in a non-routine situation

2   The cognitive problem of finding out what it is all about (beyond the level of the espoused)

3   The identity problem of adopting a contextually relevant self-position

4   The institutional problem of adapting to normative pressure and cognitive uncertainty through mimicking a standard form of expression

5   The problem (or option) of maintaining and increasing self-esteem that emerges in any situation involving examination and calling for performance

6   The motivation problem of developing an interest or rationale for active participation in the interview

7   The representation / construction problem of how to account for complex phenomena through language

8   The autonomy / determinism problem of powerful macro-discourse(s) operating behind and on the interviewee

Figure 7.1: Interview Issues (Alvesson 2003, p. 18)

■ Post-interview

This is where the researcher disengages from the field. It may be appropriate to send appreciation messages to participants. Where agreements were made to share the results of the research, fulfilment of these is advisable, both from an ethical viewpoint, and if follow-up data is required, access is more likely to be granted by the participant. It is important to transcribe recordings of interviews and organise them as soon as possible while the interviews are still fresh in mind in order not to lose any vital unspoken information.

Focus groups

Focus groups may be defined as a discussion or interview between one researcher and several participants at once. They consist of small groups of individuals who convene to communicate their opinions concerning a specific topic defined by the researcher. Focus groups are similar to individual interviews. They facilitate a detailed investigation of the observations and experiences of participants regarding a specific theme(s). However, a significant difference is that data is generated from the interaction between participants, which is managed and guided by a moderator (usually the researcher). Table 7.3 summarises the key features of a focus group.

Feature	Purpose
Deliberation	Allows for individuals with comparable experiences to come together to discuss those experiences.
Flexibility	Individuals have the opportunity to highlight issues important to them. The researcher can therefore explore ways in which people concur or diverge in relation to particular issues and the reason for this.
Emotions	Focus groups allow for an extensive understanding of the way people feel.
Moderation	Themes which may be undetected in structured individual interviews can be identified because the moderator has less control.
Freedom	Sometimes people are reluctant to discuss things on an individual basis but may feel more relaxed discussing them in a group if it becomes apparent that these ideas/sentiments are shared by the other participants. This may generate more valuable data for the study.
Challenge	Individual opinions can be queried and challenged by others. Through this process people's views can either be confirmed or amended.
Interactive	Interaction between respondents will enhance the prospect of the views expressed being accurate, and therefore, more reliable. This is because of the belief that the focus group environment means individuals are compelled to deliberate their accounts and consider their views against the experiences and beliefs of others.
Duration	Focus groups usually last from one to three hours.

Table 7.3: Key features of focus groups

■   When are focus groups applicable?

Focus groups may be used to explore under-researched issues, to investigate the origins of people's understanding of a subject; to broaden knowledge of a phenomenon unfamiliar to the researcher but familiar to the respondents, and to encourage people to converse on their understanding of an issue and expand their opinions on it. For example, Mladenovic (2000) used focus group discussions and questionnaires to explore how adopting aligned teaching environments for introductory courses in accounting could change students' negative perceptions about the accounting profession. This approach facilitated a deeper understanding of why just changing only the teaching method provided limited success in changing students' negative perception in previous studies.

Focus groups can be used alone or in conjunction with other approaches. For example, they can be used at the initial stage of a research project to gather data into an under-researched phenomenon. This data can then be used to develop a survey or interview framework for further data collection. Moreover, focus groups can be undertaken to confirm or gain reaction from findings which have been developed through the use of other techniques such as interviews, observations, and surveys.

■ Focus group process

There are several factors to consider before undertaking a focus group discussion to ensure it is viable and effective. Planning and recruiting are the first two stages before the actual focus group. In Table 7.4 the key elements of the planning and recruiting stages are summarised.

Aspect	Explanation
Planning	
Define purpose of focus groups	The research objectives must be identified. From these the moderator can identify from whom the information needs to be collected, and devise themes that can be used to direct the discussion and highlight key areas which need to be encompassed.
Develop a focus group guide	This is an outline which identifies the issues and themes that are to be explored. The guide is constructed in order to enlighten the overall research objectives and to ensure that the focus group discussions correlate with these goals. Similar to an interview guide, this ensures the discussions are useful without being led by the researcher's agenda.
Location	The location should be somewhere where the participants feel comfortable and preferably one they are familiar with. This can improve attendance and will limit distractions. The location should be accessible and where people can easily see and hear each other.
Transcription	The researcher must plan how to record the focus group. A recording device can be used to capture spoken words. There are instances when the interaction is recorded by video camera. Regardless of approach, prior consent must be obtained.

Recruiting	
How many groups?	This will depend on the nature of the research, the variation of people that need to be in involved, time restraints, and cost limitations.
Selection criteria for participants	Focus groups follow a purposive sampling strategy. As the aim is to obtain an in-depth understanding of a specific population, random sampling is unsuitable. Selection criteria must be well defined. This may relate to: age, organisational department, demographics, gender, or particular experiences.
Dynamics of the group	Groups need to be balanced so that members have a level of commonality so that the interactions will be meaningful, but sufficiently varied so they don't exactly have similar beliefs. Difficulties may occur if groups contain people from differing levels of an organisation. This can lead to views being inhibited and habitual roles emerging.
Size of groups	Groups consist of between six and ten people. More than ten can lead to difficulties in controlling the conversation, lack of substance, and individuals not contributing.
Accessing participants	Obtaining participants can be accomplished through: sampling from existing lists, advertising, snowball sampling, and gaining access and aid through organisational gatekeepers.
Inviting Participants	Possible members should be contacted and informed of the purpose of the research, the time and location of the meeting, the technique that will be used to record the discussion, and the topic of the debate.

Table 7.4: Features of the focus group planning and recruiting stages

Planning and recruiting are fundamental elements of the focus group method. Failure to do these with care can result in the process being ineffective and the data collected being poor and unrewarding.

Conducting the focus group

This may be divided into several stages: introduction, ice-breaker, initial questions, important questions, closing questions – Table 7.5 highlights these. The discussion should be driven by the focus group guide to ensure relevant information for the study is generated. However, it should not unduly constrain participants. This can uncover issues and enlighten the research through the moderator encouraging participants to raise subjects of their experiences, providing lucidity and intensity into the discussion.

Phase	Description
Introduction	It is important to create an environment which allows people to feel comfortable to talk in.
	The researcher should introduce themselves, summarise the research project, what will be done with the collected data, and confirm confidentiality.
	Ground rules may also be discussed, for example; everyone should have the opportunity to speak, and all remarks should be directed to the collective.
Ice-breaker	Participants should be given the opportunity to introduce themselves.
	When possible, allocate name badges to the group, this will allow the moderator to follow the discussion and ensure that participants can be asked questions if they are struggling to interact.
Initial questions	The research topic should be introduced in more depth.
	The group should be asked to deliberate the subject in order to clarify any difficulties and any differences in the understating of key issues.
Important questions	This is where the main debate will commence. Participants will discuss the important themes that are central to the research.
	Commonly, the moderator will probe to develop specific areas of interaction in order to gain a more in-depth understanding of issues raised or use discussion aids to instigate debate.
	It may be valuable to record physical behaviours throughout the focus group.
	There should be a constrained number of questions/themes to be addressed – usually, between two and six. Any more than this and the ability to gain an extensive insight may be diminished.
Closing questions	This is how the focus group is brought to an end.
	The closing question should give the participants the opportunity to have a final remark – this could entail them either stating something they feel has not been fully covered or stating a concluding opinion.
	The moderator can also use the closing stage to reconfirm areas of uncertainty or ask for clarification from members as to the accuracy of their interpretation on a specific matter.

Table 7.5: Phases in conducting the focus group

The moderator's role is vital within the process. They are responsible for asking questions to encourage discussions within the group. They will also try to ensure that the discussion is significant and within the parameters of the research, but without constraining the views of the participant; will use discussion aids and probes to help gain a deep understanding of the issues to be discussed or need further debate; attempt to involve all group members; and when relevant, investigate beyond facts to the feelings of participants. Moderators will also bring discussion points to close when the dialogue is going off course. Such facilitation is important to ensure that the discussion focuses on both the research interests and the relevant aspects that participants regard as important.

Dealing with challenges

Several challenges may be encountered when conducting focus groups. These challenges are highlighted in Table 7.6 with possible solutions to them.

Challenge	Solution
A small number of people are dominating the discussion	The moderator can intervene by confronting the dominant individuals. This should be done in a friendly and constructive manner to ensure that their involvement is not lost. Recognise their opinions and then ask others for their views.
The discussion is at an impasse	Intervention by the moderator can be used to either summarise the key points of the issue discussed, giving participants the opportunity to readdress specific points; or there is an agreement to focus on the next question/theme. By giving participants a choice, they feel involved.
Inactive participants	The moderator can ask the individual for their views, or can remind the group of his/her gratitude that several and contrasting views are being projected. By stating this to the group the moderator is not isolating anyone and is fostering a comfortable environment for all the participants. Through this participants can decide for themselves if they are comfortable to speak.
Multiple conversations at once	Intervention by the moderator can be used to allow a more manageable approach to resume. For example, remarking on everyone's enthusiasm on the issue but recommending that a more systematic way of expressing their views in turn would be beneficial.
Quiet groups	Participants may be asked to divide into smaller groups to discuss specific issues then asked to report back.

Table 7.6: Focus group challenges and solutions

Limitations of focus groups

Despite its usefulness in gathering qualitative data, the focus group approach has some limitations that should be considered when using it.

■ First, it could be really difficult to organise. Recruiting participants is a lengthy process and sometimes require persuasion through inducement or incentives.

■ Second, since it involves multiple viewpoints interacting simultaneously, transcribing the recordings could be complex and time consuming.

■ Third, focus groups tend to accumulate large amounts of information which can be difficult to organise and manage.

■ Fourth, unlike an interview, there is less control in focus groups. It is easy for the discussions to diverge into areas that are not relevant to the research, and constant interventions to re-direct the discussion may harm the quality of the information gathered.

■ Finally, some people are negatively influenced by the dynamics of the group. For example, a focus group of various members of an organisation may be influenced by position, gender or social standing.

Regardless of these limitations, the application of focus groups within research offers a rewarding avenue from which to collect rich multiple-perspective data which has the ability to illuminate any research project.

Ethnography and observational research

While interviews and focus groups are useful tools for understanding complex phenomena, a more immersive technique for conducting qualitative research in accounting and finance has also been used: a technique known as ethnography.

What is ethnographic research?

Let us begin by considering how one would begin to define ethnography. As Punch (2005, p.124) asserts,

> the term 'ethnography' itself comes from cultural anthropology. 'Ethno' means people or folk, while 'graphy' refers to describing something. Thus ethnography means describing a culture and understanding a way of life from the point of view of its participants: ethnography is the art and science of describing a group or culture.

Ethnography is therefore where, in your role as researcher, you attempt to describe and explain the shared patterns, values, and beliefs of a culture-sharing group. It is a form of research that involves the researcher participating in the everyday lives of people for an extended period of time. During this period the researcher watches what happens, listens to what is being said, and collects whatever data is available in order to provide evidence directly related to the issues that are the focus of the research project. The researcher is therefore viewing the phenomena under study from the point of view of the participants for a prolonged period of time. For example, McMillan, O'Gorman & MacLaren (2011) spent a three-month period in Nepal undertaking participant observations, allowing them to demonstrate how commercial hospitality has catalysed sustainable social change through empowering women.

Within the field of accounting and finance, recent methodological developments have resulted in the uptake of a number of interdisciplinary and sociologically motivated qualitative research methods. Since Dent's (1991) study of the organisational culture of Euro Rail, ethnography has emerged as a useful tool in understanding accounting operations within its institutional and organisational context (Dey, 2002). As such, the ethnographic approach to gathering data is now widely used within accounting literature (see, for example, Chua, 1995; Dey, 2000; Ahrens and Mollona, 2007) whilst ethnographic themes continue to inform the case study approach to conducting research, with a number of different ethnographic strategies being employed. With that in mind, Cunliffe (2010) describes three main forms of ethnographic research that can be employed in a research study:

- **Realist ethnography**: the realist ethnographer is concerned with factual reporting, objectivity and identifying true meanings. The observation is based on data or facts about practices and customs, structures or processes, routines and norms. An example would be the use of edited quotations without personal bias or seeking to act as an agent for change. The research report is your representation of what you have observed or heard.

- **Interpretive ethnography**: places great emphasis on subjective impressions and the likelihood of multiple meanings rather than the objectivity of identifying a single, true meaning. Those being observed are treated as participants rather than subjects. The final written account reflects the participation of both the ethnographer and those being observed through devices such as dialogue and quotations, personalisation and contextualisation.

- **Critical ethnography**: is aimed at exploring and explaining the repercussion of power and authority on those who are subject to these influences or are marginalised by them. A researcher may adopt an advocacy role to bring about changes within organisation or work group regarding problematic issues like governance, regulation, decision-making procedures and so forth.

The approach employed in your research project will depend upon the wider methodology and philosophical orientation that you are adopting as a researcher, as well as the purpose and nature of the projects you are conducting.

■ Planning ethnographic research

Ethnographic research requires a great deal of time and resources to be conducted successfully. Executed correctly within an appropriate project, however, ethnographic research can generate deep and rich insights into a social phenomenon. The required investment of time and close interactions with the subjects requires a high level of researcher commitment and the appropriate people skills. It is therefore important that the ethnographic research process is well planned from start to finish. When considering the use of ethnographic research methods for carrying out a research project the following issues should be given consideration at the planning stage.

- First, you should consult previous research and consider the problem that motivates your research, and whether the ethnographic approach is the most appropriate. Ethnographic research is useful if the problem requiring investigation involves describing and analysing the beliefs, interactions and behaviours of a particular cultural group.

- You must then consider the group that you wish to study. For undergraduate research projects, ethnographic data is often collected during part-time work or summer internships, which is a useful means of gaining access to organisations. When thinking about entering the field, remember that you will be immersed in the group under study. It is important to respect the daily lives of the participants under observation and be sensitive to their routines, especially if you are not a full participating member of the social situation (see below).

- Once in the field, data is gathered primarily through participant-observation and informal interviews and/or focus groups, supplemented by artefacts and literary sources. In these instances, keeping detailed field notes is critical. Further information on data collection is given below.

- Once collected the data will be interpreted, by identifying themes within the data; verified, through follow up interviews or triangulation techniques; and then disseminated, in the form of a report or research paper, which constructs a description of the cultural group taking into account the views of both the participants and the researcher.

Entering the field

With the parameters of your project determined, attention must then turn to issues surrounding entering the field. Giving consideration to your conduct when in the field is especially important with regards to ethnographic research, as you will be present within the group of participants for an extended period of time. Table 7.7 below highlights the three main stages to be considered when you are thinking about collecting ethnographic data, namely preparing to enter the field, being present in the field, and exiting the field.

In the field: The role of the researcher

Once in the field the next consideration is the role that you are going to take as researcher. This is based on the degree of participation you intend to have in relation to the members of the social situation that you are studying. There are five main roles that you can play as an ethnographer in the field: full member, participating observer, partially participating observer, minimally participating observer and non-participating observer.

Issue	Description
Preparation	
Access	Access must be negotiated and agreed with participants in the setting under study. The extent to which your role as researcher, either overt or covert (see below) must also be distinguished.
Knowledge	Thoroughly researching the research setting ensures familiarity with the context to be observed and allows for appropriate data to be collected. Typically this will extend to understanding the processes and behaviours required during the study.
Ethics	Informed consent should be obtained from the participants and ethical approval gained from the relevant organisations, including the university.
Data collection aims and objectives	Giving serious thought to the aims and objectives of the data collection procedure allows for a more structured approach when documenting observations in the field and ensures that as much relevant data are gathered as possible.
Observation guide	This is an important tool to remind and aid you in gathering information relating to specific themes. Should not excessively constrain the researcher by confining them to specific areas of interest. Be aware of other observations beyond the guide.
Working in the field	
Conduct	When conducting participant observations (see below) you should build affiliations with members to create trust and co-operation. As a researcher you must maintain a positive and non-intimidating self-image. This can be achieved through concise and honest self-introductions. Some amount of preparation may be required to familiarise yourself with the norms of the context in order to understand specific conventions.
Recording data	Recording data during the process can be difficult due to the persistent flows of information that could be recorded. Detailed note taking should follow pure observations. The observation guide will help in determining what to record but care should be taken when recording unstructured observations.
Arising problems	How you respond to arising problems can have implications for the project as a whole. Common challenges include: difficult individuals or groups; personal disputes; and discovering dishonesties. Tensions or unnecessary unease should not be created. Respond similarly to the expectations of the environment.
Data analysis	Typically occurs throughout the process and is rarely left to the final stages.
Departing	
When to leave	Practical necessities: time restraints require the researcher to leave the field or funds have run out or theoretical saturation has been realised. In other words, no new insights are being gained. It may also be the case that a pre-agreed period has come to an end.

Table 7.7: Entering the field

- As a **full member** you actively participate in the situation under study. Often this form of membership of the group can take the form of being a paid employee of the group, such as if you are undertaking a summer internship. This allows you to get close to the participants but carries the risk that you will begin to lose the sense of being a researcher and begin to think in terms of being an employee.

- If you take up a role as **participating observer** you are involved in the core activities of the group but you are not considered to be a full member. Often you are either employed in the setting or are, at the very least, a constant presence.

- Being a **partially participating observer** is similar to being a participating observer in that you take part in the core activities of the group but observation may or may not be the primary source of data. Often this approach is supplemented or replaced with interviews and other documentation.

- When you take up a role as a **minimally participating observer** you have less involvement in the core activities of the group. Observation may or may not be the main source of data collection and again the use of interviews and other documentation may supplement or replace observation.

- If you plan to observe the group under study from a distance, you will be considered a **non-participating observer**. In this instance observation is carried out without any direct involvement in the activities of the group under study. Interaction with participants is normally restricted to formal interviews.

■ Data collection

Observation

In carrying out ethnographic research your main data gathering technique is the observation of participants. Observation involves the monitoring and recording of naturally occurring activities and/or events within the cultural group under study. By observing situations as they occur over a set period of time you can obtain a deeper understanding of the intricate behaviours of the participants under investigations. Of interest when observing participants is how people interact and work together, and how relationships are formed and maintained.

Overt or covert observation

As mentioned in Table 7.7, the first step in the process of gathering ethnographic data is gaining access to the field. Successfully negotiating access can be one of the most difficult steps in the process. When considering the best approach for negotiating access to a setting, it is important to consider the two methods of collecting observational data: overt observation or covert observation, as these will impact on your ability to gain access to the research site.

■ With regards to **overt observation** the fact that you are joining the everyday lives of the participants for the purposes of conducting research is disclosed up front. In this instance you must therefore negotiate access to the field and explain why you want to immerse yourself in the lives of the participants. This is the most common method of participant observation applied within accounting and finance research. One issue to note here is that not everybody within a field setting may be aware that you are a researcher, even if you have negotiated overt access to the field and therefore care should be taken.

■ **Covert observation**, on the other hand, involves not disclosing the fact that you are a researcher carrying out a research project. This will help with the difficulty in gaining access to the field but carries with it a number of ethical issues such as those discussed in Chapter 11.

Structured or unstructured observation

When actively collecting data in the field, observations can also be structured or unstructured.

■ An **unstructured observation** occurs where you view and document anything you feel is meaningful or important to the study. A higher level of concentration and effort is required here as well as an increase in the amount of field notation that will be required.

■ On the other hand, **structured observation** necessitates less inclusive data collection as you only seek to document the occurrences that are of specific relevance to the research subject that you planned to explore. However, the structure must be derived from somewhere. Typically, this may be created through engagement with the literature concerning a specific topic or theoretical lens, and/or from previous frameworks used by past researchers. Structured observations are therefore collected with reference to a pre-prepared plan of framework.

In situations where there is a lack of information to create an effective structure a pilot study taking advantage of unstructured observations may help generate themes or issues to be used to devise a framework for a future, more structured study.

Field notes

Ethnographies are often conducted over a long period of time and produce a vast amount of data so the ethnographer's ability to record data through research notes is vital. Without effective field notes, pertinent data is forgotten or open to misinterpretation at a later date. Field notes should be organised, detailed and complete, to allow for effective analysis, and include the following elements. Brief notes should be written as an event unfolds, and filled-out fully shortly after. Full descriptions of everything that occurs should be written at least at the end of the day and include as many details as possible. Make sure that the notes taken are detailed but also clear so they are understandable when you return to them at a later date. Initial analytical thoughts that are relevant to the guiding research question, allowing identification of, and refinement of the project around the emerging theme is recommended. Reflection from the ethnographer's perspective, which can offer useful insights, should be included where possible.

An extension of taking field notes is the use of diaries. This can provide useful additional insights into the lives of the participants under study by allowing for the recording of more intimate, personally held views of participants, as they occur in their natural settings. By way of an example, Coulson, MacLaren, McKenzie and O'Gorman (2014) use diary inserts from soldiers serving in Afghanistan to explore Pashtunwali and tourism in the country.

In summary: The value of ethnographic research

As we have seen from the discussion above, ethnographic research involves a number of identifying features as well as diverse data collection techniques, which result in this approach offering a number of strengths and difficulties as summarised in the table below. Please note that this table contains only a few of the factors to consider and as such it should not be considered exhaustive.

Strengths	Difficulties
Rich and detailed data can be gathered due to the immersive nature of the research.	The immersive nature of the research can lead to observer bias becoming problematic.
The study takes place in natural settings rather than in created research settings.	There is the prospect that the researcher may misinterpret what they witness.
Can be used as a starting point to create themes to inform a more structured data collection process. Helpful when the information about a specific topic or context is minimal.	The vast amount of information available may result in difficulties in deciding on what is most important. This is particularly relevant for non-participant observation where information overload is possible.
By capturing the everyday lives of people, behaviours can be identified which the participants were not aware of or did not wish to reveal.	The observer effect – the participants may alter their behaviours if they know they are being watched. The participants may intentionally mislead the observer.

By combining observation with other research methods, discrepancies between what participants say and what they do can be examined.	Can be time-consuming and tiring as long periods of engagement and commitment are required. High levels of concentration and focus are therefore required.
Can be used to validate evidence gathered from other techniques. For example, as part of a case study.	Bringing together all the information collected into a coherent narrative from the wide varieties of sources can be challenging.

Table 7.8: Strengths and difficulties of ethnographic research

Chapter summary

This chapter introduced some of the most common techniques used in qualitative research methods, as illustrated in the Methods Map in Chapter 4. The approaches identified in this chapter, whether it be interviews, focus groups or observation, helps the researcher understand the environment in which their study is embedded. However, qualitative approaches require careful planning as each method has limitations. Despite this, qualitative methods, if employed wisely, can gather and expose enlightening information that can render any study fruitful and worthwhile.

References and further reading

Ahrens, T., & Mollona, M. (2007). Organisational control as cultural practice—A shop floor ethnography of a Sheffield steel mill. *Accounting, Organizations and Society*, **32**(4–5), 305–331.

Alvesson, M. (2003). Beyond neopositivists, romantics, and localists: A reflexive approach to interviews in organizational research. *Academy of Management Review*, **28**(1), 13-33.

Chua, W. F. (1995). Experts, networks and inscriptions in the fabrication of accounting images: A story of the representation of three public hospitals. *Accounting, Organizations and Society*, **20**(2–3), 111–145.

Coulson, A. B., MacLaren, A. C., McKenzie, S., & O'Gorman, K. D. (2014). Hospitality codes and social exchange theory: The Pashtunwali and tourism in Afghanistan. *Tourism Management*, **45**, 134-141.

Cunliffe, A. L. (2010). Retelling tales of the field in search of organizational ethnography 20 years on. *Organizational Research Methods*, **13**(2), 224–239.

Dent, J. F. (1991). Accounting and organizational cultures: a field study of a new organisational reality. *Accounting, Organizations and Society*, **16**(8), 735–732.

Dey, C. (2000). Bookkeeping and ethnography at traidcraft plc: A review of an experiment in social accounting. *Social and Environmental Accountability Journal,* **20**(2), 16–18.

Dey, C. (2002). Methodological issues: The use of critical ethnography as an active research methodology. *Accounting, Auditing & Accountability Journal,* **15**(1), 106–121.

Kamla, R. (2012). Syrian women accountants' attitude and experiences at work in the context of globalization. *Accounting, Organizations and Society,* **37**(3), 188-205

McMillan, C. L., O'Gorman, K. D., & MacLaren, A. C. (2011). Commercial hospitality: A vehicle for the sustainable empowerment of Nepali women. *International Journal of Contemporary Hospitality Management,* **23**(2), 189-208.

Mladenovic, R. (2000). An investigation into ways of challenging introductory accounting students' negative perceptions of accounting. *Accounting Education,* **9**(2), 135-155.

Punch, K. F. (2005). *Introduction to Social Research, Second Edition: Quantitative and Qualitative Approaches* (Second edition). London ; Thousand Oaks, Ca: SAGE Publications Ltd.

7

8 Evaluating and Analysing Qualitative Data

*Bridget E Ogharanduku, Lubaina Zakaria,
Rafał Sitko and Katherine J C Sang*

The previous chapter focused on methods of gathering qualitative data. Here we will consider possible ways of analysing qualitative data. Qualitative research often generates large amount of data that is of varying quality and usefulness. The process of navigating through this vast amount of data can be overwhelming for even the most experienced researcher. Moreover, interpreting your findings can be time consuming and difficult. This chapter provides a useful guide to analysing the data. Some common approaches to analysing qualitative data are discussed. Suggestions are made where an approach is considered more appropriate for a particular research area or data. Challenges you may encounter are highlighted. However, the most important research skill required at this stage of a research is patience and effective organising skills.

Approaches to data analysis: A reflective note

As outlined in Chapter 4, the process of developing a research design starts with locating your research paradigm. The research paradigm can be divided into two categories; ontology (i.e. the way we view the world as objective or subjective) and epistemology (i.e. the way we obtain valid knowledge either more skewed towards positivist paradigm or interpretivist paradigm).

Having reflected on your research paradigm, it is equally important to consider the approaches to analysing your data. The deductive technique is typically associated with analysing quantitative data whilst inductive approach is generally use to analyse qualitative data. Generally, a research study expressing an objective ontology with a positivist epistemological approach is particularly suited to a quantitative methodology, whilst a study expressing a subjective ontology with an interpretivist approach tends to be associated with qualitative methodology.

The interpretivist approach in the field of accounting and finance is concerned with understanding and unveiling the symbolic meaning of text or talk (Prasad and Mir, 2002), and is of particular relevance to grounded theory, thematic analysis and hermeneutics approaches to qualitative data analysis. Other important inductive techniques that can be utilised within accounting and finance research include; template, narrative, textual, content and discourse analysis each of which will be discussed in the following sections. However, before moving on it is important to be clear as to what constitutes qualitative analysis.

■ What is qualitative analysis?

Qualitative analysis involves any analysis that arrives at findings or concepts that are not based on statistical methods Glaser (1992). It involves analysing qualitative data in a non-quantifiable way. However, there are instances where researchers collect qualitative data and analyse them in a quantifiable way. A good example is Abraham and Cox (2007) where content analysis was used to count the number of words within risk-related sentences and statistical analysis to determine the relationship between the quantity of narrative risk information in the company annual reports and ownership and governance structures. Similarly, there are situations where numbers are assigned to the frequency at which a word or sentence occurs in a document or transcript.

With qualitative analysis, there are no rigid guidelines to follow but it is important that the entire process is well planned and organised to ensure the data is properly analysed and the findings or concepts that emerge are reliable and valid. Some useful steps to help are highlighted below:

- Transcribe your data if applicable
- Read, re-read and generate themes and patterns (coding)
- Interpret your findings and;
- Write your report

These steps are elaborated in the sections that follow. Writing your findings and dissertation is discussed in details in Chapter 12.

Transcribing your data

Where transcript discussions have been carried out, there is a need to reproduce the recorded voice notes into texts. This may be time consuming. It is advisable to transcribe each interview as soon as possible after the interview to avoid a pile up. Organise and label each interview appropriately in order to enhance the analysis process and avoid any mix up.

Coding

Whether it is interview or focus group transcripts, field notes taken from observations or information from documents, you will be faced with a large amount of data that you need to make sense of. Reducing qualitative data into manageable 'chunks' underpins most of qualitative data analysis. Coding involves picking elements of your data which you consider to be interesting and relevant to your research. This helps to identify categories and sub-categories emerging from the data. There are two approaches to coding qualitative data – priori and posteriori.

- **Priori** requires developing codes before collecting the data. This is often drawn from the literature and underlying theoretical framework. For example, Abraham and Shrives (2014) developed codes associated with risk disclosure from theories on risk disclosure and then used these codes to collect information from the company's annual reports.

- **Posteriori** involves codes that emerge from the data itself. This is often associated with Grounded theory.

- On the other hand, **template analysis** allows for codes to be developed before or after collecting the data. An advantage with this form is that it allows the researcher to look for specific codes while also providing the flexibility to note any emerging or unforeseen codes.

Whichever approach is adopted should be influenced by the research objectives. The rest of the section explains various approaches to coding qualitative data. What is common with all approaches is a careful reading and re-reading of the text and identification of themes and tensions within the data. The most common approaches to coding are outlined in Table 8.1.

Type of code	Description
Open	Breaking up of data into chunks or parts. May require the coding of each line of data (for Grounded Theory) Identification and refinement of concepts
Selective	Identification of relationships between codes, for example, a central category (or higher-level code) and the codes related to that.
Axial	Rebuilding of data through identifying links and cross links between codes or chunks of data

Table 8.1: Examples of types of codes (adapted from Gilbert, 2008).

Once a series of codes has been developed these can be organised into a hierarchy of codes. An example of the coding of narrative disclosures in annual reports of four food processing companies listed on FTSE 100 is provide in Table 8.2. This sample is extracted from a research paper by Abraham and Shrives (2014). Their paper examines corporate risk disclosure practices. Codes are attached to sections of the annual reports which describe risks and changes in the risk disclosure practice resulting from a negative or positive event.

Text extracted from narrative section of Annual reports	Example codes
Non–compliance with legislation can lead to financial and reputational damage. The Group is aware of the importance of complying with all applicable legislation affecting its business activities and of the potential damage to reputation and financial impact which can result from any breach.	general risk disclosure unchanged over the years disclosed in the risk report
Turnover of SlimFast declined by 21% as the entire weight–loss category was hit by an unprecedented shift in consumer preferences towards low-carbohydrate products. The impact was especially pronounced in the US, the largest market for SlimFast. SlimFast has responded by focusing on the SlimFast Plan as a proven and effective weight-loss programme with an expanded range of products, including pasta and soups. Low-carbohydrate and high-protein products were also launched at the end of 2003.	specific risk disclosure not disclosed in risk report
Prices of raw materials and commodities increased significantly throughout 2006, adversely impacting margin where we were unable to pass on increased costs. To mitigate such risks, and where appropriate, we purchase forward contracts for raw materials and commodities, almost always for physical delivery. Where appropriate we also use futures contracts to hedge future price movements; however, the amounts are not material.	general risk disclosure unchanged over the years disclosed in the risk report

Table 8.2: Sample of data obtained from documents with sample codes.

In this example, a high-level code might be 'risk disclosure practices' with lower level codes being 'general risk disclosure', 'specific risk disclosure'. This ordering of codes facilitates the analysis. However, in some cases this process can be subjective. Hence, it is necessary to consider whether another researcher would identify similar patterns or codes within the data.

8

The validity and reliability of your analysis

It is important to consider the validity and reliability of your analysis as this could significantly affect the quality of your findings, conclusions and your entire research. Reliability involves the degree to which your findings are not associated to accidental actions in the research process Kirk & Miller (1986). In other words, it is the extent to which there is consistency in assigning instances to the same category by different observers or by the same observer on different occasions. Validity is concerned with considering whether your findings and conclusions are what they appear to be. There are several threats to the reliability and validity of qualitative analysis. A careful consideration of these factors would minimize their effect and ensure the quality of your research. Based on submissions by several researchers, McKinnon (1988) classified the threats to reliability and validity into four main categories:

Observer–caused effect

This is associated with the reactive effect of the presence of the researcher on the phenomenon being investigated. This occurs when participants have an opinion about the researcher such that it significantly alters their 'natural' behaviour and conversation. As such, the researcher is no longer observing a natural setting but one that is distorted by his/her presence. For example, if participants perceive that their responses could have negative consequences for them because of their opinion about the researcher, they may provide inaccurate or untrue responses. This may affect the findings and conclusions of the study. To minimize this threat, researchers may ensure the anonymity of participants and provide sufficient information about the research and its purpose to participants.

Observer bias

This is associated with the distorted effects of the researcher's selective understanding and interpretations of the phenomenon. The potential for this threat could be present in observations, casual conversations or formal interviews with participants and in the analysis of documents. Each stage of the research is carried out at the discretion of the researcher; his/her philosophical, training and cultural background may influence this. Moreover, the researcher's prior knowledge of the phenomenon may affect his/her interpretations and perception of events. Thus, different researchers may observe, record and interpret the same event in different ways depending on their orientation. The nature of this threat limits its elimination, rather the researcher has to acknowledge the presence of his/her own biases and consider ways of managing the data collection and analysis process to ensure a minimum bias.

Data access limitations

This occurs at two levels. First it is associated with the time and happenings when the researcher enters and leaves the field. For example, if the researcher enters the field when an unusual occurrence has just happened, this could affect the data and consequently the analysis and interpretations. Further, because he/she may not know what happened previously and what happens after they exit an organization then he/she may be unable to provide a historical interpretation of the phenomenon. Second, this may originate from the researcher's host. If the researcher is restricted from accessing some data or people, then the researcher may be studying or making assumptions on less than the complete phenomenon they claim to be studying.

Complexities and limitations of the human mind

This is of two types and it is quite similar to the observer-caused effect except that it is not necessarily caused by or restricted to the researcher but it is the position that the participant seeks to maintain with all others. This threat is associated with the participant providing responses to deceive or mislead the researcher, perhaps reporting events in a manner that is impressive to himself/herself. On the other hand, the participant may be honest in providing responses but their statements are affected by natural human tendencies or fallibilities such as memory loss, personal backgrounds, philosophical positions and personal bias. Just as the researcher possesses personal bias and this could affect his/her interpretations, participants equally have personal bias that could influence their responses. Hence it is important to provide opportunities for participants to both know and say what they mean.

However, the extent to which qualitative researchers wish to ensure reliability and validity of their research is debatable (Golafshani, 2003). Nevertheless, it is important that you ensure that you are measuring what you intended to measure. Moreover, it is good practice to document all that you have done and the assumptions you have made to arrive at your findings and conclusions so as to give the reader information about why and how you arrived at your findings. The work of Abraham *et al.* (2012) provides a good example of how to ensure validity and reliability within data analysis. In their study of the usefulness of risk information disclosed by listed companies from the perspective of investment analysts and preparers of company annual reports, Abraham *et al.* (2012) provides a detail account of the stages undertaken in coding interview transcripts within their research team by applying a three-step coding system to their data analysis (see Table 8.3).

8

Stage	Action
Developing posteriori codes	Ten interview transcripts were selected and each of the three researchers analysed them in detail. A list of risk information categories and information on an ideal risk report were identified in the transcripts. Each researcher coded each interview transcript independently
Joint analysis of texts	Over a series of meetings, each list items were discussed by the three principal researchers to reach an agreement on the risk disclosure requirements of investment analysts. Codes to be used were finalised. The remaining transcripts were then coded and any additional items identified in the interviews, were appended to the coding instrument.
Verification of coding instrument	The suitability of the coding instrument was verified by an expert academic on financial reporting

Table 8.3: Stages in posterior coding of interview data adapted from Abraham *et al.* (2012)

The advice set out in Table 8.3 is appropriate to a research team of at least two people. However, for student researchers, you may be working alone on your research project. A useful suggestion would be to check with your supervisors, other academics or your participants. It is also necessary that you are aware of your own influence on the data collection and analysis process (King, 2007). This can be achieved through 'reflexivity' and keeping a detailed dairy to write down your thoughts and reflections throughout the research process. Reflexivity is based on the assumption that knowledge or the creation of knowledge cannot be separated from the knower. Hence it involves being aware of your influence as the researcher on the process and outcome of the research.

■ Thematic analysis

This is widely used in social research but it is not clearly defined because it does not have an identifiable heritage and there are few guidelines to using it. Ryan and Bernard (2003); and Braun and Clarke (2006) provide an explanation of what thematic analysis is and some useful guidelines on how to conduct it. Although thematic analysis involves similar processes applicable to other qualitative methods of analysis such as identifying codes and themes, it is different in some ways. It does not build a new theory like grounded theory, neither does it use a set of codes generated before and after the data collection like template analysis. Further, it does not highlight the use or role of language as in discourse analysis nor does it focus on unearthing the symbolic meaning of communication as in hermeneutics. Simply, it is a "method for identifying, analysing, and reporting patterns (themes) within data" (Braun and Clarke 2006, p. 79). Although, this process may seem uncomplicated it is important to follow a few rules to allow the research to be compared or synthesised with similar studies. Table 8.4, outlines key steps in thematic analysis identified by Braun and Clarke (2006).

Phase	Description of the process
1. Familiarising with the data:	Data transcription (if necessary). 'Active' reading and writing down initial ideas.
2. Generating initial codes:	Coding data (posteriori) in a systematic fashion across the entire data set.
3. Searching for themes:	Re-focusing the analysis at the broader level. Forming codes into potential themes.
4. Reviewing themes:	Checking themes against the coded extracts and in relation with each other. Forming a thematic 'map' of the analysis.
5. Defining and naming themes:	Further refinement of identified themes. Locating the overall story of the analysis.
6. Producing the report:	Writing-up the analysis results with vivid extract examples and comprehensive commentary.

Table 8.4: Phases of thematic analysis adapted from Braun and Clarke (2006).

1   According to the presented framework, the analysis should start by becoming familiar with the data particularly if a third party has done the transcription. The whole content should be read severally depending on the size of the data set. Although, it may require time, it is important to create a list of initial ideas emerging from the data.

2   The second step involves organising notes from across the entire data set into codes. While some extracts may not provide any codes others could be marked with numerals. Generally, it may prove beneficial for the next stages of analysis to generate as many relevant codes as possible. It is likely that some codes will be contradictory or seemingly unfitting but these also should be noted.

3   In the third stage codes are combined into broader patterns, i.e. potential themes. Some clusters may pile up as main themes while other more specific, will form subthemes.

4   Step four concerns revising themes. At this stage themes should be checked against the coded extracts and in relation with each other. Extracts may not fit into initially proposed patterns. Themes might not have enough evidence to support them or the underlying data may be too diverse to form a single coherent category. Furthermore, two seemingly separate patterns may concern the same topic and collapse into each other. In other cases, themes may be too different and not match meaningfully. With thoroughly revised themes it should be possible to form a 'map' similar to Figure 8.1

While Table 8.2 provides an example of coding of risk disclosure activities of four FTSE 100 companies, the figure below demonstrates how the codes identified; general risk, specific risk and unchanged disclosure can be arranged in hierarchy under the theme of 'useful risk disclosure'

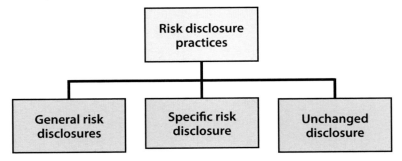

Figure 8.1: Showing the relationships between codes/themes.

5   The fifth step involves refining the themes and considering if they fit into an overall argument. The aim is to reveal any hidden relationships or interesting bits in the data. Themes have potential to expose paradoxes, differences between ostensibly similar elements and common points among very different aspects. The message the themes send should be interesting but also clear, thus their names have to be concise and catchy.

6   The final step involves writing-up the analysis. Based on identified themes the report should tell the story of the data. It is important to support the argument with examples of data extracts. However, these have to be a well embedded part of the analysis rather than an end in itself.

■ Grounded theory

Glaser and Strauss developed grounded theory in 1967 to enable researchers build theory from data rather than applying theory from the outset. This approach is very much inductive in nature. According to Elharidy *et al*. (2008), grounded theory is more popular with interpretive management accounting research because of its emphasis on deriving theory from the data, giving voice to the locals and explaining the interactions between participants in the field. It begins with empirical data; codes are then generated from these data inductively which leads to the development of theories to explain the data collected. In practice, it is not a linear process. Rather it involves moving back and forth data collection and theorisation. It involves an iterative process of developing theory by deriving assumptions from the data and then confronting these assumptions with further data leading to revised and/or new assumptions and then further data collection and so on. If you consider adopting a grounded theory approach to analysing your data, consulting Glaser and Strauss (1967) for detailed guidance is recommended. Silverman (2006, p.235) provides a simplified series of stages to a Grounded Theory approach:

- 'an initial attempt to develop categories which illuminate the data

- an attempt to 'saturate' these categories with many appropriate cases in order to demonstrate their relevance

- the development of these categories into more general analytic frameworks with the relevance outside the setting'.

The emphasis of grounded theory is on developing categories (or codes) from the data. The relevance of a category is partly dependent on the number of cases (examples, participants) attached to it. This quantification may not always be appropriate and as Silverman (2006) cautions, it may not be possible to collect or analyse qualitative data without prior knowledge of existing knowledge or theories.

An exemplar study of this approach within accounting and finance research is the work of Beattie *et al.* (2004) and their grounded theory model of auditor-client engagement. Within this study a four stage approach was applied to the interview transcripts and three types of coding applied. Several iterations were required before a stable set of concepts and categories emerged from which the analysis could be performed. It is clear from the exemplar paper that grounded theory is a time-consuming and technical process which requires a cyclical process of data collection and analysis. This may not be suitable for all qualitative research projects, particularly those with large data sets. Moreover, because of the limited time available for completing most undergraduate projects it may not be a very suitable approach.

■ Template analysis

Template analysis provides an alternative to grounded theory, particularly when the data generated is very large. A template consists of a list of codes or categories that represents the themes revealed from the data collected (Saunders *et al.*, 2009). Template analysis involves developing codes and adding these codes to units of data. These codes are analysed to identify and explore themes, patterns and relationships. With template analysis codes can be predetermined and then amended or added to as data are collected and analysed.

King (2004) sets out seven steps for undertaking template analysis as set out in Table 8.5 below.

Step	Action
Themes and codes	Identification of priori codes from the literature.
Transcription	Transcription of the data. Detailed reading of the transcriptions to ensure familiarity with the data.
Themes and codes	First round of coding the data. Identify those sections of the data, which are relevant to the research questions. Priori codes can be attached to sections of the data. At this stage, researchers can begin to identify codes emerging from the data and may need to develop entirely new codes.
Produce the initial template	The researcher can either choose to develop this following initial coding of all transcripts, or after coding a sub set. It will be necessary to provide a number of levels of codes, but not so many that the analysis becomes confusing. A hierarchy of codes may be produced during the analysis.
Develop your template	At this stage the template can be applied to the entire data set. However, there is still scope to adapt and add to the template as analysis progresses.
Interpretand write up	Data is interpreted and findings written up.
Quality checks and reflexivity	This may involve allowing another researcher check the coding or even the respondents. It is important to keep a clear diary of the steps taken during analysis and to engage in reflexivity.

Table 8.5: The seven stages of template analysis adapted from King (2007).

A benefit of template analysis is that it is more flexible as it permits the researcher to amend its use to the needs of their own research project (Saunders *et al.*, 2009). This method is used in accounting research. For example, O'Dwyer', (2003) in his study on the conceptions of corporate social responsibility by senior executives in the Irish context, developed categories/codes before conducting interviews with the senior executives and after the interviews additional categories/codes were generated inductively from the interview transcripts.

■ Narrative analysis

This is suitable for data obtained from oral history interviews and where fragmentation and condensation of the data using themes and categories could hinder an understanding of the subject under study. It involves studying a chronological series of events. Narratives could be either personal narratives of one's experience of a particular situation or life histories which describes one's personal experience over a number of years. Narrative analysis involves systematically telling and interpreting personal experiences and meanings of phenomena. This approach enables the researcher to understand and interpret how participants construct events that have either occurred in the past, present or they anticipate for the future. For example, Emery *et al.* (2002) use narrative analysis to provide an understanding of the circumstances, attitudes and feelings of women employed as professional accountants in the 1940s and 1950s in New Zealand.

Narrative analysis adopts an interpretive paradigm. Thus, analysing narratives may be influenced by the researcher's own subjectivity and interpretations. It is important to document how the narratives were analysed and the paradigm and assumptions made so that readers are aware of the basis for the conclusions. This would improve the overall validity of your research and comparability with similar studies. Findings from narrative analysis can be illustrated by using verbatim extracts from your interview transcripts however, your aim should be to interpret your findings rather than just simply describing what your participants have said. Comparing and contrasting different experiences can be interesting to readers and also illuminate an understanding of the problem you are studying. One significant feature of narrative accounts is the potential for each story to be lengthy because participants are allowed to tell their stories, hence the data may include comments, flashbacks, flash-forwards and fall asides therefore, it is important to do a systematic reduction of the data. While there are no rigid steps to follow, Reissman, (1993) suggests some guidelines (see Table 8.6).

Action	Description
Telling	Provide a facilitating context by using open-ended questions to encourage participants to provide detailed but useful narrative accounts.
Transcribing	Start with a rough transcription, a first draft of the entire interview that gets the words and other striking features of the conversation on paper (e.g. crying, laughing, and very long silence). Then go back and transcribe selected portions for detailed analysis.
Analysing	It is good to start from the structure of the narrative, how is it organized? Why does the participant develop his/her tale this way in conversation with this listener? What are the underlying propositions that make the talk sensible including those that may be taken for granted by both the speaker and listener?

Table 8.6: Guide to doing a narrative reduction adapted from Reissman, (1993, p. 54-61)

According to Reissman, (1993, p.69), "narrative analysis are quite slow and painstaking. They require attention to subtlety; nuances of speech, organisation of a response, local contexts of production, social discourses that shape what is said and what cannot be spoken". However, this method may be used in conjunction with other methods particularly when the researcher's intension is to give voice to those who have been silenced.

■ Content analysis

This method is widely used to analyse financial/accounting narratives and interview transcripts. It is a systematic, replicable technique for compressing texts into fewer content categories based on explicit rules of coding (Krippendorff, 1980; and Weber, 1990). Holsti (1969, p.14) offers a broad definition of content analysis as "any technique for making inferences by objectively and systematically identifying specified characteristics of messages". For Bowman (1984), content analysis involves the coding of words, phrases, and sentences against a particular set of schema. He suggests that this method may establish relationships, which are otherwise difficult to reveal yet, can be tested for validity.

Content analysis is widely used in accounting research to analyse risk disclosure information, social and environmental disclosure and other corporate narrative documents (Abraham and Cox 2007; Dobler *et al.*, 2011; Abraham and Shrives, 2014; Al-Tuwaijiri *et al.*, 2003; Beck *et al.*, 2010; Smith and Taffler, 2000; Brennan *et al.*, 2009). For example, Dobler *et al.*, (2011) used content analysis to analyse the management reports and financial narratives of some US, Canadian, UK and German firms to determine the quantity of corporate risk disclosure and its association with firm level risk. Priori codes were developed based on prior literature, review of regulation and pre-test analysis of sampled annual reports. In this example the unit of analysis was risk related sentences because words cannot be coded without the context of a sentence (Milne and Adler, 1999).

Berg (2004) describes two ways to approaching content analysis – manifest and latent. Manifest content analysis involves ascertaining statistical occurrence of certain elements in a given text or concept, which may result in relatively, surfaced findings that fail to acknowledge the underlying meaning of the text. Latent content analysis requires the researcher to go behind the text so that valid inferences and its underlying meaning can be ascertained. However, this may lead to an imposition of the researcher's opinion to an unacceptable extent. Similarly, Smith and Taffler (2000) suggest two approaches to content analysis – form-oriented and meaning oriented. Form-oriented involves counting the number of words, sentences or concrete references. Meaning-oriented relies on analysing underlying themes of the text under investigation. A good example of this approach can be found in Smith and Taffler (2000). They employed both form-oriented (word based) and meaning-oriented (theme based) approaches to evaluate firm financial risk in the chairman's statement of UK listed companies and explored its associations with financial distress in terms of corporate bankruptcy.

Another approach that can be considered is directed content analysis. Here the purpose is to extend or validate a theory or conceptual framework where the initial coding is based on relevant theory and research findings (Hsieh and Shannon, 2005). The researchers may then use this platform to engage with the data and consequently develop relevant themes from the data. The directed content analysis is concerned with initial coding derived from relevant theories or research findings. The prerequisite to this approach is to employ relevant prior literature and theoretical frameworks so that the initial coding can be fruitfully developed. The appropriate approach to adopt will depend on the research objectives.

■ Textual analysis

Textual analysis involves attempting to understand the likely interpretations people give to texts they use (McKee, 2003). Text in this context does not mean only written documents; it includes voice recordings, conference calls and visual images. Although textual analysis has a linguistic and communication orientation, and is common with such research, it is also used in accounting and finance research. It is used to analyse company annual reports, takeover announcements, earnings press release and merger announcements to understand the interpretations preparers and users of these reports attribute to the text and language used in the reports. This facilitates an understanding of behavioural patterns of both managers and investors and attempts an understanding or interpretation of the intentions of managers when they use certain language in the annual reports (Li, 2010).

It involves selecting and categorising words used in financial disclosure reports or narratives based on assumed meanings of the word. Usually this is obtained from dictionaries. For example, the words used in the chairman's statement could be categorised into 'optimistic' or 'pessimistic' words. Thus, any word appearing to connote positivity is categorised as optimistic while those assuming negativity are categorised as pessimistic. Such categorisation may provide an interpretation of the intensions or tone of the management, which can be compared with the financial statements to determine any correlation. Textual analysis may be done manually or with computer software packages. For example, Davis *et al.* (2012) used a textual analysis software (DICTION) to analyse the way managers directly or subtly use language in earnings press release to signal expected future performance and how such information generates a corresponding market response. The majority of researchers who use textual analysis often quantify qualitative data and use statistical software for further analysis.

8

Although this method provides a useful way for analysing the tone and sentiments in financial disclosures and announcements, its dependence on word lists developed by other disciplines often misclassifies words used in financial disclosures. English words have various meanings in different contexts, generalising the meaning and tone of a word may be misleading when the word is used in financial disclosures. This may affect the credibility of the analysis and overall findings of the research. For example, Loughran and McDonald, (2011) observed that in a sample of 10-Ks during 1998 to 2008, almost 75 percent of the words identified as negative by the widely used Harvard Dictionary are words that typically do not connote negativity in financial contexts. Hence, it is important that when categorising words used in financial disclosure texts, you ensure they have appropriate meanings in financial context.

■ Discourse analysis

Discourse and discourse analysis are termed in a variety of ways within social science literature (van Dijk, 1997a). Discourses can be defined as structured collections of meaningful texts and may take a variety of forms, including written documents, verbal reports, spoken words, pictures, symbols and other artefacts (Parker, 1992; Fairclough, 1995; Wood & Kroger, 2000). The centrality of the text provides a focal point for data collection, one that is relatively easy to access and is amenable to systematic analysis (Phillips and Hardy, 2002; van Djik, 1997b). Discourse analysis does not merely focus on individual texts but rather on bodies of texts because social reality is culminated beyond those texts per se. Discourse analysts employ an array of approaches that range from micro analyses, such as conversation analysis, linguistics, and narrative analysis, through ethnographic and ethno-methodological approaches, to the more macro study of discourse (for different categories of discourse analysis, see Alvesson and Karreman, 2000).

In this chapter, we will focus on Critical Discourse Analysis (CDA). CDA is an interdisciplinary approach to analysing written and verbal texts in which the language is viewed as a form of social practice and focuses on the way social and political power are constructed, reproduced, or challenged (Fairclough, 1995). CDA not only aims to explain society but also understanding of how discourse can maintain or challenge social inequalities and relations of power (Wooffitt, 2008; Wodak and Meyer, 2009). CDA is critical in the sense that it analyses "the way social power abuse, dominance, and inequality are enacted, reproduced and resisted by text ... in the social and political context" (van Dijk 2003, p. 253). Therefore, it provides a good fit within critical accounting research due to its concerns with notions of ideology and power, its orientation towards change and its emphasis on contextuality.

CDA particularly addresses how the linguistic features and content of texts influence and are, in turn, influenced by the contexts of text production, transmission, reception and appropriation by the wider socio-economic context. This dialectic relationship can be analysed qualitatively using a CDA's three-dimensional framework as illustrated in Figure 8.2 (Fairclough 1995, 2003). Fairclough (1995) operationalises this dialectic relationship between language and society in a framework consisting of three levels of analysis, namely (1) the text itself (micro-level), (2) the context of producing, distributing, receiving and possibly adapting texts within a discourse community (discursive practice) and (3) the dynamic socio-economic and political context in which the discourse community can be located (social practice).

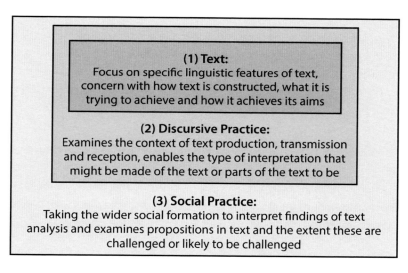

(1) Text:
Focus on specific linguistic features of text, concern with how text is constructed, what it is trying to achieve and how it achieves its aims

(2) Discursive Practice:
Examines the context of text production, transmission and reception, enables the type of interpretation that might be made of the text or parts of the text to be

(3) Social Practice:
Taking the wider social formation to interpret findings of text analysis and examines propositions in text and the extent these are challenged or likely to be challenged

Figure 8.2: A three-dimension analytical framework for CDA adapted from Fairclough (1995).

Several studies in accounting use CDA to examine legislative and corporate narrative documents (Gallhofer *et al.*, 2001; Merkl-Davies and Koller 2012; Beelitz and Merkl-Davies, 2012). For example, Beelitz and Merkl-Davies (2012) investigated the managerial discourse in CEO statements after a major incident in a German nuclear power plant. These statements were obtained from corporate narrative documents and statements made at press conferences or media interviews. The analysis revealed a shift from technocratic discourse (emphasising on facts, figures and rule compliance) to a discourse of stakeholder engagement (based on dialogue, understanding and sharing). This is to resolve conflict between organisation and its societal and political audiences. However, the results of the analysis show that changes in the discourse does not necessarily change organisational values and practices, rather it constitutes symbolic management.

CDA shares its critical realist ontology, subjective epistemology and critical stance with critical accounting research. CDA is also linked more methodologically to hermeneutics, rather than to the analytic-deductive tradition due to its emphasis on the interrelationship of text and context and its inductive approach (Wodak and Meyer, 2009). In the next section, we will explain hermeneutic approach to linking text and context through textual interpretation.

■ Hermeneutics

The Greek word *hermēneia*, meaning interpretation or understanding, encapsulated a wide range of interpretation and clarification, which covered speech, translation, and commentary. Hermeneutics has now become the theory of textual interpretation. Originally concerned with interpreting sacred texts; it has developed over time into a data analysis technique (O'Gorman, 2010). The method is dependent on the inferences made by the researcher and the meanings the researcher then attributes to elements of the text. Increasingly, hermeneutics is being adopted as a data analysis technique across social science research and is seen regularly in the core literature as an accepted and effective means of data analysis.

O'Gorman (2008) adapted and developed both the epistemological practices (Table 8.7) and the methodological principles (Table 8.8) in hermeneutical research. The first column gives the name of the epistemological practices or methodological principles whereas the second column gives a generic description of how these could be applied to any research project.

Practice	Generic description of practice
Bracketing of previous experience and turning toward lived experience	Presuppositions, biases, and any knowledge of the phenomenon obtained from personal and scholarly sources must be set aside. After data collection the researcher enters into a dialogue with the text using the understanding gathered, and drawing on their pre-understanding to interpret the phenomena.
Investigating the phenomenon	It is important to clearly define the phenomenon under investigation in order for the data collection to remain focused.
Reflecting on essential themes	Moving from data collection to data interpretation involves a process of phenomenological reflection. The first step in this is to conduct thematic analysis, which helps give a degree of order and control to the task.
Writing and rewriting	During the analysis the procedure of asking questions to the text, and listening to it, in a dialogic form is central in the writing and rewriting phase. Reflection and writing can be false dichotomies as they tend to be symbiotic tasks.

Table 8.7: Epistemological practices adapted from O'Gorman and Gillespie (2010).

Principle	Generic description of principle
Maintain a strong and oriented relation	Writing and interpretations must remain oriented to the phenomenon under investigation, thus superficialities and falsities will be avoided
Considering parts and whole	The overall interpretation is consistent with the various parts of the analysis, step back and look at the total, and how each of the parts needs to contribute towards it.

Table 8.8: Methodological principles adapted from O'Gorman and Gillespie (2010).

When the methodological principles and practices are combined they form a hermeneutic circle of interpretation, used to reflect upon, discuss and analyse data. An example of this hermeneutical process is shown in Table 8.9, taken from Prasad and Mir (2002). In this paper, the authors adopt the methodology of critical hermeneutics to analyse CEO letters to shareholders in the US petroleum industry, focusing on the country's turbulent relationship with OPEC (Organisation of Petroleum Exporting Countries). Critical hermeneutics seeks to uncover hidden and subtle meanings that serve the interest of the socially and politically powerful (Thompson, 1981). Thus, it entails not only investigating texts as formal, abstracted entities, but also analysing the socio-historical contexts in which they are embedded.

In Table 8.9, the first column shows the stages involved in hermeneutic analysis, the second column describes how that analysis took place, and finally the third column shows a summary of the results obtained from each stage of analysis.

The critical hermeneutic analysis of the CEO letters to shareholders accomplishes two methodological objectives (Prasad and Mir, 2002). First, the study completes a hermeneutic circle in the third stage of analysis, where they fuse the relationship between text (the CEO letters) and context (the legitimacy crisis faced by the oil industry). Second, the conceptual bridge of Orientalism as discussed in the fourth stage provides a coherent explanation as to how the text could be effectively used in this specific manner.

8

Stages of analysis	Description of the analysis	Summary of the results obtained from the analyses
Thematic analysis	In reading the texts to understand their manifest meaning, the paper focus on OPEC-related themes in the 64 letters to shareholders published in the annual reports of Amoco, Chevron, Exxon, Gulf, Mobil and Texaco, published between 1975 and 1986.	Two OPEC-related themes emerge from the analysis of CEO letters to shareholders: (1) The crisis image (US industry's turbulent relationship with OPEC) (2) OPEC as a dangerous national threat to the US
Laying out the context	First, the study relies on secondary sources to develop a net of contexts at the industry level and at the broader socio-historical level. Second, the narrative of contextual issues along temporal (1970s and 1980s) and thematic dimensions are developed. Secondary sources examined include: (1) industry reports, (2) trade journals, (3) business and non-business periodicals, (4) statistical sources, (5) company histories, (6) specialized analyses of the oil industry, (7) narratives of the industry intended for a relatively lay audience	Five themes emerge from the secondary texts: (1) OPEC oil embargo constituted the first oil shock in the US causing widespread shortages of petroleum products and escalating energy prices (2) US oil companies faced legitimacy threat from price escalation, in combination with overall national economic decline and industry layoff. (3) US oil companies mutual dependence on OPEC as the dominant crude oil supplier (4) The industry's resistance to OPEC's oil pricing strategies (5) OPEC as an internal threat during steep decline in oil prices
Closing the hermeneutic circle	The third stage of analysis entails discovering possible relationships of the texts and contextual story, or demonstrating the mutual implication of text and context.	The oil industry in the US was accused of profiteering and inefficiency and the US oil companies attempted to shift the blame on OPEC. CEOs of the oil companies exploited OPEC crisis to justify their corporate strategies, assuaging US public's doubts about the industry to protect its legitimacy.
A conceptual bridge to critical understanding	This stage offers a conceptual framework that provides richer explanation for the specific relationship between text and context. The focus is on the way in which the text and the producer of text constructed a specific regime of power relations and the status quo they wish to safeguard.	The notion of Orientalism is used to explain the dominant cultural self-image and the Western imperialist tendency to orientalise non-Westeners. OPEC is portrayed as the source of crisis for the US and the oil industry deploys the fear of the other through dire warnings in their letters to shareholders.

Table 8.9: Review of the hermeneutical process. Adapted from Prasad and Mir (2002).

■
Computer aided qualitative data analysis: A short note

The previous sections of this chapter introduced some useful approaches to analysing qualitative data. However, the difficulty lies in efficiently managing this form of data. Brennan *et al.*, (2009) discussed some advantages and limitations of using CADQAS over manual methods to analyse textual documents. Some of the advantages include the ability of CADQAS to manage larger data sets, reliability of coding the data, less labour-intensive and lower costs.

Linderman (2001) suggests that computers work best when categories are less complex and easy to develop, whilst manual coding is required for more complex categories. Thus, manual and computer aided analyses are not necessarily alternatives and can complement each other. Some studies dealing with the content of accounting narratives have performed their entire analysis manually (e.g. Lang and Lundholm, 2000; Clatworthy and Jones, 2003) or a mixture of both manual and computerised approaches (e.g. Abrahamson and Amir, 1996; Smith and Taffler, 2000). Others have used computer-aided programmes (e.g. Tennyson *et al.*, 1990; Rutherford, 2005). You may use any of the computer programmes or software packages available in your institution to assist qualitative research. Some studies in accounting employ sophisticated softwares (e.g. MAXQDA, NVivo, and DICTION) or even simple text-converting software to analyse qualitative data. It is important to remember that CAQDAS is primarily a data management and presentation tool, rather than a substitute for careful reading of the text or theory development.

8

■
Qualitative data management

While it is necessary to have a strategy to sort, summarise and analyse your data, it is equally important to consider a data management plan to store, secure, backup, preserve, and where applicable, share your data. This means that in qualitative research, data management and data analysis are both important (Meadows, 2004). Data management is an important and valuable component of the responsible conduct of your research. You are personally responsible for the management of the research data you create. Effective data management is important for both funded and non-funded research projects. With respect to funded projects, many research funders have data policies which specify the research data management practice expected from fund holders. In many cases, submission of a data management plan is part of research funder's requirements. For example, UK Research Councils require grant holders to manage and retain their research for re-use and have set out a number of requirements for the management of research data by institutions and individual researchers. Your institutions may also provide useful resources to help you with managing your research data.

Whether your project is funded or non-funded, a data management plan should be developed at the beginning of your research project so that good practices are established early. The earlier you start thinking about managing your research data, the easier it will be. Indeed, managing your research data well will "facilitate interpretation just as good orchestration facilitates good dance music" (Meadows and Dodendorf, 1999, p. 196). Your research also may span the related areas of data management, curation, and preservation (Whyte and Tedds, 2011).

- **Research data management** is about organising the data, from its entry to the dissemination and archiving of valuable results. It aims to establish reliable verification of results, and allows further innovative research based on existing information.

- **Preservation** is concerned with ensuring that what is submitted to a repository or publisher remains fit for secondary use in the longer term (e.g. 10 years post-research project).

- **Curation** is about ensuring that research results can be archived, and that valued research data remains fit for future use.

Chapter summary

This chapter introduced the reader to some of the common qualitative data analysis techniques as illustrated in the Methods Map in Chapter 4. Qualitative data analysis focuses on analysing non-numerical and non-standardised data set, and generally involves the use of non-statistical methods to analyse the data. There are different approaches to analysing qualitative data, including inductive and deductive approaches. A number of analytical procedures for qualitative data have been discussed from an inductive perspective; these include grounded theory, thematic analysis, template analysis, narrative analysis, textual analysis, discourse analyses, content analysis and hermeneutics.

These inductive approaches begin with reducing vast amount of data through coding which facilitates qualitative analysis. Procedures for analysing qualitative data usually share a number of common characteristics. These include: the reciprocal nature of data collection and analysis; the categorisation and unitisation of research data; conceptualization of relationships and the development of analytical categories and concepts; and developing testable propositions to build or test theory. Whichever approach you adopt for your research it is important that you recognise that there are no definitive processes to the analysis of qualitative data, however, the whole process should be planned and well organised in order to ensure an effective analysis of the data.

The use of CADQAS can help you manage, organise, explore and retrieve your research data, as well as building propositions, theorising, and recording your thoughts systematically. It is equally important to consider other aspects of data management including preservation and curation (i.e. how to manage and retain your research data for future use) as they are also an integral and vital part for a qualitative research to be successful.

References and further reading

Abraham, S., & Cox, P. (2007). Analysisng the determinants of narrative risk information in UK FTSE 100 annual reports. *The British Accounting Review*, **39**(3), 227-248.

Abraham, S., Martson, C., & Darby, P. (2012). *Risk Reporting: Clarity, Relevance and Location*. Institute of Chartered Accountants of Scotland (ICAS), Edinburgh.

Abraham, S & Shrives, P. J. (2014). Improving the relevance of risk factor disclosure in corporate annual reports. *The British Accounting Review*. 46(1), 91-107.

Abrahamson, E. & Amir, E. (1996). The information content of the president's letter to shareholders. *Journal of Business Finance and Accounting*, **23** (8), 1157-1182.

Al-Tuwaijiri, S.A., Christensen, T.E., and Hughes II, K.E. (2003). The relations among environmental disclosure, environmental performance, and economic performance: a simultaneous equations approach. *Accounting Organisations and Society*, **29**, 447-471.

Alvesson, M., & Karreman, D. (2000). Varieties of discourse: On the study of organizations through discourse analysis. *Human Relations*, **53**, 1125–1149.

Beattie,V., Fearnley, S., & Brandt, R. (2004). A grounded theory model of auditor-client engagement. *International Journal of Auditing*, **8**, 1-19

Beck, A.C., Campbell, D., & Shrives, P.J. (2010). Content analysis in environmental reporting research: Enrichment and rehearsal of the method in a British–German context. *The British Accounting Review*, **42**(3), 207-222.

Beelitz, A. and Merkl-Davies, D.M. (2012). Using discourse to restore organisational legitimacy: 'CEOspeak' after an incident in a German nuclear power plant. *Journal of Business Ethics*, **108**(1), 101-120.

Berg, B.L. (2004). *Qualitative Research Methods for the Social Sciences*, 5th ed., Pearson Publication.

Braun, V., & Clarke, V. (2006). Using thematic analysis in psychology. *Qualitative Research in Psychology*, **3**(2), 77-101.

Brennan, N.M., Guillamon-Saorin, E. and Pierce, A. (2009). Methodological Insights: Impression management: Developing and illustrating a scheme of analysis for narrative disclosures – a methodological note. *Accounting, Auditing and Accountability Journal*, **22**(5), 789–832.

Bowman, E.H. (1984). Content analysis of annual reports for corporate strategy and risk. *Interfaces*, **14**, 61–71.

Clatworthy, M. and Jones, M.J. (2003). Financial reporting of good news and bad news: evidence from accounting narratives. *Accounting and Business Research*, **33**(3), 171-85.

Conway, M. (2007). The subjective precision of computers: a methodological comparison with human coding in content analysis. *Journalism and Mass Communication Quarterly*, **83** (1), 186-200.

Davis, A. K., Piger, J. M., & Sedoe, L.M. (2012). Beyond the numbers: measuring the information content of earnings press release language. *Contemporary Accounting Research*, **29** (3), 8450-868

Dobler, M., Lajili, K., & Zeghal, D. (2011). Attributes of Corporate Risk Disclosure: An International Investigation in the Manufacturing Sector. *Journal of International Accounting Research*, **10**(2), 1-22.

Duriau, V.J., Reger, R.K. & Pfarrer, M.D. (2007). A content analysis of the content analysis literature in organization studies: research themes, data sources, and methodological refinements. *Organizational Research Methods*, **10**(1), 5-34.

Elharidy, A. M, Nicholson, B. & Scapens, R. W (2008). Using grounded theory in interpretive management accounting research. *Qualitative Research in Accounting & Management*, **5**(2), 139 – 155.

Emery, M., Hooks, J., & Stewart, R. (2002). Born at the wrong time? An oral history of women professional accountants in New Zealand. *Accounting History*, **7**(2), 7-34.

Fairclough, N. (1995). *Critical Discourse Analysis: The Critical Study of Language.* Longman, London.

Fairclough, N. (2003). *Analysing Discourse: Text Analysis for Social Research.* Routledge, London.

Ferguson, J. (2007). Analysing accounting discourse: avoiding the 'fallacy of internalism'. *Accounting, Auditing & Accountability Journal*, **20**(6), 912-34.

Gallhofer, S., Haslam, J. and Roper, J. (2001). Applying critical discourse analysis: struggles over takeovers legislation in New Zealand, *Advances in Public Interest Accounting*, **8**, 121-55.

Glaser, B. (1992). *Basics of Grounded Theory Analysis: Emergence vs Forcing?* Sociology Press, California.

Gilbert, N. (Eds.). (2008). *Researching Social Life*. Sage Publications, London.

Glaser, B. G., & Strauss, A. L. (1967). *The Discovery of Grounded Theory: Strategies for Qualitative Research*. Transaction Publishers.

Golafshani, N. (2003). Understanding reliability and validity in qualitative research. *The Qualitative Report*, **8**(4), 597-607.

Holsti, O.R. (1969). *Content Analysis for the Social Sciences and Huma*nities. Addison-Wesley, Reading.

Hsieh, H. F. and Shannon, S.E. (2005). Three approaches to qualitative content analysis. *Qualitative Health Research*, **15**(9), 1277-1288.

King, N. (2004). Using templates in the thematic analysis of text. In Cassell, C. and Symon, G. (Eds.), *Essential Guide to Qualitative Methods in Organizational Research*, Sage Publications, London, 256-270.

King, N. (2007). *Template Analysis* http://hhs.hud.ac.uk/w2/research/template_analysis/ last accessed 19th February 2014.

Kirk, J. & Miller, M. (1986). *Reliability and Validity in Qualitative Research*. Sage Publications, London.

Krippendorff, K. (1980). *Content Analysis: An Introduction to Its Methodolog*y. Sage Publications, Newbury Park.

Lang, M. & Lundholm, R. (2000). Voluntary disclosure and equity offerings: reducing information asymmetry or hyping the stock? *Contemporary Accounting Research*, **17**(4), 623-662.

Li, F. (2010). Textual analysis of corporate disclosures; a survey of the literature. *Journal of Accounting Literature*. **29**(2) 143-165

Linderman, A. (2001). Computer content analysis and manual coding techniques: a comparative analysis. in West, M.D. (Ed.), *Theory, Method and Practice in Computer Content Analysis*, Ablex, Connecticut, 97-109.

Loughran, I. & McDonald, B. (2011). When is liability not a liability? Textual analysis, Dictionaries and 10-Ks. *The Journal of Finance*. **66** (1), 35-65.

McKee, A. (2003). *Textual Analysis; a beginner's guide*. Sage Publication, London

McKinnon, J. (1988). Reliability and Validity in field research; some strategies and tactics. *Accounting, Auditing and Accountability Journal*. **1**(1), 34-54.

Meadows, L.M. (2004). Qualitative data management. In Lewis-Beck, M.S., Bryman, A., & Liao, T.F. (Eds.), *The SAGE Encyclopedia of Social Science Research Methods*, Sage Publications, London.

Meadows, LM., & Dodendorf, DM. (1999). Data managment and interpretation using computers to assist. In Crabtree, B.F. & Miller, W.L. (Eds.) *Doing Qualitative Research*, Sage Publications, London, 195-220.

8

Merkl-Davies, D. & Koller, V. (2012). 'Metaphoring' people out of this world: A Critical Discourse Analysis of a chairman's statement of a UK defence firm. *Accounting Forum*, **36**(3), 178-193.

Milne, M.J., & Adler, R.W. (1999). Exploring the reliability of social and environmental disclosures content analysis. *Accounting, Auditing & Accountability Journal*, **12**(2), 237-2

Morris, R. (1994). Computerized content analysis in management research: a demonstration of advantages and limitations. *Journal of Management*, **20**, 903-31.

Oakes, L.S., Considine, J. & Gould, S. (1994). Counting health care costs in the United States: a hermeneutical study of cost benefit research. *Accounting, Auditing & Accountability*, **7**(3),18-49.

O'Dwyer, B., (2003). Conceptions of corporate social responsibility; the nature of managerial capture. *Accounting, Accountability and Auditing Journal*, **16**(4) 523-557

O'Gorman, K. D. (2008). *The Essence of Hospitality from the Texts of Classical Antiquity: The Development of a Hermeneutical Helix to Identify the Philosophy of the Phenomenon of Hospitality*, University of Strathclyde, Glasgow.

O'Gorman, K. D. (2010). *The Origins of Hospitality and Tourism*. Goodfellow, Oxford.

O'Gorman, K. D. & Gillespie, C. H. (2010). The Mythological Power of Hospitality Leaders? A hermeneutical investigation of their reliance on storytelling. *International Journal of Contemporary Hospitality Management*. **22**(5), 659-680.

Parker, I. (1992). *Discourse Dynamics: Critical Analysis for Social and Individual Psychology*. Routledge Publications, London.

Phillips, N., & Hardy, C. (2002). *Understanding Discourse Analysis*. Sage Publications, California..

Prasad, A., & Mir, R. (2002). Digging Deep for Meaning: A Critical Hermeneutic Analysis of CEO Letters to Shareholders in the Oil Industry, *International Journal of Business Communication January*, **39**(1), 92-116.

Reissman, K. C. (1993). *Narrative Analysis*. Sage Publication, London

Ryan, G. W., & Bernard, H. R. (2003). Techniques to identify themes. *Field methods*, **15**(1), 85-109.

Rutherford, B. (2005). Genre analysis of corporate annual report narratives. *Journal of Business Communication*, **42** (4), 349-378.

Saunders, M,. Lewis, P,. and Thornhill, A. (2009). *Research Methods for Business Students* (5th ed.) Pearson Education, Essex.

Silverman, D. (2006). *Doing Qualitative Research: A Practical Handbook.* Sage Publications, London.

Smith, M. & Taffler, R.J. (2000). The chairman's statement: a content analysis of discretionary narrative disclosures. *Accounting, Auditing & Accountability Journal,* **13**(5), 624-46.

Tennyson, B., Ingram, R.W. & Dugan, M.T. (1990). Assessing the information content of narrative disclosures in explaining bankruptcy. *Journal of Business Finance and Accounting,* **17**(3), 391-410.

Thompson, J. B. (1981). *Critical Hermeneutics: A study in the thought of Paul Ricoeur and Jurgen Habermas,* Cambridge University Press, New York.

Thompson, J.B. (1990). *Ideology and Modern Culture: Critical Social Theory in the Era of Mass Communication.* Polity Press, Cambridge.

Thompson, J.B. (1995), *The Media and Modernity: A Social Theory of the Media,* Polity Press, Cambridge.

Van Dijk, T. A. (1997a). The study of discourse. In T. A. van Dijk (Ed.), *Discourse as Structure and Process,* 1–34. Sage Publications, London.

Van Dijk, T. A. (1997b). Discourse as interaction in society. In T. A. van Dijk (Ed.), *Discourse as Social Interaction.* Sage Publications, London, 1-37.

Van Dijk, T. A. (2003). Critical discourse analysis. In D. Schiffrin, D. Tannen, & H. H. Hamilton (Eds.), *The Handbook of Discourse Analysis.* Wiley-Blackwell, Malden and Oxford.

Weber, R. P. (1990). *Basic Content Analysis,* 2nd ed. Newbury Park.

Whyte, A., & Tedds, J. (2011). Making the Case for Research Data Management. DCC Briefing Papers. Edinburgh: Digital Curation Centre. Available online: http://www.dcc.ac.uk/resources/briefing-papers.

Wodak, R. & M. Meyer (2009). Critical discourse analysis: History, agenda, theory and methodology. In R. Wodak & M. Meyer (Eds.), *Methods for Critical Discourse Analysis.* 2nd ed. Sage Publications, London.

Wood, L. A., & Kroger, R. O. (2000). *Doing Discourse Analysis: Methods for studying action in talk and text.* Sage Publications, California.

Wooffitt, R. (2008). Conversation analysis and discourse analysis in Gilbert, N. (Eds.). *Researching Social Life.* Sage Publications, London, 441-461.

8

9 Quantitative Data Gathering Methods and Techniques

Ahmed Salhin, Anthony Kyiu, Babak Taheri, Catherine Porter, Nikolaos Valantasis-Kanellos and Christian König

Researchers are concerned with analysing and solving problems. These problems come in many forms, can have common features and often include numerical information. It is therefore important that researchers should be competent in the use of a range of quantitative methods. Data is required in order to perform quantitative analyses. This chapter focuses on methods of collecting quantitative data, sampling and measurement issues, surveys, collecting secondary data and experimental research.

The nature of quantitative research

According to our Methods Map (see *Chapter 4*), quantitative methods are part of an **objective** ontology and a **positivist** epistemology. Social science research is mainly influenced by the hypothetico-deductive paradigm (a research approach that starts with a theory about how things work and derives testable hypotheses from it). According to Malhotra (2009), quantitative research aims at quantifying the collected data and employs some kinds of statistical analysis based on a representative sample. The following phrases are linked with quantitative methodology and are often used interchangeably: deductive approach, etic view, objective epistemology, structured approach, systematic approach, numerically based data collection, statistical analyses and replicable research design.

In other words, quantitative studies have four main characteristics:

1   systematic/reconstructed logic and linear path (step-by-step straight line);

2   data which is hard in nature (e.g. numbers);

3   a reliance on positivist principles and an emphasis on measuring variables and testing hypotheses and

4   they usually verify or falsify a pre-existing relationship or hypothesis.

Advantages of using quantitative data relative to qualitative data include the broad comparability of answers, speed of data collection and the 'power of numbers'. Qualitative questions can be asked in a quantitative survey, but responses (and resultant data) are much more structured (and, some may say, restrictive).

The data that you need to collect will very much be driven by the research question you are trying to answer (see Box 9.1). This needs to be very specific and will drive both your data collection *method* and *sampling*. We discuss these terms below.

Box 9.1: Examples of research questions suited for quantitative analysis

In its simplest form, a quantitative research question will try to quantify the variables you wish to examine.

> e.g. 'What is the average change in a company's value after merger and acquisition transactions?'

Another researcher might wish to identify the differences between two or more groups on one or more variables.

> e.g. 'What is the difference in value between financial and non-financial companies after merger and acquisition transactions?'

Finally, a researcher might wish to explore the relationship between one or more variables on one or more groups. This type of research is mostly associated with experiments and the identification of causal relationships as will be discussed later in the chapter.

> e.g. 'What is the relationship between leverage and the value of a company after merger and acquisition transactions?'

9

■   Defining dependent and independent variables

Data analysis and design involves measuring variables, which can be dependent or independent. We define dependent and independent variables as follows: a **dependent** variable is one which the researcher thinks will be affected by another variable (or by an experiment), while an **independent** variable is one which the researcher thinks will affect the dependent variable. These will be identified directly from the research question. For example, if you are studying the effects of stock liquidity on firms' performance, firms' performance is the dependent variable and liquidity is the independent variable. Other independent variables, called **control** variables, may include firm size, capital structure and other factors that may affect performance. These control variables are included in order to provide a clear understanding of the role of the independent variable on the dependent variables. In the example above, stock liquidity is not the only variable that affects the performance of the firm: size, capital structure and some other factors might also have an impact on performance. The power of the relationship between the dependent and the independent variables under investigation can be understood more reliably through the inclusion of control variables in the model.

For all quantitative studies, a crucial component of design is the selection and measurement of the dependent variable. It is crucial because the usefulness of the research depends upon the relevance of the dependent variable and its representation on the outcome of interest. Researchers must be cautious, as dependent variable selection reflects the problem definition process and can thus influence the decision-making. Our example suggests the aspect of performance to be considered and the method of measuring it should be carefully selected. For example, if the researcher is interested in the 'financial' aspect of performance, he/she has to choose a suitable measure of financial performance, e.g. accounting measures, such as return on assets (ROA) and return on equity (ROE), or market measures, such as Tobin's Q and market return. To use a different example, if a researcher studying the relationship between board of directors' diversity and capital structure were to choose 'the ratio of male/ female directors in the board' as the dependent variable, he/she would have to justify why that ratio is considered to be a more appropriate indicator of diversity than, for example, the ratio of independent directors in the board.

■   Primary and secondary sources of data

In quantitative research, data can be gathered from either a primary or a secondary source. Primary data refers to data that has been collected directly through first-hand experience. The most common means of gathering primary data for quantitative research is through the use of experiments and surveys, which will be explained in detail later in this chapter. Secondary data, on the other hand, is pre-existing available data collected from second-hand sources. The type of data which will be collected depends on a number of factors, such as (1) the objectives of the research and (2) time and resources constraints, as primary data collection can be time consuming and expensive.

Gathering primary quantitative data

■ Sampling and measurement

Population and sample size

The collection of primary data requires that the researcher clearly define the population under investigation, as well as the units of analysis that constitute that population. '*Population*' refers to all the concerned units (e.g. people, companies) within a particular problem space and at the specified time that the researcher would like to study. For example, in a study looking to ascertain the level of compliance to the UK code of corporate governance, the population would be all public UK companies. However, because it is often impossible to investigate all members of the population (usually for legitimate reasons, such as time and resources constraints), a portion of the population, known as a '*sample*', is studied. Samples are therefore used to make inferences about the population. In trying to draw a sample from a population, a number of techniques are used. Broadly, there are two types of sampling techniques: probability/random sampling and non-probability/non-random sampling.

- Probability sampling uses a random selection process and gives every member of the population an equal chance of being included in the sample. There are two main requirements for probability sampling: first, an adequate sample frame, comprising a comprehensive list of all members of the population of interest, and second, an ability to randomly select based on features present in the sample frame (Walter 2013).

- Non-probability sampling involves a specific sample chosen on the basis of particular characteristics or similar differentiating features relevant to the study; therefore, it cannot be used to determine whether the results of the study are representative of the entire population. Table 9.1 provides a summary of the various types of probability and non-probability sampling techniques.

9

Table 9.1(a): Types of sampling: Probability sampling

Simple random sampling: Every unit of the population has an equal and independent chance of being selected; the selection of one unit does not affect the selection of another. A good sampling frame is therefore required. Usually the population is geographically concentrated; for example, in order to study the investment strategies of Small and Medium Enterprises (SMEs) in a market that has a population of 20,000 SMEs, a simple random technique to select 500 companies implies that, in the first selection, each company has a 1 in 20,000 chance of being selected. In the next selection, the remaining units have a 1 in 19,999 chance of being selected, and so on.
Systematic sampling: This is a variation of the simple random sampling. A starting point is first chosen at random and subsequent units are chosen at regular intervals. The population is first divided by the desired sample. To use the previous example, the 20,000 SMEs would be divided by 500, the number required for the sample, which gives 40; this is the interval. Next, choose a number less than 40 as the starting point for your selection. If, for example, the number 9 is chosen as the random starting point, and the interval is 40, the companies selected are 9, 49, 89, 129, 169, etc., continuing until the sample size of 500 is reached. Although members of the population are not selected independently, the sample chosen is spread more evenly across the population.
Stratified random sampling: The population is divided into strata (groups), and these strata make up the final sample in the study. It is mainly based on homogeneous subgroups. For example, if investment strategies will be analysed according to size and return on assets levels, the stratified random sampling technique ensures that there is a good representation of SMEs, as well as companies with both low and high return on equity. The size of each stratum can be taken in proportion to its size in the population; this is known as proportional stratified random sampling. If there are 3,200 small companies with high return on equity in a population of 20,000 (16%), 7,200 small companies with low return on equity (36%), 2,800 medium-sized companies with high return on equity (14%) and 6,800 medium-sized companies with low return on equity (34%), the sample of 500 should reflect these percentages, taking sample sizes of 80, 180, 70 and 170, respectively
Multi-stage cluster sampling: The sample is selected according to groups within the population. It is mostly used when it more feasible to select groups of individuals than individuals themselves from the defined population. In this sense, the unit of sampling becomes the group. For example, if a researcher wanted to study the spending patterns of students in all UK universities, it would be inefficient to randomly select students given that the researcher was in the possession of a registry list of all British universities. A more sensible approach would be to divide the country into several regions and select some of them for further exploration. The researcher would then create a list of all universities within these selected regions (and might focus the sample even more by selecting particular departments/schools within those universities) and then select a sample of students from those universities. Each decision towards a more specific selection in every step of this process is made randomly. Thus, this is a multistage sampling technique that aims to break the entire population into multiple clusters in order to make the study effective from a cost and time perspective

Table 9.1(b): Types of sampling: Non-probability sampling

Convenience sampling: Also called accidental, haphazard, chunk and grab sampling. The selection of the sample is based on proximity, how accessible the participants are to the researcher and how easy it is to select the participants. For example, in selecting a sample of 500 companies out of the population of 20,000, for convenience, the researcher could aim to select companies that featured in a certain database.
Purposive sampling: The researcher makes decisions about who/what study units will be involved in the research. This is based on who the researcher thinks will be in a better position to provide the required information to meet the objectives of the study. For example, if a researcher would like to examine investing strategies of SMEs in a certain market but decides that he/she is going to select only manufacturing companies because they have a higher level of investment in fixed-assets than companies in the services sector, it will be deemed to be a purposive sampling technique.
Snowball sampling: The sample is selected using networks between and among members of the population. First, a few individuals in the population are selected and the necessary information is gathered from them. They are then asked to help identify other people in the population who could also become part of the sample. This process goes on until the required number has been obtained. It is a useful technique when very little is known about the population, as persons within the group act as links to other participants. A major drawback, however, with this technique is that, if the persons who help to identify other participants are biased in their recommendations, the sample may be biased.
Expert sampling: The researcher identifies some people as experts with demonstrable experience in the subject matter of the study being conducted. For example, the researcher wants to study how the latest changes to accounting standards are perceived among expert accountants. The researcher could aim to include only those individuals who are Chartered Accountants. As experts, their opinion would be considered to be more valuable in comparison with others who hold a lesser certification. The same would also apply to years of experience in a particular role in cases where the researcher would like to include professionals from a particular industry in his/her sample.
Quota sampling: The researcher divides the population in categories according to common characteristics then specifies the minimum number of sampled units in each category. Although members of the population are sampled by convenience, they must possess the specified characteristics in order to be included in the sample. For example, a researcher who wants to identify spending patterns among male and female students with UK, German, French and Greek origin could use quota sampling to include a particular proportion of male and female students of those ethnicities in the sample and thereby be able to provide a comparison among them.

A small sample is unlikely to produce results that accurately represent the entire population. It is possible to pick, strictly by chance, a group whose members happen to be different in some attributes from the population as a whole (this is referred to as the sampling error). This draws attention to the systematic bias (i.e. extraneous sampling factors) that affects survey results and reduces data validity, including frame bias (a wrongly chosen population), selection bias (under-representing certain parts of the population), non-response bias (data skewed according to who from the chosen sample actually engaged with the study), interviewer bias, questionnaire bias, respondent bias and processing bias (interviewer writes down the wrong answers); see De Vaus (2007) for more information.

There is considerable debate over what constitutes an acceptable sample size for results to be statistically valid, but there is no golden rule for determining a suitable sample size; it will often depend on your budget. It is generally accepted that the larger the sample is, the more generalizable are the results of the study. Different authors make diverse recommendations of sample sizes appropriate for quantitative research, including an absolute sample ranging from 200 to 300 participants (De Vaus 2007; Hair, Black, Babin and Anderson 2010).

In the real world, some respondents may decide not to participate in the survey at all. This might be an issue when non-respondents differ to respondents in a non-random manner in terms of demography and other characteristics, which consequently introduces sampling bias (Walter 2013). For example, the responding members of any sample may be more educated and older than the actual education and age distribution represented in the population from which the sample is drawn. The portion of respondents who participate in the survey is referred to as the response rate. Researchers generally use a formula to calculate response rate:

■ Main measurement types

Measurement is the process of assigning values to objects in a study so as to represent attributes and quantities (Nunnally and Bernstein 1994). Unless the objects in a study can be measured according to some category or criteria, variations in them cannot be identified. There are two classifications of means of measuring quantitative data, which are described by Hair *et al.* (2010): *nonmetric* and *metric* measurement scales.

- ■ **Nonmetric** measurement scales describe differences by indicating the presence/absence of a characteristic (i.e. nominal and ordinal scales).

- ■ **Metric** measurement scales are used when subjects differ in degree with regard to a particular attribute (i.e. interval and ratio scales). Table 9.2 shows the main measurement types.

Table 9.2: The measurement types

Measure	Description
Nonmetric measurement scales	
Nominal	The numerical values only 'name' the attribute uniquely. It normally presents categories or classes, including demographic attributes (e.g. sex, gender, religion), forms of behaviour (e.g. purchase activity) or action that is discrete (e.g. invests in the stock market or does not invest in the stock market). For example, in a study of a basketball team a player is identified by the number they have on their shirt; this number identifies the individual player. However, this number is a nonmetric representation – a player who wears number 20 is not considered to be twice as good as a player who wears number 10 on their shirt
Ordinal	The attributes can be rank ordered. The distances between attributes do not have any meaning. For example, on a survey you might code educational qualification as 1 = basic education; 2 = Higher diploma; 3 = A-level/Advanced Higher and college; 4 = university education. In this measure, higher numbers mean more education but, for example, a Higher diploma is not considered to be twice as good as basic education
Metric measurement scales	
Interval	The distance between attributes does have meaning, the interval between values is interpretable and the steps between the values/scores are equal in size. The values can be added, calculated, computed to gain an average, etc. For example, the difference between the year 2000 and 2001 equals 1 year, which is the same as the difference between the years 2014 and 2015
Ratio	There is always an absolute zero that is meaningful. This means that you can construct a meaningful fraction with a ratio variable. In social research, most 'count' variables are ratios, for example, the return on equity. This is because it is possible to have zero return and it is meaningful to be able to say 'we had twice as much return this year as we did in the last year'

Finally, it is important to state that, considerable effort should be put into determining the appropriate method sampling and measurement of variables for the research. Not only will this ensure that the research objectives are achieved and conclusions drawn are valid, it will also save time and resources.

Experiments

We will now briefly discuss experimental design. Experiments are often viewed as the 'purest' way to establish an association between two variables and they therefore score well on the concept of internal validity. We will then extend our concepts to consider non-experimental (or survey-based) data.

Experiments have a wide range of applications in social science and are considered to be a reliable and efficient means of collecting data to verify or refute theories. The main purpose of experiments is to study causal links. In particular, researchers aim to identify whether one change in an independent variable, caused by manipulation (of data), will affect a dependent variable. The main difference between experiments and surveys is that researchers have increased control over the conditions and events of an experiment, as in many cases they are conducted in laboratories. Moreover, according to Oehlert (2000), experiments enable direct comparison between treatments of interest and can offer minimised comparison bias and error. In addition, experiments provide researchers with the ability to observe variables of interest that might be unobservable in the real world. The sampling unit of the experiment, which provides measures based on experimental manipulation, is referred to as the subject of the experiment.

Experimental design process

Experimental design involves four main design elements (Zikmund, Babin, Carr and Griffin 2010).

- The first is **manipulation of the independent (experimental) variable**. Moreover, the way an independent variable is manipulated is defined as experimental treatment. This fact creates two groups. The experimental group is the first and is represented by participants exposed to planned treatments.

- The second is called **the control group** and is represented by participants on whom none of the planned treatments are carried out. It should be stated that the control group is therefore used to highlight the outcomes that occur among the experimental group. For example, if we are studying investor trading behaviour in an environment where there is more/less information available on the stocks being investing in, we would first need to run the study in an environment where there is a normal level of information (a control group), so that it could be demonstrated that it was indeed the change in the availability of information that was the cause of increased/decreased level of trading in the experimental group. The second step is selection and measurement of the dependent variable (see *Diversity of board members*).

- The third step is **selection and assignment of experimental subjects** or test units.

- The fourth is **control over extraneous variables** (environmental variables affecting the dependent variable). See Adams, Edelman, Valentin and Dowling (2009) for more details. Box 9.2 shows an example of research that used experiments in order to address the research aim.

Box 9.2: Experiment design example

How noise trading affects markets: An experimental analysis (Bloomfield, O'Hara and Saar 2009)

Bloomfield *et al.* (2009) conducted an experiment to examine how noise traders have an impact on the stock market different to that of informed traders and liquidity traders. They defined an informed trader as a trader who has fundamental information about the stock being traded, a liquidity trader as an investor who trades because of external circumstances (liquidating for a reuse of the fund for a purpose not related to the stock being traded) and a noise trader as one whose trading is neither based on fundamental information nor depends on external reasons.

The experiment was designed to identify how six groups (compositions) of traders, containing noise traders and trading two blocks of securities (block 1 and block 2), affect the laboratory market compared to another six groups (composition), which consist of only informed and liquidity traders trading the same blocks of securities. In order to rule out the effect of transaction taxes on the behaviour of different types of traders, one half of each composition is allowed to trade the block of securities in the presence of taxes, while the other half is allowed to trade the block of securities in the absence of taxes.

The results of this experiment suggest that noise traders have both positive and negative effects on the market. On one hand, they reduce bid–ask spreads, which results in more liquidity of stocks in the market. However, on the other hand, they increase prices' deviation from their intrinsic values, particularly in less efficient markets. For a detailed discussion of this experiment and the tests used, as well as the approach used to achieve the results, please consult Bloomfield et al. (2009)

9

Surveys

As mentioned earlier, surveys are the main means by which primary quantitative data is collected. A survey is simply a structured method of asking different respondents the same questions in the same order and creating a database of answers. While under an experimental approach variables are manipulated to observe their impact on other variables, the use of surveys allows natural variations in the variables to be explored. Generally, surveys include oral questioning (interviews) or the use of questionnaires to elicit written responses from participants (Sarantakos 1988).

■   Survey design

The design of a survey involves six main processes:

1 Formulating the research questions/conceptual framework;

2 Making a list of the information requirements;

3 Deciding on the research strategy;

4 Designing a draft survey;

5 Conducting a pilot study; and

6 Carrying out the final design.

According to Oppenheim (2000), there are two main types of survey design: *descriptive* and *analytical* (or *exploratory*). The descriptive survey is meant to establish the proportion of any given population who share particular characteristics. It is mainly used to provide answers to such questions as 'who' (demographic characteristics of individuals), 'what' (activities carried out by individuals) and 'how' (social and economic status of the individuals). The descriptive survey is therefore used to examine how attitudes and behaviours of respondents can be used to explain variability in different phenomena. Analytical surveys, on the other hand, are used to investigate the relationships and differences between sample groups and to describe cause-and-effect relationships.

When gathering survey data using questionnaires, these can be administered in two ways: *researcher-administered* or *self-administered*.

■ Questionnaires are said to be **researcher-administered** when they are filled in by the researcher through some form of communication with the respondent. This can be by face-to-face communication, telephone or via media such as Skype. Some advantages of researcher-administered questionnaires are that they allow the researcher to clarify questions by addressing the concerns of respondents directly, they help the researcher to ensure that the questionnaire is fully completed and they are usually associated with a higher response rate. Equally, there are some downsides to the use of researcher-administered questionnaires. The researcher might potentially influence the respondents' answers by his or her presence and behaviour; the respondents' honesty may be decreased by a motivation to base their reply on what they interpret to be the 'right' answer or thing the researcher expects to hear.

■ **Self-administered questionnaires** involve the respondents completing the questionnaires on their own and handing them back to the researcher, either through post, hand delivery, fax, email or the use of web surveys. They are cheaper and therefore could be used for a large number of respondents. In addition, respondents are not subjected to the problem of researcher influence. However, they are associated with lower response rates, more missing data and possible misinterpretation of questions by respondents.

What questions should be asked?

The key guide to determining the questions to ask in a questionnaire should be the objectives of the study. It is therefore important that you have a clear idea about what you want to achieve w ith your research. This will enable you think about the information you will need to elicit from respondents to achieve your goals. In terms of style, questions should be kept short and straightforward, as questions of this nature are easier to pose and answering them will not be viewed as overly time consuming by respondents, who may be unwilling to invest a significant amount of time. Finally, you should consider the feasibility of the questionnaire in terms of costs, facilities, time and sensitivity. This final point should not be taken lightly. We often are drawn toward questionnaires as a preferable method of investigation because they seem more manageable, straightforward and achievable, particularly when there are time constraints and limited resources available for the research. However, poorly designed questionnaires can yield a distinct lack of useful data and information gathered from questionnaires is only useful if the sampling is done appropriately and an adequate number of responses are achieved (i.e. non-random sampling).

Constructing a questionnaire

Constructing a questionnaire is an art in itself. The main purpose of the questionnaire is to translate the research objectives into a specific formulated/structured format, in which theory or constructs can be tested using quantitative data. In addition, an important issue in developing a questionnaire is the sequential formation, clarity and readability of the questions. You should therefore try to motivate respondents and grab their attention by using a well-formatted questionnaire with an appropriate sequence of questions. A wording check-list for formulating questions is provided by De Vaus (2007), which is shown in Box 9.3.

There are two broad types of questions: *unstructured* and *structured*. Unstructured or open-ended questions allow the respondents to freely express themselves, as they do not require categories pre-defined by the researcher. They place a responsibility on the respondents to think harder to come up with answers and as such may lead to lower response rates. In addition, open-ended questions are much more difficult to answer and assess using quantitative methods, without further categorisation. Structured questions, on the other hand, use closed-ended categories that are pre-determined by the researcher. They therefore reduce the depth of thought required by the respondents to complete the questionnaire, as respondents are given a limited set of options from which to select an answer. There are a variety of available formats of closed-ended questions, including numerical rating scales, ranking, binary choice and multiple choice. Figure 9.1 shows examples of closed-ended questions.

Box 9.3: Checklist to assist in the wording of questions

1. Is the language simple? It should be.

2. Can the question be shortened? It should be as short as possible.

3. Is the question double-barrelled? There should be one 'clause' in your question.

4. Is the question leading? It should not direct the respondent toward a specific answer

5. Is the question negative? It should be as neutral as possible.

6. Is the respondent likely to have the necessary knowledge? It should be based on accurate assumptions about the respondent's ability to answer it.

7. Will the words have the same meaning for everyone? Some phrases/words can have loaded meanings for certain groups – beware of this.

8. Is there a prestige bias? It could be embarrassing for respondents to answer honestly or they could attempt to project a sense of status through their answers.

9. Is the question ambiguous? e.g. "How often do you wear Chanel?" The respondent may wear Chanel clothing once a month but Chanel perfume every day, thus they may not be sure how to answer.

10. Is the question too precise? You could be asking something so specific that you may be excluding the individual from effectively participating.

11. Is the frame of reference for the question sufficiently clear? e.g. "How long do you spend commuting?" This could mean: from your house to your place of work; the actual travel time spent in a car/plane/bus; the total time spent commuting in a whole working day (to and from work); and many other variations.

12. Does the question artificially create options?

13. Is personal or impersonal wording preferable?

14. Is the question wording unnecessarily detailed or objectionable? See points 1 & 2

15. Does the question contain gratuitous qualifiers? e.g. "When you are driving your kids to school in the morning do you play music?"

16. Is the question a 'dead giveaway'? Does it betray your research agenda and objectives thus potentially skewing the respondent's entire set of responses?

Figure 9.3: Closed-ended questions

Type of closed-choice question	Example
Dichotomies questions	Do you smoke cigarettes? ☐ Yes ☐ No Sex: Male Female

Multiple choice formats	How often do you visit museums and art galleries?
	  ☐ At least weekly
	  ☐ Two or three times a month
	  ☐ About once a month
	  ☐ Once every three months
	  ☐ Never
	Age:
	  ☐ 18-25
	  ☐ 26-35
	  ☐ 36-45
	  ☐ 46-55
	  ☐ 56-64
	  ☐ 65 and older

Likert scales
Note: The use of longer scales (a ten-point) allows for the detection of finer differences between respondents that would not be possible with a five-point scale
	Please indicate your level of agreement with following statements:
	Visiting this museum is an enriching experience for me
	  ☐ Very strongly disagree
	  ☐ Strongly disagree
	  ☐ Disagree
	  ☐ Neither agree nor disagree
	  ☐ Agree
	  ☐ Strongly agree
	  ☐ Very strongly agree
	Visiting this museum helps me to express who I am
	  ☐ Very strongly disagree
	  ☐ Strongly disagree
	  ☐ Disagree
	  ☐ Neither agree nor disagree
	  ☐ Agree
	  ☐ Strongly agree
	  ☐ Very strongly agree

9

Semantic differential	Please rate your emotions according to the way the experience made you feel

	1	2	3	4	5	6	7	
Unhappy								Happy
Annoyed								Pleased
Unsatisfied								Satisfied

Ranking format	Please identify the top three aspects you most enjoyed at this visit (Use each of the numbers only once. 1 indicates the most-enjoyed aspect and 3 indicates the third most-enjoyed aspect) People …………………..( ) Climate ………………..( ) Open space……………( ) Heritage………………..( ) Beaches……………….( ) Lifestyle and culture…..( ) Safe to travel ………….( ) Wildlife………………..( )
Filter or contingency questions	Have you ever booked a holiday? ☐ Yes ☐ No If yes, about how many times have you booked a holiday? ☐ Once ☐ 2 or 5 times ☐ 6 to 10 times ☐ More than 10 times

Internal and external validity of quantitative results

The concepts of validity and reliability have a significant impact on how researchers think about their work. Reliability focuses on it being possible to repeat the study (to be carried out by an independent researcher) and expect the same results. The validity concept can be seen in quantitative-based studies as both internal and external. *Internal validity* poses the question: can researchers be reasonably sure that the change/lack of change or association was caused by the treatment or independent variable? *External validity* is the extent to which the results are generalizable and can be applied to other samples. This is less clear for experiments, but more likely in, for example, the case of research using a randomly chosen survey sample.

In terms of surveys, a well-sampled and well-executed quantitative survey can still have high internal validity (though the researcher must be more careful about asserting causality rather than associations), as well as external validity if it has findings that can be generalised outside of the immediate sample. Internal validity also can be achieved through a pilot study, which can be carried out at the data collection stage to ensure that the questions and measurements are appropriate. A pilot survey can be useful in various ways, including for testing the wording of questionnaires, the sequencing of questions, the questionnaire layout, fieldwork arrangements and analysis procedures, gaining familiarity with respondents and estimating response rate and interview time.

In terms of experiments, validity is about ruling out factors which raise doubt as to whether change in the dependent variable can be attributed entirely to the independent variable or treatment. Internal validity (experimental design-related) can be compromised in various ways, including by change to subject during the study period (maturation); an external change during the study, for example weather conditions (history); the observation process itself may influence subjects (instrumentation); control groups could be significantly different (selection bias); and attrition of subject from research (motility). External validity (generalised beyond the research subjects and setting) has two main threats: reactive effects of testing (i.e. observation may sensitise subjects) and effects of selection (i.e. subjects may not be representative of wider population).

Gathering secondary quantitative data

As mentioned earlier in this chapter, secondary data is data that is already available and need not be collected from first hand sources. This can either be data collected earlier by other researchers, data assembled by institutions for research purposes or data that has been collected for purposes other than research, such as official statistics and administrative records. When primary data is archived and made available, it can serve as secondary data. For example, the British Household Panel Survey (BHPS) serves as secondary data to researchers who retrieve it and use it for their research.

■ Finding and retrieving secondary data

One major source for the obtainment of secondary data is official data archives. These are organised by both private and public institutions whose purpose is to collect/acquire, archive and disseminate data for secondary research. For example, the UK Data Archive is a national institution that archives and provides data for research in mainly the social sciences and humanities through the UK Data Service. In addition, the Institute of Social and Economic Research (ISER) at the University of Essex provides data on the British Household Panel Survey that is used as secondary data for quantitative studies in accounting and finance and other disciplines. These days most data archives are electronic and can be obtained via the internet.

Again, most higher education institutions, such as universities, usually subscribe to one or more established databases, thus giving their staff and students access to the data available in them. Some of the notable databases which you may have access to are presented in Table 9.4. Information and training on how to use to these databases to retrieve data for your research can be acquired from your subject librarian at your university.

Table 9.4: Some databases for retrieving secondary data in accounting and finance research

Database	Description
Thomson Reuters Datastream	Provides data on equity securities, such as share prices, accounting information and stock indices. It also provides economic data, such as exchange rates and interest rates, as well as data on bonds and investment trusts
Thomson One Banker	Provides data on companies across the globe. These include data on share prices, earnings estimates, company fillings and company deals, such as mergers and acquisitions
Bankscope	Contains detailed accounting information of about 30,000 banks worldwide
Osiris	Provides financial information, data on ownership and corporate actions for over 55,000 publicly listed companies
Boardex	Contains detailed information on the boards of over 150,000 listed companies
Fame	Provides detailed information of Small and Medium Size companies (SMEs) in UK and Ireland

■ Evaluating secondary data

Once secondary data has been retrieved, it is necessary to evaluate it in order to ascertain its suitability for the research. The first step is to find out whether the original source from which the data was obtained is credible. In the case of survey data, for example, it will be useful to verify the sampling techniques that were used. Hox and Boeije (2005) assert that evaluating secondary data requires additional information which normally should be part of the data itself. This includes the purpose of the study, details of entities that were studied and any known biases that occurred in the course of collecting the data. It is also important to check the accuracy of the data by looking out for errors in computations or, if possible, by comparing data from other sources. Finally, ascertain the validity and reliability of the data by examining whether it actually represents what is supposed to be measured and whether any alterations have been made to it.

Summary

In this chapter, we have discussed primary quantitative data collection, following an experiment or a survey strategy. However, secondary quantitative data can be also useful in a research project. The use of primary data gives the researcher the ability to control the formation of the sample, as well as control over the nature of the data that collected. Consequently, the researcher can be more confident that the data will fit the aim and objectives of the study. However, the collection of primary data can be a time-consuming process that requires great effort from the researcher. This is a fact that can prove to be problematic for projects with tight time limits. This obstacle can be overcome by the use of secondary data, which can be collected in a more time-efficient way and, in many cases, will lead to larger sample sizes (compared with primary data). The issue with this approach, however, is that the data might not be a perfect fit for the research aim and objectives. Additionally, some issues might occur with the quality of the data, as the researcher will not be actively involved either in the sample selection or the data collection process (Easterby-Smith, Thorpe and Jackson 2012).

We have also introduced the tools that are needed for collecting quantitative data. The key issues that should be related to your research question are a) defining your dependent and independent variables, b) how to sample your participants and c) how to design appropriate questions to elicit the data you need to answer your research question. The next chapter discusses the quantitative methods that are at your disposal for analysing the data that you have so painstakingly collected.

9

References and further reading

Adams, H., Edelman, B., Valentin, D. and Dowling, W. J. (2009) *Experimental design and analysis for psychology*, Oxford University Press Oxford.

Anderson, D. R., Sweeney, D. J., Williams, T. A., and Martin, K. (2010) *An Introduction to Management Science: Quantitative Approaches to Decision Making*, South-Western Cengage Learning.

Bloomfield, R., O'hara, M., & Saar, G. (2009). How noise trading affects markets: An experimental analysis. *Review of Financial Studies*, **22**(6), 2275-2302.

Canavos, G. C. and Koutrouvelis, I. A. (2008) *An Introduction to the Design and Analysis of Experiments*, Prentice Hall Higher Education.

De Vaus, D. (2007). *Surveys in Social Research (5th ed.)*. Australia: Routledge.

Easterby-Smith, M., Richard Thorpe, & Jackson., P. (2012). *Management Research (4th ed.).* London: Sage.

Hair, J. F. J., Black, W. C., Babin, B. J., & Anderson, R. E. (2010). *Multivariate Data Analysis: A Global Perspective (7th ed.).* USA: Pearson.

Hox, J. J., and Boeije, H. R. (2005). Data collection, primary vs. secondary. *Encyclopedia of Social Measurement*, **1**, 593-599.

Malhotra, N. (2009). *Basic Marketing Research; a decision-making approach* (3rd ed). New Jersey: Pearson.

Neuman, W. L. (2014). *Social Research Methods: Qualitative and Quantitative Approaches* (7th ed.). England: Pearson

Nunnally, J. C., and Bernstein, I. H. (1994). The assessment of reliability. *Psychometric Theory*, **3**: 248-29

Oehlert, G. W. (2000). *Design and Analysis of Experiments: Response surface design;* Freeman and Company: New York, NY, USA

Oppenheim, A. N. (2000). *Questionnaire Design, Interviewing and Attitude Measurement.* London: Pinter.

Sarantakos, S. (1988). *Social Research (2nd ed.).* Melbourne Macmillan

Walter, M. (2013). *Social Research Methods (3rd ed.).* Australia: Oxford.

Zikmund, W. G., Babin, B. J., Carr, J. C., & Griffin, M. (2010). *Business Research Methods (8th ed.):* South-Western Cengage Learning.

10 Approaches to Quantitative Data Analysis and Evaluation

*Stephen Rae, Ahmed Salhin, Babak Taheri,
Catherine Porter, Christian König and
Nikolaos Valantasis-Kanellos*

To understand data and present findings appropriately, researchers need awareness of statistical techniques. This chapter discusses the statistical tools used to analyse data. It focuses on two sets of the most widely used statistical tools, as shown in the 'Deductive' section in the data analysis area of the Methods Map (see Chapter 4): (1) exploring relationships and (2) comparing groups. In addition, we briefly explain 'Big Data'.

Data preparation

Real-life data are generally unorganised and filled with problems and errors that impede analysis. We discuss two pre-processing steps that prepare data for further analysis: data entry and data cleaning.

■ Data entry

Data is commonly organised using tables, with *records* as rows and *attributes* as columns. A record is an identifiable piece of information which contains a set of attributes. For example, one may organise questionnaire data so that each record corresponds to all the answers from a respondent and each attribute is answer to one question.

It is difficult to ensure complete accuracy when entering data. *Double data entry* reduces data entry errors by having two individuals enter the same content and compare their inputs; when discrepancies are found, the correct copy is verified and maintained. Another accuracy-improving method is to use encoding to avoid entering text data directly. For example, when entering gender information such as 'male' or 'female' in text form, typographic errors, such as 'mael' could be introduced and inconsistent capitalisation (e.g. 'Female' versus 'female') could cause the same words to be interpreted as different. Numerical encoding (e.g. 'male' as 0 and 'female' as 1) eliminates these problems. Encoding functions are provided in many data analysis software packages, including SPSS (IBM Corporation). Figure 10.1 illustrates a snapshot of variable view and data value in SPSS. Table 10.1 explains information required for each variable.

	Name	Type	Width	Decimals	Label	Values	Missing	Columns	Align	Measure	Role
1	Gender	Numeric	8	0	14: Gender	{1. male}	99	8	Right	Nominal	Input
2	Age	Numeric	8	0	15 Age	{1. 18-25}	99	8	Right	Nominal	Input
3	Marital	Numeric	8	0	16 Marital status	{1. single}	99	8	Right	Nominal	Input
4	Visit_group	Numeric	8	0	17 Did you visit	{1. alone}	99	8	Right	Nominal	Input
5	residence	Numeric	8	0	18 Where is yo	{1. local are	99	8	Right	Nominal	Input
6	Education_	Numeric	8	0	19 Highest level	{1. no educ	99	8	Right	Nominal	Input
7	Job	Numeric	8	0	20: Your curren	{1. Manager	99	8	Right	Nominal	Input
8	Souvenir	Numeric	8	0	21 Did you buy	{1. yes}	99	8	Right	Nominal	Input
9	Recommend	Numeric	8	0	22: Would you	{1. yes}	99	8	Right	Nominal	Input
10	visit_time	Numeric	8	0	23 Have you vis	{1. never}	99	8	Right	Ordinal	Input
11	Q1_1	Numeric	8	0	Relax mentally	{0. no opinio	99	8	Right	Scale	Input
12	Q1_2	Numeric	8	0	Discover new pl	{0. no opinio	99	8	Right	Scale	Input
13	Q1_3	Numeric	8	0	Be in a calm at	{0. no opinio	99	8	Right	Scale	Input
14	Q1_4	Numeric	8	0	Increase my kn	{0. no opinio	99	8	Right	Scale	Input
15	Q1_5	Numeric	8	0	Have a good ti	{0. no opinio	99	8	Right	Scale	Input
16	Q1_6	Numeric	8	0	Visit cultural att	{0. no opinio	99	8	Right	Scale	Input
17	Q1_7	Numeric	8	0	Visit historical	{0. no opinio	99	8	Right	Scale	Input
18	Q1_8	Numeric	8	0	Interest in history	{0. no opinio	99	8	Right	Scale	Input
19	Q1_9	Numeric	8	0	Religious motiv	{0. no opinio	99	8	Right	Scale	Input
20	Q2_1	Numeric	8	0	Visiting this sit	{0. no opinio	99	8	Right	Scale	Input
21	Q2_2	Numeric	8	0	Visiting this sit	{0. no opinio	99	8	Right	Scale	Input
22	Q2_3	Numeric	8	0	Visiting this sit	{0. no opinio	99	8	Right	Scale	Input
23	Q2_4	Numeric	8	0	Visiting this sit	{0. no opinio	99	8	Right	Scale	Input
24	Q2_5	Numeric	8	0	I get a lot of sat	{0. no opinio	99	8	Right	Scale	Input
25	Q2_6	Numeric	8	0	Visiting the site	{0. no opinio	99	8	Right	Scale	Input
26	Q2_7	Numeric	8	0	I find visiting thi	{0. no opinio	99	8	Right	Scale	Input
27	Q2_8	Numeric	8	0	Visiting this sit	{0. no opinio	99	8	Right	Scale	Input
28	Q3_1	Numeric	8	0	Visited a Japan	{1. Not at all	99	8	Right	Scale	Input
29	Q3_2	Numeric	8	0	Watched a TV	{0. no opinio	99	8	Right	Scale	Input
30	Q3_3	Numeric	8	0	Read a book or	{0. no opinio	99	8	Right	Scale	Input
31	Q3_4	Numeric	8	0	Attended any c	{0. no opinio	99	8	Right	Scale	Input
32	Q3_5	Numeric	8	0	Taken a tourist	{0. no opinio	99	8	Right	Scale	Input
33	Q3_6	Numeric	8	0	Played an activ	{0. no opinio	99	8	Right	Scale	Input
34	Q4_1	Numeric	8	0	The overall arch	{0. no opinio	99	8	Right	Scale	Input
35	Q4_2	Numeric	8	0	I liked the pecul	{0. no opinio	99	8	Right	Scale	Input
36	Q4_3	Numeric	8	0	I liked the way t	{0. no opinio	99	8	Right	Scale	Input
37	Q4_4	Numeric	8	0	I liked the infor	{0. no opinio	99	8	Right	Scale	Input
38	Q5_1	Numeric	8	0	I liked special a	{0. no opinio	99	8	Right	Scale	Input
39	Q5_2	Numeric	8	0	This visit provid	{0. no opinio	99	8	Right	Scale	Input

Data View   Variable View

Figure 10.1(a): Example of variable view in SPSS software

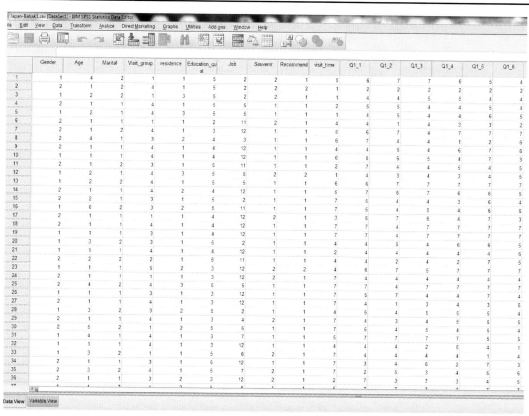

Figure 10.1(b): Example of data view in SPSS software

Table 10.1: Information required for each variable in variable view in SPSS

Variable Label	Short Description
Name	Up to 8 characters (no spaces), starting with a letter Not allowed: ALL, AND, BY, EQ, GT, LE, LT, NE, NOT, WITH, OR, TO Can be: short version of item description e.g., var01, Q1a
Width	Max. no. of characters
Decimal places	Decimal places for numbers
Label	Longer version of name
Values	Values for coded variables
Missing	Blanks, no answer, etc
Columns	No. of columns in data view screen
Alignment	Left, right, centre
Types of measure	Nominal, ordinal, scales

10

■   Data cleaning

Real-life data need to be cleaned because they are often *incomplete, noisy* and *inconsistent* (Han, Kamber, & Pei, 2011). Incompleteness arises when the values for some attributes are missing for some records. One approach is to delete the whole record that has missing data. This is viable when the number of records with missing data is relatively small compared to the whole data set, but may cause the deletion of observations that would be usable aside from a single missing attribute. Another approach is to impute the missing values using the expected value of the corresponding attribute or regression on other attributes. Noisiness refers to random factors that can only be quantified in a probabilistic way. Noises confound observations and cause outliers that are far away from normal observations (however, note that outliers may be the correct values and not caused by noise). A primary objective of data cleaning is to identify and 'smooth' outliers. Inconsistencies often arise when data from different sources are combined, e.g. combining sources using American and British dating formats (e.g. 3 April 1990 could be displayed as either 4/3/90 or 3/4/90).

In addition, data might take *impossible* or *unrealistic* values. A stock price of £2000 is possible but rather unrealistic, while a negative price is impossible. Examining data for abnormal figures can be performed on a record-by-record basis, although this is only suitable for small data sets. For larger data sets, there are some techniques which are suitable for diagnosing data for any error. Missing, impossible or unrealistic values could be found by sorting data into ascending/descending or by calculating frequencies, using any statistical package. Plotting the data will reveal most of the errors in the data set and provides a preliminary impression of its structure. Figure 10.2 illustrates a plot of 100 values with some missing values, a negative value and an outlier.

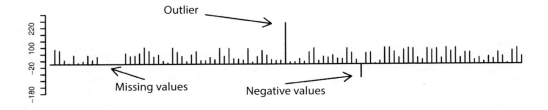

Figure 10.2: Example of plotting data to check for errors

Preliminary analysis

■ Describing data

To present a sample in an illustrative way, one can use descriptive statistics, graphs or both.

For a nonmetric variable (e.g. an ordinal scale), *frequency* and *ratio* are the two commonly used descriptive statistics. Frequency counts the number of occurrences of a specific category, while ratio calculates the corresponding percentage of frequency in the sample. Nonmetric data can be visualised through pie charts or bar charts. Here we give an example which considers the size category of companies (based on Singhvi and Desai, 1971). Table 10.2 summarises the frequencies and ratios of all eight size groups. Figure 10.3 plots these with a bar chart and a pie chart.

Table10.2: Company size category: frequencies and ratios

Size category ($m)	Frequency	Ratio (%)
<10	19	12.26
10–20	19	12.26
20–80	20	12.90
80–130	21	13.55
130–200	15	9.68
200–300	20	12.90
300–500	13	8.39
>500	28	18.06

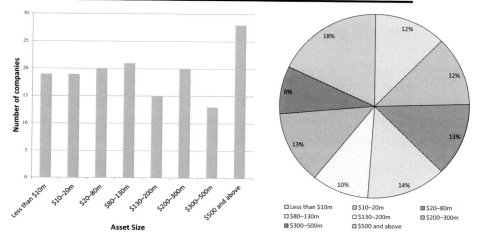

Figure 10.3: Size category of companies: bar graph and pie chart

10

If the sample is of a metric type, researchers normally calculate a variety of statistics measuring the basic characteristics of the sample. The *central tendency* measures provide a typical value that represents the entire sample. Examples of these measures include the mean (arithmetical avverage), median (the value of the middle case), and mode (the most frequent value) of a particular sample. Dispersion measures (e.g. variance, standard deviation) assess the spread of values away from the central tendency variation across the sample. See Wisniewski (2010) for more details.

Many of the techniques discussed in this chapter assume a Normal distribution of data. For this reason, two additional descriptive statistics are often very important: *skewness* and *kurtosis*. *Skewness* is a measure of the asymmetry of a variable's distribution. *Kurtosis* measures the weight of tails of the distribution. Figure 10.4 demonstrates these concepts using hypothetical probability distributions.

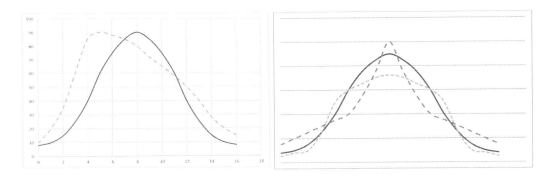

Figure 10.4: Skewness (left) and Kurtosis (right)

The left diagram demonstrates skewness. The solid line represents a Normal distribution with skewness 0. The dashed line is asymmetric and represents a positively skewed distribution with a thick right-hand tail. Negative skewness (not pictured) would have a thick left tail.

The right diagram demonstrates kurtosis. Again, the solid line represents a Normal distribution with kurtosis 0. The dashed line represents positive kurtosis (leptokurtosis), a higher, narrower peak and thicker tails at both ends. The dotted line shows negative kurtosis (platykurtosis), a broader, flatter peak.

A Normal distribution should have both skewness and kurtosis close to 0. If this is not the case, many statistical techniques will lead to inaccurate conclusions due to the underlying assumption of Normal data (see *Parametric and Non-Parametric Data*, below). In these cases, the researcher may search for alternative methods or ways to work around the non-Normal data.

Histograms, boxplots, and line charts are means of visualising metric measurements. Histograms and bar charts are very similar as both are used to describe the distribution of a sample, but in a histogram the scale of the horizontal axis must be equally spaced. Using the same data set on company sizes, we have plotted the distribution of size categories using a boxplot in Figure 10.5.

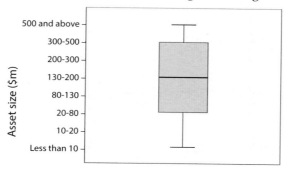

Figure 10.5: Size of companies: boxplot

Figure 10.6 shows a line chart used to visualize the FTSE100 stock market index over a 30-year period, which has a particular value for time series analysis.

Wooldridge (2009) provides further information on preliminary tests of data.

Figure 10.6: FTSE100 stock index values from 1985 to 2014

■   Data types

The type of data collected determines the techniques, estimation methods and models that the researcher may use to find an answer to the research question(s). Data might have a cross-sectional dimension, time dimension or both. Cross-sectional data represents data on individuals, countries, firms, regions or any other subjects, which is collected at, approximately, the same point of time. The purpose of cross sectional analysis is to understand how the differences between the units or subjects affects the phenomenon that researcher is investigating. Time series analysis concerns the evolution of the phenomena over time and observes variables across a period. Data that has both cross sectional and time series dimensions can be either pooled cross sectional data or panel data. The difference is that pooled cross sectional data observes the variables on a random sample of subjects that might change over time, while panel data observes the same sample of subjects over time. The type of data is likely to depend on the intended research question as this will define whether a cross-section or time element is required.

The appropriate analysis technique(s) for a project depends on the type of data and the type of measurement (nominal, ordinal, interval or ratio). It is therefore important to correctly identify the type of data and the type of measurement before analysis. Examples of how data type and measurement type influence the appropriate methods are included in some of the sections later in the chapter.

■ Statistical significance, null and alternative hypotheses

There are three terms used frequently in quantitative analysis: statistically significant, null hypothesis and alternative hypothesis.

- ■ **Statistically significant**: The observed results are unlikely to have happened by chance (highly improbable). The level of significance is influenced by sample size (not by population size). Statistical significance is usually measured with a p-value of the appropriate test. Researchers commonly believe that the results are probably true if the statistical test has a p-value lower than 0.05. For example, Aebi *et al.* (2012) showed that banks which had a Chief Risk Officer (CRO) on the board of directors achieved better performances during the 2007/2008 financial crisis than banks which did not. The difference in outcomes was considered to be statistically significant because $p = 0.0455$.

Significance testing relies on the probability of observations, which means there is a small chance that the conclusion drawn is incorrect. At the 5% significance level, there is a 5% probability that the results are caused by chance alone. A lower p-value is better in this regard as it means there is a lower chance of drawing an erroneous conclusion, although 5% is generally considered to be a low enough risk (some fields require 1% or lower). There are two possible errors that can occur: A Type I error is a false positive – a result that appears significant but is the result of chance alone. A Type II error is a false negative – a result that appears insignificant but is caused by the subject being studied.

- **Null hypothesis**: There is no significant difference or relationship (H_0).
- **Alternative hypothesis**: There is a significant difference or relationship (H_1). There might be more than one alternative hypothesis in a study based on the research question and aim. The paper mentioned above could have used the following hypotheses:

H_0 (the presence of a CRO makes no difference to performance during the financial crisis) versus H_1 (banks with a CRO performed better than those without during the financial crisis).

■ Parametric versus nonparametric analysis

There are two commonly known statistical techniques in social science research: *parametric* and *nonparametric analyses*. Parametric tests have four main features: normally distributed data (data are from one or more normally distributed populations), homogeneity of variance (each group of participants comes from a population with the same variance), interval data, and independence (the behaviour of one participant does not influence the behaviour of another) (see Field 2009 for more information). For example, partial correlation, multiple regression, factor analysis, paired simplest *t*-test, analysis of variance (ANOVA) and multivariate analysis of variance (MANOVA) are parametric techniques. On the other hand, nonparametric techniques, which include Chi-square, Spearman's rank order correlation, the Wilcoxon signed rank test, the Kruskal-Wallis test and the Friedman test, do not have such stringent requirements. Table 10.3 shows the nonparametric alternative techniques. This chapter mainly focuses on parametric data analysis.

Table 10.3: Nonparametric techniques, parametric alternative and variables

Non-parametric	Parametric alternative	Independent/dependent variable
Chi-square	None	One categorical dependent variable/ One categorical independent variable
Spearman's Rank Order Correlation	Correlation coefficient	Two continuous variables
Wilcoxon Signed-Rank	None	One categorical independent variable (two levels)
Kruskal-Walls	One-way between groups ANOVA	One categorical independent variable (three or more levels)
Friedman Test	One-way between measures ANOVA	One categorical independent variable (three or more levels)

10

Statistical techniques I: Exploring relationships

The techniques introduced in this section are based on the analysis of independent and dependent variables and address multiple purposes, such as testing theories and models, predicting future outcomes and trends and assessing the reliability and validity of primary and secondary data scales.

- **Correlation analysis** explores the association and relationship between two variables in terms of strength and direction.

- **Partial correlation analysis** explains the relationship between a pair of variables, which are or might be influenced by a third variable.

- **Multiple regression analysis** is used to predict the value or score of a single dependent variable from multiple independent variables.

- **Factor analysis** explores the structure of relationships within a large group of related variables. It reduces them to a limited number of dimensions and determinants.

■ Correlation analysis

Correlation analysis quantifies the strength of a relationship between two variables. There are various measures of correlation available, with the Pearson correlation being the most common (if the type of measure used is unspecified, it is usually Pearson). Correlation measures generally take the form of a correlation coefficient (or ρ) that ranges from -1 (strong negative relationship) to $+1$ (strong positive). $r = 0$ indicates no correlation between the two variables. In addition, r^2 represents the proportion of variation in one variable that can be explained by the other variable and is more accurate in determining any correlation. Figure 10.7 illustrates a sample of different relationships between two independent variables which represent different values of the correlation coefficient; see Cohen *et al.* (2013) for more information.

The Pearson correlation coefficient measures the strength of a straight line relationship between two normally-distributed variables. Where a curvilinear relationship or non-normality is involved, rank-based correlation measures are available. Spearman's correlation and Kendall's tau are two examples. While the two measures calculate the correlation coefficient through different processes, they each start by ranking observations from highest to lowest, and the rankings are used to calculate the correlation rather than the actual variable values.

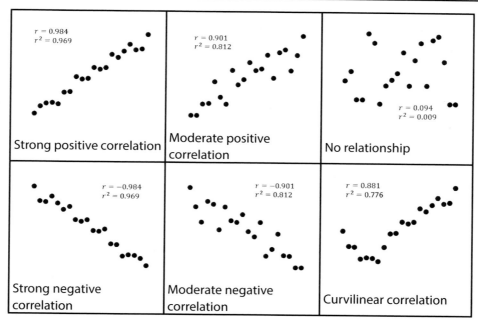

Figure 10.7: Interpreting scatterplots

Example: A student asks him/herself if he/she will get better exam results if he/she studies longer hours. After collecting data from a sample, the data is displayed in a scatter plot with the hours of study on the y-axis and the exam grade on the x-axis. The resulting diagram will look similar to one of the above diagrams. A strong positive correlation in this example means that, according to the data set, the longer the student studies, the better his/her exam grade will be. A strong negative correlation means that the longer he/she studies, the worse his/her exam grades will be. No relationship in this case means that the number of hours the student studies is not associated with his/her grade. A moderate correlation means that there is a weaker relationship. In all cases other factors might be relevant and may need to be included in a more complex model.

Note that correlation analysis does not show a cause-and-effect relationship. Two variables may be highly correlated either by chance or if both are caused by a third.

Partial correlation

As an extension to the Pearson correlation, partial correlation analysis allows us to explore the relationship between two variables which are or might be influenced by a third variable. The analysis focuses on removing the impact of any additional variables on the two variables of the researcher's interest. Sometimes a third variable might influence a relationship to some extent, thereby increasing

10

or decreasing the value of the correlation coefficient. If variables A and B appear to be strongly related to each other, their relationship might be under the influence of a third variable, C. The statistical control of variable C may show that the original correlation between A and B is much weaker that it appears to be.

The partial analysis of correlation requires at least three continuous variables and addresses the issue of whether there is still a significant relationship between two variables after controlling for the impact of the additional factor. The objective of this technique is to identify any correlations that can be explained by the effect of external variables not related to the unit of analysis.

Example: In the above example of determining the effect that of studying on an exam, partial correlation considers the effect that other factors have on the outcome of the exam, e.g. previous education or learning environment.

■ Multiple regression analysis

Multiple regression analysis is a technique to explore the relationship between one dependent variable and various independent variables. Similar to correlation analyses, multiple regression measures the association between variables. However, the main concern of the regression analysis is not only the strength and sign (positive or negative) of the relationship, but also the causal relationship between variables. In addition, multiple regression analysis is not limited to two variables but allows the exploration of interrelationships between a larger number of variables. In particular, multiple regression can be used to interpret the relationship between two variables (e.g. financial performance and capital structure) while controlling for all other factors that may also influence the dependent variable (e.g. size, industry, etc.). A more detailed description and explanation of assumptions can be found in Tabachnick and Fidell (2012).

Multiple regression analysis determines a formula for the dependent variable, taking the form:

$$Y = \alpha + \beta_1 X_1 + \beta_2 X_2 + \ldots + \beta_t X_t$$

Where Y is the dependent variable, α is a constant, each X represents one of the independent variables, and each β is a coefficient for the relevant X.

Research that aims to predict a particular outcome of a phenomenon usually uses these kinds of techniques. Complex constructs based on theoretical or conceptual models can be measured easily; therefore multiple regression analysis is capable of dealing with more complex real-life problems. Analysing a theoretical model gives detailed insight into a phenomenon and the individual contributions of variables and constructs by considering the whole. Multiple regression analysis measures how much of the variance in the dependent variable can be explained by the independent variables. Each variable needs to be evaluated individually in order to find out its contribution to the whole, based on the value of its coefficient.

There are a number of assumptions made in multiple regression that limit its application in some circumstances. However, it is a widely used and well-studied method. The effects of violating most assumptions are known and there are advanced techniques for working around many of the potential problems that would otherwise result for multiple regression.

Example: In the same scenario used for the previous two examples, the dependent variable in this case would be the exam grade, while the independent variables could be the hours of study, the previous education of the student, the student's gender, age or any other factor that distinctly characterises the sample population or that the researcher hypothesises would affect exam grade.

Regression analysis is a family of methods. The appropriate version to use in a given research project depends on the types of data. Examples of data types and useful statistical models used in each case can be found in Table 10.4.

Table 10.4: Examples of different data types and suitable regression models

Data type	Example
Cross sectional data	Understanding the impact of research and development expenditure (R&D) on the financial performance of UK companies in a certain year. The data collected has no time element.
Time series data	The values of some variables might be affected by their values in the past. For example, stock market prices and interest rate in a specific point of time might be driven by their past events and the research question might be how much these past events affects current values. The model used here is different than the one used in the cross sectional analysis. The researcher might decide to use a Vector Auto-Regressive model (VAR) to regress current values of the variable on past values (lags) of the same variable. Other example of time series models are ARIMA, ARMA, ARCH, GARCH, EGARCH, etc.
Pooled cross-sectional data and panel data	The researcher might be interested in looking at the same relationship between R&D and the financial performance; however, he/she has chosen to collect data on companies over a certain period of time (e.g. 10 years). The data on R&D and firm performance will be collected for each subject (company) in each of the 10 years within the chosen time period. The important issue here is that, for pooled cross-sectional data, the sample of companies is not required to be the same for every year of the 10 years. In panel data, the sample of companies is constant over the period. The models suitable in analysing this type of data are called Fixed-effect and Random-effect models.

10

The nature of the data also has an effect on the chosen model and estimation method. For example, *Probit* and *Logit* regression models are suitable for categorical dependent variables. In addition, some estimation methods will be more suitable than others depending on the nature of the data and the underlying assumptions about the population. For a categorical dependent variable, the Maximum Likelihood Estimation method (MLE) is more appropriate than an Ordinary Least Square method (OLS). Another example to consider could be a case in which the chosen model suffers from a potential *endogeneity* problem (i.e. independent variables may be correlated with error term in the model). The researcher in this case might use the Generalized Method of Moments (GMM) estimation method to overcome that specific problem. The ability to answer research questions depends on choosing the correct models, techniques, methods, tests, etc. for the type and nature of the data at hand.

Full details of different kind of models and estimation techniques are beyond the scope of this book. For further details, see Wooldridge (2012).

■ Factor analysis

Factor analysis does not measure correlations for testing hypotheses but rather evaluates a large set of variables in order to synthesise it into a smaller, more set of factors or components. Factor analysis is based on the comparison of inter-relationships among variables in order to identify groups that belong together, and is applied to problems that cannot be directly measured. However, the valuable information is still retained in the smaller data set. The resulting number of variables or factors is more manageable and can be used for other methods, such as regression or correlation analysis. The main concerns of factor analysis are threefold.

1 It helps the researcher to understand the structure of certain variables.

2 It helps to build constructs and questionnaires to test variables.

3 It reduces the number of variables from a large set to one with a more manageable number of components.

For example, Ludvigson and Ng (2007) used factor analysis to generate three factors that summarise a large amount of economic information, and used them to explain excess stock market return.

The *R-matrix* is the commonly used arrangement including correlation coefficients (such as those used in the correlation analysis) between each pair of variables or factors. The analysis focuses on exploring the maximum level of common variance in a correlation matrix utilising the smallest number of explanatory scales.

■ Time series analysis

A time series is a series of observations of one or more variables made across successive periods of time. Analysis of such series often focuses on how the value of a variable at time *t* is related to the value of the same variable at time *t-1*. Time series analysis extracts meaningful information from a time series. This commonly involves looking for trends in the data, which can in turn be used to forecast likely future values.

Finance provides many examples of time series. The value of a stock index or commodity may rise or fall on a daily basis, but over longer periods a general movement trend will be apparent. A time series may also experience seasonality, a regular cycle of rising and falling value. For example, items used in an annual celebration are in low demand for most of the year but high demand leading up to the celebration.

Time series data has a number of additional qualities to test for in addition to those described in *Describing Data* above. Testing for *stationarity, co-integration, autocorrelation, heteroscedasticity*, etc. might be required.

- *Stationarity* means the probability distribution of a time series does not change over time.

- Two time series are said to be *co-integrated* if they are non-stationary but a linear combination of them is stationary.

- *Autocorrelation* refers to the correlation between the value of a variable at one time and the value of the same variable at an earlier time (its lagged value).

- *Heteroscedasticity* occurs when the variance of the error term from a regression model is not constant.

Time series analysis encompasses many techniques and models. A detailed description is far beyond the scope of this chapter. Hamilton's (1994) book is a useful guide for beginners.

10

■ Summary: statistical techniques to explore relationships

Table 10.5 summarises the main characteristics of the required variables and gives an example of a research question for each statistical technique that is used to compare groups. The general assumptions for statistical analysis are discussed in the previous section.

Table 10.5: Summary of statistical techniques to explore relationships

Variables	Example question
Correlation	
Two continuous independent variables	Ils there a relationship between company size and level of leverage?
Partial correlation	
Three continuous independent variables	Is there a relationship between a company's recent financial performance and its level of leverage after controlling for company size?
Multiple regression	
Two or more independent variables; one continuous dependent variable	What is the causal relationship between disclosure of information, company size, accounting volatility and recent financial performance?
Factor analysis	
Set of related continuous independent variables	What is the underlying structure of the items that make up the excess stock market return and how many factors are involved?

Statistical techniques II: Comparing groups

The aim of this section is to describe and explain the main statistical techniques that are used to explore differences between groups or conditions in social science research. The purpose of testing and comparing a set of two or more groups is to identify statistically significant differences in the means of the analysed groups. Using these kinds of techniques helps to make statistical inference about any population from a randomly chosen sample.

■ *t-test analysis* compares the value of the mean scores (variables) for only two groups.

■ *ANOVA* compares the values of one or two independent variables for more than two groups with different or independent participants.

■ *MANOVA* is used to compare the mean scores for two or more groups with more than one dependent variable.

■ *Analysis of covariance (ANCOVA)* explains the difference between independent variables and one dependent variable influenced by an additional variable that has to be controlled for.

■   # *t*-test analysis

The *t*-test analysis shows whether or not there is a significant difference in the means of two groups, based on the analysis of one categorical independent and one continuous dependent variable. The *t-statistic* is the ratio of the difference between two sample means (μ_1-μ_2) divided by an estimate of the standard error (SE). The SE is a measure of the dispersion of both samples and is calculated by a formula that includes the variance of each sample and the total sample size. The size of the *t*-statistic relative to a benchmark ascertains whether the difference between two means is statistically significant. For example, Chan *et al.* (2012) conducted a series of *t*-tests using different benchmark portfolios and found that Chinese Initial Public Offering (IPO) shares of type A underperform their non-IPO benchmarks, while type B IPOs outperform their non-IPO benchmarks.

The different levels of significance are described by Hair *et al.* (2010). The calculation of the statistic is:

$$\text{t statistic} = \frac{\mu_1\text{-}\mu_2}{SE_{\mu_1\text{-}\mu_2}}$$

The *independent-sample t*-test compares the difference in the means for two dissimilar population groups, such as males and females, or children and adults, meaning that independent sample groups are compared under different conditions. The *paired-sample t*-test is used to compare measurements of the same sample under different conditions. For further details on the different techniques see Field (2009).

To summarise, *t*-testing is used to determine whether two groups are different in some regard. It could be used to investigate whether oil industry companies produce significantly more environmental reporting information than companies in the financial services industry. Taylor *et al.* (2010) use *t*-testing to investigate changes over time by comparing the mean level of risk reporting in one year to the level of risk reporting in the next.

■   # Analysis of variance

Comparing the means of two different groups or conditions is not always sufficient and needs to be extended in order to compare the means of three or more sample groups. The use of ANOVA is adequate for these reasons, as it compares the variance between different groups with the variability within each of the groups. The *F-statistic* expresses the differences in the variances of different groups as a ratio (see Field (2009) and Hair *et al.* (2010) for more details). ANOVA tests the null hypothesis that the means of different groups are

10

not equal. If the *F-statistic* is significant, the null hypothesis can be rejected and the population means are equal.

ANOVA is similar to *t*-testing in that it compares the means of different populations and could be replaced by a series of *t*-tests comparing two groups at a time. However, each *t*-test has a small chance of a Type I or Type II error, increasing the total error probability. ANOVA performs a single test and therefore reduces error chances.

One-way between-groups ANOVA compares different groups or conditions and tests the impact of one independent variable (or factor) on one continuous dependent variable. *Two-way between-groups* ANOVA compares different groups or conditions and tests the impact of two independent variables on one continuous dependent variable.

Continuing the example, ANOVA would be appropriate if the researcher was comparing the environmental reports of three or more industry sectors.

Multivariate analysis of variance

Multivariate ANOVA (MANOVA) extends the previous approach to situations in which there are several dependant variables. Analysing multiple variables at the same time reduces the risk of errors, but models should be based on good theoretical or conceptual constructs. Instead of ANOVA models for individual variables, MANOVA represents a more complex, single method of testing a wider range of questions (Hair *et al.* 2010). In real life, finding a significant result is more likely if you run a series of individual analyses at the same time. Therefore, MANOVA gives more realistic results that are not inflated by errors.

Continuing the example, MANOVA would be appropriate for comparing both environmental and the risk management information.

Analysis of covariance

In situations where an additional variable (the covariate) may influence the value of the dependent variable, ANCOVA is a useful technique. ANCOVA combines regression analysis and ANOVA and therefore removes the influence of any additional variable in order to control the score of the dependent variable. Stevens (2012) recommends the use of two or three covariates in order to reduce errors and increase the significance between the groups. The right choice of covariate is crucial to eliminate errors that bias results. An effective covariate is highly correlated with the dependent variable(s) but not correlated with the independent variables. As a result, the influence of differences between individual groups will be reduced and controlled, increases the power of the (Tabachnick and Fidell 2012).

■ **Summary of techniques to compare groups**

Table 10.6 summarises the main characteristics for the required variables and gives an example research question for each statistical technique. The general assumptions for statistical analysis have been introduced in the previous sections.

Table 10. 6: Summary of statistical techniques to compare groups

Technique	Variables	Example question
z- or-test analysis	One categorical independent variable and one continuous dependent variable	Is there a change in tourists' satisfaction scores from time 1 to time 2?
ANOVA (one-way)	One categorical independent variable and one continuous dependent variable	Is there a difference in satisfaction scores for different age groups of tourists?
ANOVA (two-way)	Two categorical independent variable and one continuous dependent variable	Is there a difference in satisfaction scores for different age groups and genders of tourists?
MANOVA	One or more categorical independent variables and two or more related continuous dependent variables	Is there a difference between genders, across different age groups, in terms of their scores on satisfaction and motivation measures?
ANCOVA	One or more categorical independent, one covariate variable and one continuous dependent variable	Is there a significant difference in tourist motivation between three age groups, while controlling for the scores on repeated visits at time 1?

Structural equation modelling

10

The data analysis techniques described so far can only analyse one layer of linkages between independent and dependent variables at a time. Structural equation modelling (SEM) is one of several more recent methods that can answer research questions in one single systematic and comprehensive analysis by modelling the relationships among multiple independent and dependent variables at the same time.

SEM has been used to study a range of topics including economics and finance. SEM combines factor analysis and regression and fits two models. One tests the construction of latent variables (factor analysis), while the other tests the relationships between them (regression).

Hair *et al.* (2010, p.634) define structural equation modelling as "a family of statistical models that seek to explain their relationships among multiple variables". It can make use of latent variables – those that cannot be measured directly but have observable indicators. Figure 10.8 illustrates these relationships.

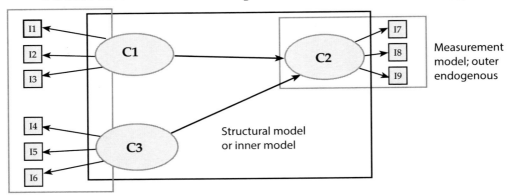

Measurement model; outer exogenous

Figure 10.8: Visual demonstration of SEM

Information about Figure 10.8:

Exogenous variables are independent variables not presumed to be caused by other variables in the model. Endogenous variables are variables assumed to be caused by other variables in the model. Unlike regression tools, SEM assesses the structural model and in the same analysis evaluates the measurement model, loadings of observed items (measurements) on their expected latent variables. C1, C2 and C3 are the constructs or latent variables: they represent an abstract concept.

SEM relaxes many regression assumptions, including variable independence. In Figure 10.8, variables C1 and C3 could be connected.

SEM is sometimes executed using specialised software packages, such as AMOS and SmartPLS. There are two methods to estimate the relationships in a structural equation model: component-based SEM (PLS-SEM) and covariance-based SEM (AMOS-SEM). Each of these methods may be appropriate for different research contexts and researchers need to understand their dissimilarity before using them. Unlike covariance-based SEM, which uses the structure of variables, PLS is a component-based approach suitable for both predictive applications and theory building (Hair *et al.*, 2014). PLS can be modelled in formative (i.e. based on classical test theory where the measured indicators are assumed to be caused by the construct) and reflective (i.e. indicators cause changes in the construct) modes (Taheri *et al.*, 2014). Table 10.7 illustrates the main differences between component-based SEM and covariance-based SEM. For further information on the method, see Schumacker and Lomax (2004).

Table 10.7: Differences between component-based SEM and covariance-based SEM

Basis of comparison	PLS-SEM (e.g. SmartPLS)	CB-SEM (e.g. AMOS)
Objective	Prediction oriented	Theory oriented
Approach	Variance based	Covariance based
Assumption	Predictor specification (nonparametric)	Multivariate normal distribution and independent observations (parametric)
Relationship between a latent variable and its measures	Can be modelled in either formative or reflective mode	Usually only reflective indicators
Implications	Optimal for prediction accuracy	Optimal for parameter accuracy
Model complexity	Large complexity (e.g. 100 constructs, 1000 indicators)	Small to moderate complexity (e.g. < 100 indicators)
Sample size	Power analysis based on the portion of the model with largest number of predictors. Recommendations for minimum number of observations can range from 30 to 100 cases	Ideally based on power analysis of specific model. Recommendations for minimum number of observations can range from 200 to 800

Large scale – big data

■ Nature of big data

Big data is a type of secondary data that can be utilised in research projects. The use of big data can be seen as a deductive or inductive analytical approach based on the nature of a potential study. Big data are generated by various methods and means, every second of every day, in forms that are beyond imagination. According to Gartner's report, "big data is high volume, high velocity, and/or high variety information assets that require new forms of processing to enable enhanced decision making, insight discovery and process optimization" (Laney, 2012).

Using big data presents new challenges. The term 'big data' refers to cases in which the data set is unmanageably large. As a result, big data require the user to find ways to extract meaning from vast quantities of information before any analysis can commence.

10

■   Forms of big data

Big data can be sourced by various means. A main distinction lies between the data type (structured or unstructured) and source (machine or human generated):

- *Structured data* are those data with precise length and format.
- *Unstructured data* are those that do not follow any specified format.
- *Machine-generated data* are created by machines without human interaction.
- *Human-generated data* are created by the interaction of humans with machines.

It must be mentioned that both machine- and human-generated data can be created in structured and unstructured ways. For example, sensor data (RFID, GPS), web log data, point of sale and financial data are characterised as structured machine-generated data, while input data (age, sex, income, etc.), click stream data and gaming-related data can be characterised as structured human-generated data. On the other hand, satellite images, scientific data, photographs and videos, radar or sonar data are perceived to be unstructured machine-generated data, while a company's internal documents, social media data and website content are unstructured human-generated data.

A framework that shows the most relevant sample of technological companies is provided by Nair and Narayanan (2012), which adds the internal/external dimension to the data source classification; this is depicted in Figure 10.9. According to this framework, the nature of the company and its main strategic focus will determine what kind of data should be considered in their decision making. However, a complete analysis of these choices does not fall into the scope of this book. For more information, consult Nair and Narayanan (2012).

■   Big data application and analysis tools

Big data enable managers to measure and directly enhance their understanding of their business. They are then able to convert this quickly gained knowledge into valuable information that helps to make decisions and potentially creates a competitive advantage (Bughin, Chui, and Manyika 2010). The company's finance and management accounting functions are able to benefit from this analysis and predictions (Bhimani and Willcocks 2014).

Some companies that use big data have created tools to handle huge amounts of data in efficient, cost-effective and time-sensitive ways (e.g. BigTable, MapReduce, Hadoop). A thorough description of these tools falls outside the scope of this book. For a comprehensive discussion about advanced analytic tools see Zikopoulos *et al.* (2012). For simplicity, a more basic analysis tool, such as Google Analytics, can be used.

	Structured		Unstructured	
External	Mobile phone/GPS	Public surveys	Google + Twitter	Facebook
	Purchase History	Credit history	Pinterest	Instagram
			Personal life events	Blogs
	Travel History	Life event records		
	Real Estate Records			Foursquare
		Census data	External sensor data	
Internal	Customer relationship management (CRM)	Web profiles	Online company forums	Web feeds
		Sales records		
			SharePoint	
	HR records	Expense records		
	Financials	Customer profiles	Text documents	Sensor data

Structured · **Unstructured**

Data type

Figure 10.9: Four dimensions of Big Data (Source: Nair and Narayanan 2012)

(Data source axis shown on left)

Summary

In this chapter, we have discussed the researcher's data preparation approach and preliminary (descriptive) analysis. We have also introduced some of the main statistical techniques used in quantitative research in accounting and finance. The key issues that should be related back to your study question are: a) how to prepare data; b) how to use preliminary data analysis; c) the most appropriate analyses for comparing groups; and d) the most appropriate techniques for exploring relationships.

10

References and further reading

Aebi, V., Sabato, G., & Schmid, M. (2012). Risk management, corporate governance, and bank performance in the financial crisis. *Journal of Banking & Finance*, **36**(12), 3213-3226.

Bhimani, A., & Willcocks, L. (2014). Digitisation,'Big Data'and the transformation of accounting information. *Accounting and Business Research*, **44**(4), 469-490.

Brooks, C. (2014). *Introductory Econometrics for Finance*. Cambridge University Press.

Bughin, J., Chui, M., & Manyika, J. (2010). Clouds, big data, and smart assets: Ten tech-enabled business trends to watch. *McKinsey Quarterly*, **56**(1), 75-86.

Chan, K., Wang, J., & Wei, K. J. (2004). Underpricing and long-term performance of IPOs in China. *Journal of Corporate Finance*, **10**(3), 409-430.

Cohen, J., Cohen, P., West, S. G., & Aiken, L. S. (2013). *Applied Multiple Regression/ Correlation Analysis for the Behavioral Sciences*: Taylor & Francis.

Field, A. (2009). *Discovering Statistics using SPSS* (Vol. 3). London: SAGE Publications Ltd.

Hair, J. F. J., Black, W. C., Babin, B. J., & Anderson, R. E. (2010). *Multivariate Data Analysis: A Global Perspective* (7th ed.). USA: Pearson.

Hair, J. F. J., Hult, G. T. M., Ringle, C. M., & Sarstedt, M. (2014). *A Primer on Partial Least Squares Structural Equation Modeling (PLS-SEM)*. UK: Sage.

Hamilton, J. D. (1994). *Time Series Analysis*. Princeton: Princeton University Press.

Han, J., Kamber, M., & Pei, J. (2011). *Data Mining: Concepts and Techniques*. USA: Morgan Kaufmann.

Laney, D. (2012). The Importance of 'Big Data': A Definition. Gartner. Available at: https://www.gartner.com/doc/2057415/importance-big-data-definition

Ludvigson, S. C., & Ng, S. (2007). The empirical risk–return relation: a factor analysis approach. *Journal of Financial Economics*, **83**(1), 171-222.

Nair, R. and Narayanan, A. (2012). Getting Results From Big Data: A Capabilities-Driven Approach to the Strategic Use of Unstructured Information. Florham Park, N.J.: Strategy&. Available at: http://www.strategyand.pwc.com/media/ file/Strategyand_Getting-results-from-big-data.pdf [Accessed 6 Nov. 2015].

Schumacker, R. E., & Lomax, R. G. (2004). *A Beginner's Guide to Structural Equation Modeling*. Psychology Press.

Singhvi, S. S., & Desai, H. B. (1971). An empirical analysis of the quality of corporate financial disclosure. *Accounting Review*, **46**(1), 129-138.

Stevens, J. P. (2012). *Applied Multivariate Statistics for the Social Sciences*, 5th Edition: Taylor & Francis.

Tabachnick, B. G., & Fidell, L. S. (2012). *Using Multivariate Statistics*. Boston: Pearson Education.

Taheri, B., Jafari, A., & O'Gorman, K. (2014). Keeping your audience: Presenting a visitor engagement scale. *Tourism Management*, **42**, 321-329.

Taylor, G., Tower, G., & Neilson, J. (2010). Corporate communication of financial risk. *Accounting & Finance*, **50**(2), 417-446.

Wisniewski, M. (2010). *Quantitative Methods for Decision Makers*, Essex: Pearson Education, Limited.

Wooldridge, J. (2012). *Introductory Econometrics: A Modern Approach*. Cengage Learning.

Zikopoulos, P., deRoos, D., Parasuraman, K., Deutsch, T., Giles, J., & Corrigan, D. (2012). *Harness the Power of Big Data The IBM Big Data Platform*: McGraw-Hill.

11 Ethics, Moral Philosophy and Accounting and Finance Research

*Audrey Paterson, David Leung
and William Jackson*

> *Oh, what a tangled web we weave,*
> *When first we practice to deceive.*
>
> (Sir Walter Scott, 1808)

So far within this text book, we have discussed the nature of research, how to find a suitable research topic, the literature review, research traditions in accounting and finance, and a variety of ways in which to collect and analyse data. However, an aspect of the research process that we have not addressed so far concerns ethics and codes of conduct. As outlined in earlier chapters, researchers have a wide variety of ways in which to collect data for their study, each of which raises questions with respect to ethical and moral principles. In Chapter 1, we determined that research is essentially about the production of knowledge but in the pursuit of generating this knowledge we must also take into consideration that the research community has a responsibility, not just to pursue knowledge or objective truth but also to the subject of their enquiry and its participants.

Given that the results of research are inevitably made public or published, there is almost always a risk or potential threat to the research subjects or public rhetoric as the research findings may produce accounts of social situations, which may conflict with the interests or beliefs of some individuals or social groups. The researcher must therefore be accountable for their actions, and the possible effects of such actions, on their research subjects. Keeping this in mind, it is therefore important when conducting any research project to review the ethical position regarding your study and to be aware of and adhere to ethical and professional codes of conduct.

The field of accounting and financial ethics has grown considerably in recent years in both the educational and professional context and has taken on an interdisciplinary aspect. This can be attributed to philosophers and scholars within accounting and finance successfully connecting ethical theory to real world problems. Within this chapter, we introduce you to the notion of ethics and moral philosophy and its importance to everyday life. We begin by first considering what ethics is and why it's important. This is then followed with examples that demonstrate questionable ethical and moral behaviour from both research and professional practice. We deliberately draw in both as the outputs of research also inform the corporate world, the activities of which affect society as a whole. Following this we introduce a selection of key moral philosophies and their application to academic and professional practice within accounting and finance. The chapter includes examples of important issues that require careful reflections and consideration when determining approaches to data gathering and ensuring professional integrity. Finally, some practical advice and the fundamental principles of good research conduct and codes of ethics are put forward.

What is ethics and why is it important?

The notion of ethics concerns our moral conduct, our duties and responsibilities towards other people, society, animals, plants and the environment; and whether we are good or bad, or right or wrong. This of course is a subjective, fuzzy and at times murky area. After all, what is good or bad? And who decides? Unfortunately, there isn't a natural or universal scale for the weighing of good or bad, or some authority which we can refer to that can definitively determine an action as morally good or bad.

Cavan (1982) defines ethics "as a matter of principled sensitivity to the rights of others. Being ethical limits the choices we can make in the pursuit of truth. Ethics say that while truth is good, respect of human dignity is better, even if, in the extreme case, the respect of human dignity leaves one ignorant of human nature" (Cavan, in Bulmer 1982, p810). While in society we learn ethical and moral behaviour through childhood, civil society, religion and other social settings, the teaching of ethics and moral philosophy fell out of favour for a significant period of time. During the nineteenth century, ethics and moral philosophy featured prominently in the university curriculum and was viewed as essential to the development of the student's character. By the twentieth century, however, the teaching of ethics and moral philosophy in many universities had lost its appeal. This arose mainly due to organisational changes within academic institutions and the development of Faculties that covered a much broader range of academic disciplines and vocational subjects. The main focus was turned to educationally based programmes that provided vocational credentials in which little room remained for ethics and moral philosophy. While this remained the case well into the twentieth century there has been a gradual shift towards reintroducing ethics and moral philosophy into educational programmes such as accounting and finance in recent years, triggered mainly by the numerous scandals that have come out of the corporate world, and the financial services industry.

Ethics, research and the corporate world

Indeed, we do not need to stray too far in the corporate world and the financial services industry to come across examples that demonstrate a complete lack of moral or ethical consideration for society, the environment or human life. The activities of business and the financial services industry and their decision making processes are heavily driven by the profit maximisation criteria which can often lead to highly questionable decisions being made. The case of the Ford Pinto is one such example. Ford's engineers discovered before the assembly of the vehicles had started that the fuel tanks of the Ford Pinto would explode if caught up in a rear end collision. Ford determined after researching the cost benefit of replacing faulty fuel tanks, that it would be more cost effective to pay the damages for any deaths caused by the exploding fuel tanks than to delay assembly and reconfigure the design of vehicles. More than twenty-four people were killed due to exploding fuel tanks before the company issued a recall notice to fix the problem (Bazerman and Tenbrusel, 2011).

The tobacco industry provides another interesting ethical case. Tobacco companies in general claim not to target youths and children in their marketing campaigns. The Altria Group, which is the world's largest and most profitable tobacco company, and includes brands such as Marlboro, has very active marketing campaigns for its products in developing countries. Criticisms of the Marlboro brand relate to their hiring of young girls known as 'Marlboro Girls' to distribute free cigarettes to youths at sponsored concerts and events (Winter, 2001). A recent study conducted by ACT in 2014 found 22% of five and six-year-old children in low to middle income countries could identify the Marlboro brand. Additionally, research on the international reach of tobacco marketing campaigns suggests that children as young as thirteen are targeted (Borzekowski and Cohen (2013). Furthermore, despite the tobacco industry's

11

own research demonstrating the addictive and health damaging effects of the products, many companies have been accused of conducting marketing campaigns in a way that suggests their cigarettes with lower tar content are safer thus portraying it as a healthier option when it makes little difference (ILRF, 2005).

Within agriculture, the Monsanto Company is the largest producer of genetically modified seeds in the world. It is also the world leader in the production of the herbicide glyphosate which is marketed as 'Round Up'. Monsanto's innovations in seed technology were heralded as the world's best hope of tackling the looming global food crisis. The genetically modified seeds are argued to produce healthier and bigger crop yields while the use of 'Round Up' is marketed as a pesticide that is not harmful to the soil. Both products are patented and argued to be aggressively marketed to farmers and sold at inflated prices (Hockridge and Tomlinson, 2010). Research into genetically modified seeds, suggest that the higher yields predicted have not transpired (Gurian-Sherman, 2009). With respect to the soil toxicity of 'Round Up', research indicates that the toxins from the pesticide accumulate in the soil which ultimately harms the crops, renders the plants infertile and is linked to some serious health issues (Baden-Mayer, 2015). Moreover, farmers who have used genetically modified seeds are reported to have found extreme difficulty in growing non-genetically modified crops on that land without the crop becoming contaminated. Additionally, farmers who sign up to the GM technology agreement forgo the right to farm seeds saved and thus have to buy GM seed, the cost of which has escalated dramatically in recent years (Folger, 2013). Interestingly, Monsanto have also produced a genetically modified seed known as 'Round Up Ready Seeds' that are capable of resisting the herbicide. Anderson, 2014, suggests that farmers who experience problems of infertile plants due to contaminated soil from continued use of Round Up are thus forced to purchase these seeds thereby creating a dependency on Monsanto products.

Within the accounting and financial services industry we can point to examples such as the collapse of Enron which arose primarily out of malpractice, dodgy dealings, and the misrepresentation of financial information resulting from individual and collective greed that developed from an atmosphere of market excitement and corporate arrogance (Clikeman, 2013). Other examples of aggressive accounting practices include Tesco, the UK's largest retailer, who are reported to have purposefully tampered with the financial accounts in order to outwardly portray the company revenues as being higher (to a sum of £263 million) in order to increase the market value presented to prospective investors (ACCA, 2015). In a similar vein, Toshiba understated their costs on long term projects which led to an overstatement of their operating profits by $1.2 billion between 2008 and 2014. Indeed, it is thought that the full extent of Toshiba's aggressive accounting is still yet to be revealed (Addady, 2015).

Within finance examples include price-fixing, insider trading; the pursuit of short-term profit by assigning investors' money in questionable investments, misrepresentation of financial positions and rogue trading in the futures market. The collapse of Barings Bank for example was a direct result of unauthorized, speculative and aggressive trading in futures and options on the Singapore International Monetary Exchange by rogue trader Nick Leeson. Likewise, the Libor scandal that emerged following the 2007/8 financial crisis was a direct result of malpractice on a large scale across a range of investment banks and practitioners (Adams and Angus, 2015) who engaged in a series of fraudulent actions to inflate or deflate interest rates in order to protect their credit worthiness impression within the financial markets.

While these are extreme examples, the potential for researchers and professionals that use research information to act in questionable and unethical ways exists in all disciplines. Indeed, we do not need to delve too far into history to come across research projects within areas such as medicine and psychology that are highly questionable. For instance, German physicians working for the Nazis during the Second World War (1945-1949) ruthlessly used Jewish prisoners of war without their consent for medical experiments, which included deliberately infecting them with a disease or inflicting a wound to observe the effects.

Within psychology, John B. Watson from the Johns Hopkins University conducted an experiment on a 9-month old boy, Albert, in a study of classical conditioning. The experiment involved introducing the boy to a white rat which he initially loved. Later in the experiment each time the rat was introduced a hammer was used to cause a loud bang. The child quickly came to associate the rat with the loud noise and began to fear the rat and other furry animals (Watson and Rayner, 1920).

Anthropologists and ethnographers have a long tradition of researching all aspects of human culture. As such, their research skills are particularly useful to government intelligence agencies, and many anthropologists and ethnographers have conducted research on behalf of such organisations. Indeed, Franz Boas in his address to The Nation in 1906 expressed concern over the fact that he had found evidence that anthropologists were representing themselves as social science researchers when in fact they were acting as government spies. Project Camelot, a military funded project in 1964 by the United States of America (USA) Army, had the remit to gain an understanding of different societies and cultures in order to assist in the prediction and influence of social developments

11

in foreign lands and was later suggested to be a counterinsurgency project (Horowitz, 1967).

Ethical and moral philosophy

According to Douglas (1976), the nature of contemporary society is best described by a conflict model that is riddled with profound conflicts of interest, in which conflict is the reality of life; suspicion is the guiding principle and no one gives anyone anything for nothing, especially truth. Such a view is rather depressing and damning of society and the corporate world, but as the aforementioned examples demonstrate, we cannot assume adherence to high ethical or moral standards by individuals or organisations. The challenge for individuals and indeed organisations as well as the law, is how to balance conflicts, competing rights and obligations.

The study of ethics and moral philosophy is a vast area and extensive history. It is not our purpose or indeed possible to cover every aspect of ethical and moral philosophy in this chapter. We leave that to specialist academics in the area (see suggested further readings at end of the chapter). Rather we introduce you to three prominent but contrasting theories to demonstrate the continued relevance of ethics and morality in educational research and its application to the corporate world: consequentialism, non-consequentialism in the form of individual rights, and deontology.

■ Consequentialism

Utilitarianism is the best known form of consequentialism. While the concept of utilitarianism can be traced back to the earliest thinking on ethical matters, the classical formation can be attributed to Jeremy Bentham (1748-1832). Utilitarianism is an approach to morality that treats pleasure or desire-satisfaction as the sole element in human good and regards the morality of actions as entirely dependent on consequences or results for human well-being (Boatright, 2003). For utilitarians, motives are irrelevant as they cannot be seen but the consequences can be, therefore they count. Thus under this system, actions are classified and measured in terms of the pain or pleasure it will produce and can only be justified if it produces what Bentham called "The General Good" or "The greatest happiness of the greatest number" (Robinson and Garratt, 1988, p.71). Within this doctrine an act is then morally right, or not wrong, if it produces as great a balance of pleasure over pain as any alternative action open to the agent.

An obvious criticism of this view concerns the question of how happiness can be measured. Bentham had hoped to develop a precise method of scientific calculation, however, this proved unrealistic. That is not to say that happiness cannot be measured at all. It is possible, for example, to develop a set of measures that provides estimates of happiness. Within economics, for example, the measurement of consumption of goods and services to satisfy our wants and needs provides some quantification that can be linked to happiness. The greater our wants and needs are satisfied, the greater happiness is achieved which has obvious parallels with utilitarianism. However, Bentham was very clear that it is the common good that we should seek, not the individual, in order to ensure the maximum human happiness. Within this, Bentham made the common good the sole arbiter of right or wrong (Singer, 1994).

■ Non-consequentialism

While consequentialism is concerned with the results of actions to determine good or bad, right or wrong, non-consequentialism asserts that duties must be obeyed irrespective of the outcome. From this perspective a non-consequentialist holds the view that the end does not justify the means rather it is the intention to do the right thing that is of importance and not the result (Dellaportas *et al.*, 2005) but how do we determine what the right thing is? In order to address this question we can consider it from the perspective of the theory of rights.

From the theory of rights perspective, a good action is one in which the rights of the other is respected. Conversely, a bad action is one that violates another person's right. The principle holds that people have natural worth which must be respected and thus imposes a moral obligation on individuals to respect the rights of others when confronted with a moral dilemma (Singer, 1994). Aspects that fall within the theory of rights include, freedom of choice, right to the truth, freedom of speech, right to life, right to due process and right to what is agreed. A difficulty that arises with this theory is how to handle two or more equally convincing rights as it does not give weight to the various rights.

■ Deontology

11

According to deontological ethics, certain acts are right or wrong in themselves. Deontologists tend to concentrate on those acts which are wrong. Thus, according to deontologists such as Kant, acts of promise breaking, lying, stealing, invasion of privacy etc. are wrong independently of their consequences. Kant's moral theory centres around the categorical imperative which states that one should "act only on the maxim which you can at the same time will to be universal law" in other words "do unto others as you would have others do unto you". Kantian ethics involves choosing duties, not wants or desires. Motives are the central feature of moral actions and not the consequences (Want and

Klimowski, 1996). Goodwill is the motive that drives our desire to be good people and it is through practical reasoning that it is achieved. Kant advocates that moral actions are those which affirm this principle – acts which are done from a sense of duty as opposed to doing what we want.

Criticism of deontology concerns its inability to provide a credible explanation of what constitutes our moral obligations and how to reconcile moral conflicts. It also puts trusts in authorities for rule setting but authorities can be wrong. Furthermore, it is based on moral absolutes such as lying is wrong, however is lying always wrong? In times of serious conflict lying may be necessary in order to save lives. It is also heavily influenced by religion but religions have different beliefs which are not always compatible with each other (Boatright, 2003).

Conducting research

As discussed in earlier chapters of this book, researchers have open to them a variety of ways in which they can conduct research and gather data. A good deal of research conducted within social science is conducted with the consent of the study participants. Whether the data is gathered through archival sources, data banks, questionnaires or direct engagement with study participants, the researcher has an obligation to conform to ethical codes of practice. The rights of individuals perform an important role in research and indeed all moral issues. Within the doctrine of informed consent, the research subject must be competent, informed about the purposes of the research, understanding what he or she is told and give consent voluntarily and not under any form of duress. They should also have the right to withdraw from the research if they start to feel uncomfortable or threatened with the direction that the researcher is taking.

However, even within research that is more overt (open) and has the consent of the participant, ethical considerations can still arise. For example, studies that involve some form of participant observations that are conducted over a long period of time run the risk of the researcher becoming too involved with the study participants. The researcher may inadvertently cross the boundary into the participant's private space which might compromise the study findings, introduce bias and cross ethical boundaries.

Likewise, in longitudinal studies where the researcher is present over many months or longer there is a risk that the study participants become so used to the researcher being there that they stop thinking of them as a researcher but as part of the team and may thus start to unwittingly reveal inappropriate information. The researcher therefore has an obligation to keep the participants reminded of their position, to not do so, is unethical. Additionally, how such information then is used raises some ethical questions as such information may have been concealed if the study participants had been reminded of the purpose of the researcher's presence.

Another issue lies in the area of informed consent for observations conducted within organisations. While access may be granted and consent given to observe practices, if this is given at the higher level, questions then arise as to how compliant the study participants are at the lower levels. For example, have they been ordered to participate by their manager? If so, this is not informed consent. From an ethical point of view, such participants should not be observed or included in the study findings.

Additionally, where informed consent has been given for the research to be conducted, the researcher needs to establish a bond of trust and therefore must be careful with respect to self-representation, demeanour and exercise caution when given access to sensitive data to ensure the safety for the participants is secure and the trust bond is not violated. For example, it would be unethical to give the impression that the research was focussed a non-sensitive aspect of organisational documents when in fact the research was looking to expose some unsavoury aspects of the organisational activities. The withholding of information, manipulation of the research focus and deception to gain access to data therefore would be considered unethical.

Within social science research, there has been a tendency towards considering overt and covert research practices as opposites. However, as discussed above, while overt research involves participant consent, the approach also provides opportunities for data to be collected covertly. Some of the issues with covert research will be discussed next.

Covert research

Covert research is an exploratory approach in which the researcher's true identity, purpose and academic intentions are not disclosed (either fully or partly) to the subject under study. Within covert research it is possible to separate this into two forms, passive and active. The distinction between the two forms is however, somewhat meaningless as both forms involve the collection and use of data without the fully informed consent of the subjects of study.

However, one distinction that we can draw for passive forms of research is that within this it does not necessarily involve the active attempt to conceal the researcher's identity or true purpose. As discussed above, a researcher may have legitimate access to participants to conduct a study but may find that during the course of that study opportunities arise to gather data on a separate angle of the research topic or the possibility to gather data for a completely new study. In such circumstances, if the researcher gathers the data and uses it without the consent of the study participants, the agreed informed consent and ethical code will have been breached.

Alternative examples of passive covert research include observations of social activity in public places such as supermarkets, shopping malls, parks, cinemas, art galleries, cafes, bars and restaurants. The growth of social media and internet sites is another way in which passive covert research can be conducted. Through such channels it is possible to monitor and observe social interaction without contributing or divulging the researcher's intention or purpose. Such forms of research typically emerge as a result of a particular contextual aspect of fieldwork rather than an outright desire to conceal the researcher's identity or need for deception. For example, studies of social spaces that are inhabited by large amounts of individuals for a short time would render getting informed consent of every individual who passed through that space unfeasible. Likewise, research conducted via social media and other internet sources and the fluid membership of such space may prove problematic in gaining informed consent as opportunities for explanation and consent may be limited.

In contrast, active covert research involves the researcher engaging in data collection methods, where the researcher spends an extended period of time in a particular research setting concealing his identity as a researcher and pretending to play some other role. For example, playing the role of a patient to observe the medical practices and treatment of patients, or taking up a job as a cleaner in a factory to observe the activities and productivity of the workforce. In essence the researcher is presenting himself as something that s/he is not, involving deceit and subterfuge, which is contradictory to the usual norms of empirical research which builds upon the relationships, informed consent and trust of the subjects been researched.

Despite the ability of covert research to overcome fundamental research difficulties such as the expectation that individuals who are the objects of open research will behave differently under the gaze of the researcher, it is a method subject to much debate and controversy. Arguments in defence of the use of covert research suggest that significant potential benefits to individuals and/or society could result from its practice. For example, it permits investigation into aspects of social behaviour that are morally contentious or illegal activities that would under more overt research methods be difficult or impossible to study. However, this leads to a fundamental conflict on the one hand, between the rights of an individual not to be the object of covert research and the duty of the researcher not to violate those rights, and on the other hand the consequential benefits which could emerge from the practice of covert research.

One of the main arguments against covert research is that the subject of the research has rights to be both aware that research is proposed and able to give or refuse consent that they should be involved; however, the very nature of covert research does not permit informed consent, thus because of the underhand way in which the evidence is gathered, covert research has been accused of being unethical.

Additionally, the wearing of such masks in social research not only compromises the subjects but also the researcher, his colleagues, students and data. Consequently, covert research presents the researcher with ethical and political dilemmas as it almost always involves the researcher being exposed to areas of the participants' life, which for some, may be considered as being part of their private domain and thus an intrusion on their individual rights. Furthermore, as the researcher is inevitably wearing an alternative identity and role this may lead to the researcher questioning his own sense of self. Likewise, in order to be fully integrated into the research setting, the researcher might end up engaging in activities that are against their own sense of morality and result in psychological harm. There is the additional risk that the activities may be illegal which may expose the researcher to physical, moral, legal and professional harm.

■ Individual rights

As we have seen so far, individual rights feature highly in various aspects of ethical and moral philosophy. The rights of the individual are comprehensive and can be found in papers such as the UN Declaration of Human Rights, US Bill of Rights, the Magna Carta and the UK and the European Court of Human Rights which covers many aspects of individual rights. Included in these rights is the right of individuals not to be deceived by others; the right not to be treated as less than autonomous, mature adult; the right to full knowledge and intentions of all participants; the right not to be embarrassed; the right to a private personality; and the right prior to contributing to any type of research activity, an opportunity to provide informed consent. Clearly the rights of the individual are somewhat problematic for any researcher who wishes to observe human behaviour either overtly or covertly, as the issue of individual rights gives rise to conflicts between the rights of the researcher and the rights of participants as citizens.

■ Codes of ethics

Such conflicts and the ability of social scientists to engage in unethical or morally questionable behaviour have led to a debate over the establishment of a code of ethics for social science researchers. Reynolds points out that social science researchers are not unaware of the uncertainty about their personal and moral worth and suggests that the establishment of ethical standards of procedures to guide personal behaviour would perhaps help them to determine if they are morally good (Reynolds, 1982 p193). Such a code has in fact been established by the American Sociological Association (ASA). Galliher, provides a re-examination of the professional code of ethics as presented by the ASA. In particular, he looks at Rule 3 "every person is entitled to the right of privacy and dignity of treatment. The sociologist must respect these rights", Rule 4 "all research should avoid causing personal harm to subjects used in research", and Rule 5 "confidential information provided by research subjects must be treated as such by the sociologist" (Galliher, 1973). Those who defend the establishment of rules or codes of conduct appeal to general ethical principles and believe that not to adopt them can result in unethical behaviour. While these rules reflect the values of most social researchers they also impose limitations on the research profession and have not been without opposition on the grounds that "all research is seated in some way and to some degree, we never tell the subject everything" (Roth in Bulmer, 1982, p155).

■ Reflections

From the foregoing discussion it is clear the ability to engage in unethical or morally questionable behaviour is present not just for those operating in the corporate world but for researchers as well. Furthermore, it can be seen that there are many ethical and moral aspects that need to be considered when engaging in research not only from the point of view of the effects on the research subjects but also the effects on the researcher and their professional association.

Reflecting back on the earlier examples within this chapter, it would seem that the rights of individuals do not appear highly on the corporate agenda or the researchers acting on their behalf. The Ford Pinto case for example demonstrates a clear conflict between the rights of the individual to be sold a safe and roadworthy vehicle and the economic application of cost benefit analysis to put a value on human life. While many of us would argue that such decisions are morally wrong, application of utilitarian ethical principles would conclude that if the monetary benefit exceeds the monetary amount of damages claims then the correct decision has been made. Likewise, the activities of the tobacco industry, Monsanto, Tesco, Toshiba etc. could be argued to be just good business. Indeed, Bazerman and Tenbrunsel (2011) suggest managers may believe they are making sound business decisions that such decisions are not necessarily consciously unethical, but rather occur as a result of their attention being diverted by organisational factors and the need to meet immediate targets.

Similarly, while medical and psychological experiments conducted without consent have raised moral outrage in society strict application of utilitarian ethics would suggest it was justified as the advances made in medical and psychological treatments serve the greater good. Indeed, any attempt to take individual rights into consideration within the concept of utility proves problematic as the theory in general is incapable of accounting for rights. However, others have argued that such practice casts doubt on the truthfulness of science and that such practice is a great disservice to scientific inquiry. Indeed, the classical conditioning experiment conducted on Albert is deemed unethical today because Watson made no attempt to desensitize Albert to the phobias that he produced in him (Fridlund *et al*, 2012).

Consequentialists, non-consequentialists and deontologists are always at odds in ethical debates. For some, morality is pragmatic and takes personal fulfilment and happiness into account while others believe that it should be pure and above human desires. Consequentialism is clearly more flexible than deontology, but deontologists may perhaps protect morality more vigorously and take duties such as promise breaking, lying etc. more seriously. However, these doctrines, despite their differences usually arrive at the same moral ends – "the individual is considered the major cause of effects upon others" (Reynolds, 1982, p194). Additionally, deontology is based on the assumption that a moral action is one which is done from a sense of duty, rather than treating people as and ends and never as a means. From the Project Camelot example, we could argue that the researchers were lying about their true purpose but could perhaps justify such actions by arguing that they were acting from a sense of duty to their country. However, if everyone took this view and lied all the time, then truth and meaning would disappear. Studies such as this provoke debate over the allowable limits of deception in the name of research. Inevitably such research produces results of controversy as features of the accounts can give rise to conflicts over people's beliefs, values and norms. The more morally dedicated a person is to these beliefs etc. the more threatening the attentions of the researcher are likely to prove. Thus a major problem in the development of strategies to cope with ethical and moral issues in researching human participants, including covert participation, is ensuring that the individuals acting on behalf of society (political representatives, researchers etc.) do not infringe upon the rights of ordinary citizens for personal benefit or some presumed good for society.

For Brazerman and Tenbrunsel (2011), many of the aforementioned problems, whether corporate or research, stem from ill-conceived goals which lead employees and managers to engage in questionable practices to meet immediate organisational targets. The desire to meet immediate pressures can result in motivation blindness which is a failure to recognise contradictory information

11

and ethical dimensions in the decision making process. Likewise, managers who make statements such as "do whatever it takes" can unconsciously trigger unethical behaviour. Similarly, the acceptance of seemingly trivial lapses in ethical behaviour can result in future ethical transgressions being overlooked. If such transgressions continue then before long, trivial ethical transgressions become the norm and can lead to more serious unethical behaviour in the long run. In a similar vein, overvaluing outcomes (good results/profits) that may have been achieved by engagement in some unethical practice, unconsciously rewards and encourages unethical behaviour. The challenge is how to balance conflicts, competing rights and obligations within ethical and moral codes of practice.

Research and professional codes of practice

As our previous sections demonstrate, there are good and valid reasons for the implementation and adherence to both professional and research codes of conduct. There are many useful organisations which provide sound principles and guidelines for the researchers. Of particular relevance are the British Educational Research Association, British Psychological Society, British Sociological Association, Chartered Association of Business Schools, Economic and Social Research Council and the Social Research Association – the ethics codes of which are all freely available on their websites (see further suggested readings below).

Many accounting and finance students take up membership of a professional association within their field such as the Institute of Chartered Accountants Scotland (ICAS); the Chartered Institute of Management Accountants (CIMA); the Association of Chartered Certified Accountants (ACCA); the Certified Institute of Public Finance and Accounting (CIPFA); the Institute of Chartered Accountants for England and Wales (ICAEW) or the Chartered Institute for Securities and Investment (CISI). Each of these professional associations has a code of practice to which any member regardless of their status (student or professional), are required to conform (Hellier and Bebbington, 2004).

While the codes of practice of the professional association take a more practice based orientation they are also useful points of reference when conducting research. For example, the professional codes of practice contain five fundamental principles (See Box 11.1): integrity, objectivity, professional competence and due care, confidentiality and professional behaviour which are entirely consistent with principles of research ethics.

Box 11.1. Five fundamental principles of ACCA and CIMA*

A. Integrity – to be straightforward and honest in all professional and business relationships.

B. Objectivity – to not allow bias, conflict of interest or undue influence of others to override professional or business judgments.

C. Professional Competence and Due Care – to maintain professional knowledge and skill at the level required to ensure that a client or employer receives competent professional service based on current developments in practice, legislation and techniques and act diligently and in accordance with applicable technical and professional standards.

D. Confidentiality – to respect the confidentiality of information acquired as a result of professional and business relationships and, therefore, not disclose any such information to third parties without proper and specific authority, unless there is a legal or professional right or duty to disclose, nor use the information for the personal advantage of the professional accountant or third parties.

E. Professional Behaviour – to comply with relevant laws and regulations and avoid any action that discredits the profession.

*Based on the Handbook of the Code of Ethics for Professional Accountants by the International Ethics Standard Board of Accountants (2015).

Practical advice and good research principles

In the following section we provide some practical advice that will enable you to conduct your research within the principles of ethical research. This includes a reminder of the need for ethical approval from your institution to conduct your project and the importance of accountability and transparency to be embedded within your research plan/study. Things to consider when initiating contact, the provision of information sheets to study participants and the importance of informed consent are also highlighted. This is then followed with a reminder of the pitfalls of engaging in deception and covert research. Issues relating to anonymity, confidentiality and data protection and the need to maintain honesty and professional integrity are also discussed. A handy checklist to which you can refer is also provided.

■   Ethical approval

Academic institutions and organisations have, as part of their internal structure, an Ethics Committee which is responsible for ensuring the activities of the organisation and its members are conducted within the bounds of professional codes of practice and ethical guidelines as laid down by their organisation, profession and law. Universities, in particular, have specific ethical standards with respect to the conduct of research that are monitored and enforced through the University Ethics Committee. The rules and codes of conduct laid down by the committee apply to staff as well as students.

University Ethics Committees generally include:

- A Lay Member of the University Court
- One member from outside the University
- The Deputy Principal for Research
- A representative of the Director of Research of each School and Institute
- The Chair of the Animal Ethics Committee or his/her representative
- The University Secretary

Additionally, in some universities a representative of the local regional council's Ethics Committee may have the right to attend meetings of the University Research Ethics Committee.

Before engaging in any research project you must make yourself aware of your institution or organisation's research ethics policy and approval process, complete and submit all appropriate paperwork and ensure compliance with your institution's regulations.

■   Accountability and transparency

Within any research project, whether it is from a professional organisation or an individual such as a research student, we must take into consideration the influence or potential impact of the research outputs on the study participants and society. It is an ideal of ethical and moral philosophy that research is founded on a sound evidence base with clear accountability and transparency processes embedded into the research project plan and study.

Throughout the research process, the researcher will form relationships with different stakeholders and participants. Some of the engagement between the researcher and participants may trigger the need for accountability, based on normative principles. The term 'accountability' is somewhat chameleon in nature. However, within the research context we consider accountability to be formal in nature and based on contractual commitments to the study participants with respect to their individual rights, thus the ethical roots of accountability lie in the contract or formal rules which creates them.

Within research accountability we have four guiding principles: participation, evaluation, transparency and feedback.

- *Participation* concerns the way in which the researcher involves stakeholders and study participants in the research processes and activities.

- *Evaluation* enables reflection on and learning from their experiences. Furthermore, only through a transparent evaluation process can a researcher report on its activities to its stakeholders and participants.

- *Transparency* refers to the way in which we make available information relating to the study to stakeholders and other interested parties including the study participants.

- *Feedback* mechanisms offer the stakeholders and study participants opportunities to comment on, and if necessary seek redress for, the researcher's prior acts.

The accountability relationship creates a link to the researchers and provides a mechanism for recourse in situations where the study participants may have been adversely affected by the research process or outputs. For example, accountability relationships may be triggered when a researcher makes a claim of a particular sort that cannot be substantiated or has been based on deceptive access to data and thus may compromise the study participants. If the research has an impact on a person or group, particularly if it is in a negative way, then the researcher should be accountable to the person or group for harm that they cause, especially if there are no other means of recourse. Researchers who are accountable, participative, transparent, conduct evaluations and invite feedback, are more likely to be effective than those who are unaccountable.

■ Initiating contact

To help you enlist participants in your project you will need to create a 'participant information sheet'. This document, which could be in the format of a covering letter or leaflet, should include the aims of the project, an explanation of the data collection method(s) and the time it involves, a statement about anonymity, confidentiality and data security, a statement of the participant's right to withdraw and the benefits of participation. For ease of distribution, via email or post for example, and to maximise participation uptake, the information sheet should be as short as possible – perhaps just one page long. (Warning: anything longer risks deterring prospective participants.) Accordingly, it is a good idea to include 'contact details for further information' at the bottom of

11

the sheet, especially when the project is complex and you are struggling to keep the words down. For an example of an information sheet, see Appendix 4. For further examples, simply type 'participant information sheet' into an Internet search engine and select from the thousands of templates!

■ Informed consent

As a general principle you should obtain 'informed consent'. Put simply, this means that you need to provide sufficient information about the research (which you should have already done in the information sheet) and ensure that there is no coercion or undue influence. Ideally you should ask the participant to sign a 'consent form' which includes a statement that the participant understands the details of the study as outlined in the information sheet and that the participant can withdraw from the project at any time. If possible you should use your own university's consent form but if your university does not have one, it is perfectly acceptable to use a consent form from another institution. Simply type 'consent forms' in an Internet search engine and select a consent form from a university website or alternatively use the one in Appendix 4.

However, there are certain situations where consent forms may be unnecessary. If the participant agrees to the project in an email or letter, there is little point in subsequently requesting a completed consent form. It is also reasonable to assume that consent has been given when questionnaires are returned. Where there are multiple participants it may not be practicable to issue out consent forms. In the case of a corporate governance project, consider the practicalities of asking permission from all the shareholders at an Annual General Meeting of a listed company. Or in the case of an accounting education study, imagine trying to obtain signed consent forms at a first-year university lecture with hundreds of students. Street surveys also pose a problem. Shoppers and commuters for example just do not have the time or inclination to read through the information sheet or listen to a researcher explaining in detail the importance of his/her research.

Similarly, it is not always possible or desirable to hand out consent forms before chatting (informally) with participants or their colleagues. Imagine how you would be perceived by prospective participants if you carried around a pile of consent forms! You would most certainly miss out on the often colourful and revealing discussions at the water cooler, during tea breaks or lunch for instance.

Another consideration relates to the issue of working with children. It is likely that your participants will be adults, however if your participants are children (you may be doing a finance education project for example) you will need to obtain consent from their parents and teachers. As a further precaution you will most probably be checked against some kind of disclosure register. In the UK for example, you will be checked against the Disclosure and Barring Service (formerly Criminal Records Bureau) for any criminal records, including spent and unspent convictions, cautions, reprimands and final warnings. If you are on the barred list then you will not be able to work with children.

■ Deception and covert research

To many researchers the idea of gathering data through deceptive means is unacceptable both ethically and morally. However, there is a significant difference between being economical with details of the hypothesis under test for example and the deliberate withholding or falsifying of information regarding the true nature or purpose of the research.

As discussed earlier, covert research involves undertaking research without the participant's knowledge and approval. It is a data collection method favoured by undercover journalists and sometimes by doctoral students in the social sciences. However, it is a relatively uncommon method in undergraduate accounting and finance research. There are material risks for both you and your university – consider the rollercoaster of emotions you will experience when undercover, together with the danger of a defamation claim. And as the method also involves a degree of deception (you will need to hide the true aims of your research in the information sheet) your supervisor will probably recommend other means of data collection.

That said, there are certain situations where it is appropriate to use deception or to be economical with the truth, especially if knowledge of the true aims of the project is likely to alter normal behaviour and thereby compromise the findings. If participants were aware that your project is about earnings management, tax evasion, fraud, corruption or some other sensitive area, they will of course be careful in their interactions with colleagues when being observed by you, in what they say during interviews and what they write when responding to questionnaires. As no right-minded person will want to implicate themselves, there will be nothing in the data that will be of use for your dissertation and you will have wasted your time.

Concealing the true aims of the project may therefore be justified in certain situations. Indeed, projects which explore earnings management, corporate governance or critical studies of budgetary control for example, may not even get off the ground if the detailed aims of the project were made explicit at the outset. Thus you will need to be pragmatic in your approach, bearing in mind the advice of your supervisor and the risks and rewards of using covert research.

11

And of course there is no need to do a full-blown undercover project. Instead you may do a standard ethnography with all the normal ethical safeguards in place but also include some data collected from covert research for example, unguarded conversations about customers, management control, remuneration, auditors; tax authorities and so on.

Although less of an issue for undergraduate dissertations, a final point is that it is considered good practice to reveal the true aims of the research after the study. For professional undercover journalists revealing the true aims of the research and eliciting a response from participants will be a normal part of the project. This is because the journalist will invariably want to disseminate their findings to a public audience. However for undergraduate dissertations it is advisable to pay heed to normal confidentiality rules, unless of course there is some legal obligation to disclose the data to an appropriate authority as discussed below. Before gathering data through deceptive or covert means, consideration must also be given to the potential reaction of the study participants when the deception is revealed to them. If it is likely to instil anger, objections, embarrassment or discomfort then such an approach is inappropriate and should not be followed.

■ Anonymity, confidentiality and data protection

The nature of research of course requires the acquisition of data; however this should not be at the expense of the participant's private life. Most accounting and finance projects are more to do with work than play. Thus, when contacting prospective participants or conducting telephone interviews, you should use work telephone numbers rather than personal (home/mobile) numbers; and you should only conduct interviews at the participant's workplace or neutral location such as a café rather than at the participant's home.

With respect to data security, you should of course comply with the country's data protection laws. The UK Data Protection Act (1998) for example, requires that data is used for limited, specifically stated purposes, kept for no longer than is absolutely necessary, and kept safe and secure. You should therefore password-protect your electronic documents, secure paper documents under lock and key and, at some point after the project, destroy the data such as interview recordings and transcriptions.

In certain circumstances, research participants may only agree to engage with your study if they have assurance that the data and their identification be kept anonymous. You may also wish to inform participants that your dissertation is for supervisors' eyes only; that there will only be a certain number of hardcopies of the dissertation, that the dissertation will be withheld from the university library and that the dissertation will not be digitalised for public access. Understandably, these options are particularly welcome when the project is of a personal or sensitive nature, for example where the student has done a case study of his/her family business and there are discussions about financial issues and their secrets of success.

Indeed, it is standard practice to anonymise participants and their organisations (see information sheets, above) with real names replaced with pseudonyms (unless they waive their right to anonymity). Purists may baulk at the practice as it risks distorting the data; however, any impact on research findings from the use of pseudonyms is more than offset by the obligation to protect the participant, that is preventing harm, including hurt feelings, reputational and career damage and defamation claims. At the very least, you should be making it difficult to identify organisations, interviewees, survey respondents, observed participants in ethnographies and so on in your dissertation.

You should also be aware that you may have a legal obligation to report suspicious unlawful activity. For example, in the UK, if you suspect that the participant organisation is engaged in money laundering and that there are reasonable grounds for your suspicions, you must inform the National Crime Agency. But before you contact such authorities it is imperative that you first seek advice from the dissertation supervisor as allegations of illegality or bad practice are of course highly consequential. For a start you do not want to be sued for defamation!

It is important that you are aware of the potential dangers as well as the benefits of using online media in the research process. Such platforms (for example, newsgroups, forums, chatrooms and blogs) are prone to security attacks, 'trolling', online harassment and other abuses it is not sensible to use them for formally discussing your project or eliciting data from participants. In such dynamic environments, it is all too easy to reveal accidently real names of participants and organisations. Moreover, there is very little guidance for such issues as ethical standards relating to the use of the Internet are not yet well developed (Chartered Association of Business Schools, 2015, section 6.g).

■ Honesty and professional integrity

Whether or not you are affiliated to a professional body, you are obliged to behave in a 'professional' manner. As a researcher you must comply with your institution's ethical code of conduct, be honest; and make an impartial, objective assessment of the data and report faithfully the 'truth'. Thus you should not falsify or fabricate data. You must not make up the data to increase your questionnaire response rate for example! (Warning: fabricating data is not only dishonest and unethical but invariably leads to nonsensical analysis and meaningless results. Examiners will detect it.)

Obviously, you must not remove private data without the owner's consent. For example, if you came across a corporate governance manual during your ethnographic research and you find it particularly useful for your dissertation then you should formally request a copy from the participant organisation rather than just walk out with it. Similarly, you should not be attaching company documents (for example, spreadsheets and internal memorandums) to emails and sending them to external email addresses or forwarding internal emails to people unconnected with the company, without prior consent. Put simply, you must not steal data – it is not only unethical, it is unlawful!

Honesty means you must not plagiarise and claim credit for work that you have not done yourself. Cutting and pasting blocks of text from articles and copying datasets, analyses and so on from someone else's project is of course wrong. Nor should you 'self-plagiarise' and claim credit more than once for a piece of work. This means you should not be importing text from previous assessed coursework, for example, essays and research proposals, into your dissertation. In addition, you should acknowledge all the contributors in your research. The dissertation is normally an individual piece of work, however if your project does involve other fellow students, collaborators and others, then you must fully acknowledge their contributions. That way the examiner is able to assess the work that is yours and yours alone.

Also, you should not omit relevant data where its inclusion would have materially affected your findings. Excluding anomalies from your dataset without justification, to support a hypothesis that you personally like, is just plain wrong. It is also plain amateur as it is a lost opportunity. Anomalies by their very nature are interesting and therefore worth discussing in the dissertation, and as any creative (social) scientist will tell you, anomalies may just be the spark that opens up a new field of inquiry. It follows that you should be open about your dataset (subject to confidentiality issues). If you have not included all the data in your dissertation and your supervisor needs to see the complete dataset, you should of course be able to provide it. If subsequently the supervisor requires you to discuss your findings, you should again be able to oblige.

As an objective researcher you should be trying to avoid any potential bias. This means you should decline any gifts from participants or, at least, disclose any gifts which you have accepted (in some contexts it may be normal business custom to accept gifts). Likewise, you should disclose the gifts that you give.

Although providing incentives is generally a good idea given the 'no' default position of many participants (*Initiating contact*, above) its use has the potential to create bias in sampling or in participant responses (British Educational Research Association, 2011, para. 22). In a similar vein, you should disclose any sponsorship arrangement and potential conflicts of interest. Consider for example the potential conflicts of interest faced by the sports scholar who is doing a dissertation on athlete funding. Is it in the student's interest to report that athlete funding is adequate or indeed over-funded? A more common example is the potential bias in ethnographical research conducted during internships where there is the real possibility of a subsequent job offer. Can the student report openly on issues such as gender (im)balance and (mis)treatment of trainees – that is, anything that could upset the company and scupper a job application?

Finally, it is worth stating clearly again that you should not harm the participant, either physically or emotionally. For example, if the participant falls ill during an interview you should of course stop and reschedule. As noted above, you have an obligation to prevent hurt feelings as well as reputational and career damage and defamation claims. In practice this means that you will need to have your wits about you. For example, consider how easy it is to reveal accidently participants' (negative) opinions of each other during interviews which may lead to embarrassment, anxiety or even distress; and to overlook the cultural context, for example Friday prayer, religious holidays, local traditions, business customs and so on, which may offend participants.

Checklist

Before, during and after the project you should consider the following questions:

1 Have you consulted your university's ethical guidelines?

2 Have you checked your professional body's ethics code (if applicable)?

3 Is your information sheet sufficiently informative?

4 Are the consent forms signed?

5 Are you working with children or vulnerable adults? If you are, have you obtained consent from parents and teachers?

6 Can you justify covert research (if applicable)?

7 Have you anonymised the participants and the organisations?

8 Have you intruded into the participant's private life?

11

9 Have you harmed any participants?

10 Have you secured the data?

11 Is the data used for its intended purpose?

12 Have you made an impartial assessment of the findings?

13 Have you addressed any conflicts of interest?

14 Have you acknowledged all sources in your references?

15 How is the data to be stored in the long term?

16 At what point will the data be destroyed?

17 Have you considered all material ethical issues?

Summary

Within this chapter we have introduced you to the notion of ethics and moral philosophy and its relevance to research, the corporate world and the financial services professions. As we have seen, researchers and practitioners alike are susceptible to transgressions of ethical behaviour. Three prominent but contrasting ethical theories, consequentialism, non-consequentialism and deontology have been put forward to illustrate the complexity of determining good moral and ethical behaviour (many more could be applied). As demonstrated, when engaging in research and corporate activity there are many ethical and moral aspects that need to be considered. The challenge is how to balance conflicts, competing rights and obligations. The codes of ethics and good research principles put forward in this chapter provide a good platform on which you can develop an ethical research plan that has clear accountability and transparency embedded within it.

References and further reading

ACCA, (2015) Section 3: Code of Ethics and Conduct, Rulebook, *Association of Chartered Certified Accountants,* Available at: www.accaglobal.com/content/dam/ACCA_Global/Members/Doc/rule/acca-rulebook-2015.pdf

ACCA (n.d) Tesco scandal – the perils of aggressive accounting. http://www.accaglobal.com/zm/en/student/sa/features/tesco-scandal.html

Adams, A., and Angus, R., (2015), Ethics in the City, *The Journal of the CFA Society of the UK,* www.cfauk.org

Addady, M., (2015), Toshiba's accounting scandal is much worse than we thought, *Fortune Magazine,* Available at: http://fortune.com/2015/09/08/toshiba-accounting-scandal/

ACT Brazil, (2014), Maybe, You're the Target: New Global Marlboro Campaign Found to Target Teens, Alliance for the Control of Tobacco Use, Brazil, Available at: http://www.fctc.org/images/stories/Report_Youre_the_Target.pdf

Altria (n.d.) http://www.altria.com/Responsibility/Tobacco-Product Issues/Pages/default.aspx?src=highlights

Anderson, L., (2014, Why Does Everyone Hate Monsanto? *Modern Farmer,* http://modernfarmer.com/2014/03/monsantos-good-bad-pr-problem/

Aras, G., and Crowther, D., (2012), *Governance and Social Responsibility: International Perspective,* Palgrave, Basingstoke.

Baden-Mayer, A., (2015), 15 health related problems linked to Monsanto, *Eco Watch,* Available at: http://www.ecowatch.com/15-health-problems-linked-to-monsantos-roundup-1882002128.html

Bazerman, M.H., and Tenbrunsel, A.E., (2011), Ethical breakdowns, *Harvard Business Review,* Available at: https://hbr.org/2011/04/ethical-breakdowns

BERA, (2011), Ethical guidelines for educational research, *British Educational Research Association,* Available at: www.bera.ac.uk/wp-content/uploads/2014/02/BERA-Ethical-Guidelines-2011.pdf

Boatright, J.R, (2003), *Ethics and the Conduct of Business,* 4th edition, Prentice Hall, London.

Borzekowski, D.L.G., and Cohen, J.E., (2013), International reach of tobacco marketing among young children, *Paediatrics,* **132**, 825- 831.

BPS, (2014), Code of Human Research Ethics, *British Psychological Society,* Available at: www.bps.org.uk/system/files/Public%20files/inf180_web.pdf

BSA, (2002), Statement of Ethical Practice for the British Sociological Association, *British Sociological Association,* Available at: www.britsoc.co.uk/media/27107/StatementofEthicalPractice.pdf

11

Bucholz, R. A. (1989), *Fundamental Concepts and Problems in Business Ethics*, Prentice-Hall, Englewood Cliffs, NJ.

Bulmer, M., (1982), *Social Research Ethics: An examination of the merits of covert participant observation*. Macmillan, London.

CABS, (2015) *Ethics Guide: Advice and Guidance*, Chartered Association of Business Schools. Available at: charteredabs.org/wp-content/uploads/2015/06/Ethics-Guide-2015-Advice-and-Guidance.pdf

CIMA, (2015), Code of Ethics for Professional Accountants, Chartered Institute of Management Accountants. Available at: www.cimaglobal.com/Professional-ethics/Ethics/CIMA-code-of-ethics-for-professional-accountants/

Clikeman, P.M., (2013), *Called to Account: Financial Frauds that Shaped the Accounting Profession*, Routledge, London.

Chryssides, G.D., and Kaler, J.H., (1993), *An Introduction to Business Ethics*, Chapman & Hall, London.

Dellaportas, S., Gibson, K., Alagiah, R., Hutchinson, M., Leung, P., and Van Homrigh, D., (2005), *Ethics, Governance & Accountability: A professional perspective*, Wiley, Sydney, Australia.

Denscombe, M., (2002), *Ground Rules for Good Research: A 10 Point Guide for Social Researchers*, Open University Press, Buckingham and Philadelphia.

Douglas, J. D., (1976). *Investigative Social Research: Individual and Team Field Research*, Sage, London

Erikson, K., (1967). A comment on disguised observation in Sociology. *Social Problems*, **14**, 366-373.

ESRC, (2015), Framework for research ethics, Economic and Social Research Council, Available at: www.esrc.ac.uk/files/funding/guidance-for-applicants/esrc-framework-for-research-ethics-2015

Folger, T., (2013), The next Green Revolution, *National Geographic Magazine*, Available at: http://www.nationalgeographic.com/foodfeatures/green-revolution/

Fridlund, A. J., Beck, H. P., Goldie, W. D., and Irons, G., (2012), Little Albert: A neurologically impaired child, *History of Psychology*. doi: 10.1037/a0026720

Galliher, J.F., (1973), The Protection of Human Subjects: A re-examination of the Professional Code of Ethics, *The American Sociologist*, **8**(3), 93 100.

Gilligan, C., (1982), *In a different voice: psychological theory and women's development*, Cambridge, Massachusetts, Harvard University Press, Available at: https://hbr.org/2011/04/ethical-breakdowns

Gray, R., Owen, D., and Adams, C., *Accounting and Accountability: Changes and challenges in corporate social and environmental reporting*, Prentice Hall, Harlow, England.

Gurian-Sherman. D., (2009), Failure to yield: Evaluating the performance of genetically modified crops, *Union of Concerned Scientists*, Available at: http://www.ucsusa.org/sites/default/files/legacy/assets/documents/food_and_agriculture/failure-to-yield.pdf

Helliar, C., and Bebbington, J., (2004), *Taking Ethics to Heart*, Institute of Chartered Accountants of Scotland Monograph, Edinburgh.

Hockridge, E., and Tomlinson, I., (2010), Warning shot, Available:http://www.warmwell.com/farming_of103-warningshot.pdf

Horowitz, I.L., (1967), The rise and fall of Project Camelot: Studies in the relationship between social science and practical politics, *The Hispanic American Historical Review*, **49** (1), 116-118.

International Ethics Standards Board for Accountants (2015), *Handbook of the Code of Ethics for Professional Accountants*, International Federation of Accountants, Available at: www.ethicsboard.org

ILRF, (2005), The 14 Worst Corporate Evildoers, *International Labour Rights Forum*, http://www.laborrights.org/in-the-news/14-worst-corporate-evildoers

Leeson, N. (n.d.) http://www.nickleeson.com/

Montsano (n.d.) Who we are, http://www.monsanto.com/whoweare/pages/our-commitments.aspx

MacIntyre, A.D., (1998). *A Short History of Ethics: A History of Moral Philosophy From the Homeric Age to the Twentieth Century*. Routledge, UK.

McMillan, K., and Weyers, J., (2008), *How to Write Dissertations and Project Reports*, Pearson, London.

O'Connell, V., (2008), Philip Morris readies aggressive global push, *The Wall Street Journal*, Available at: http://www.wsj.com/articles/SB120156034185223519

Reynolds, P.D., (1982), Moral judgements: strategies for analysis with application to covert participant observation. In: Bulmer, M., ed, *Social Research Ethics: An examination of the merits of covert participant observation*. London: Macmillan, pp. 185-213.

Richards, J., Wimalasena, L. and MacLean, G., (2015), Managing ethics in research projects, in O'Gorman, K. and MacIntosh, R. (eds.) (2015), *Research Methods for Business & Management: A Guide to Writing Your Dissertation*, 2nd edition, Goodfellow, Oxford.

Robinson, D., and Garratt, C., (1988), *Introducing Ethics*, Cambridge: Icon Books.

Saunders, M., Lewis, P. and Thornhill, A., (2012), *Research Methods for Business Students*, 6th edition, Pearson, Harlow.

Scott, Sir, W., (1808), *Marmion, Canto VI, Stanza 17*, Available at: http://izquotes.com/author/walter-scott

11

Singer, P., (1994), *Ethics*, Oxford Reader, Oxford: Oxford University Press.

SRA, (2003), Ethical Guidelines, *Social Research Association*, Available at: the-sra. org.uk/wp-content/uploads/ethics03.pdf

Thomas, W.C., (2002), The Rise and Fall of Enron: When a company looks too good to be true, it usually is, *Journal of Accountancy*, Available at: http://www. journalofaccountancy.com/issues/2002/apr/theriseandfallofenron.html

UK Research Integrity Office (n.d.) Code of Practice for Research. http://ukrio.org/ publications/code-of-practice-for-research/

Want, C., and Klimowski, A., (1996), *Introducing Kant*, Cambridge: Icon Books.

Watson, J.B., and Rayner, R., (1920), Conditioned emotional reactions. *Journal of Experimental Psychology*, **3**, 1-14.

Winter, G., (2001), Enticing Third World youth: Big tobacco is accused of crossing an age line, *New York Times*, August 24th, Available at: http://www.nytimes. com/2001/08/24/business/enticing-third-world-youth-big-tobacco-is-accused-of-crossing-an-age-line.html

12 Writing Up: A Tool Kit for Constructing your Written Project

Robert MacIntosh, Thomas Farrington, John Sanders and Mercy Denedo

For many people, their dissertation represents the largest piece of written work they will have had to produce to date. Writing tens of thousands of words is a qualitatively different problem than writing shorter essay or assignment style pieces. With scale comes the challenge of making sure that the document as a whole flows, is clearly structured and reads like a single integrated piece. In reality, you will find yourself writing different sections at different times sometimes months apart. It is not uncommon for these different sections to vary slightly in focus, structure or tone and this can mean that the final project reads as somewhat disjointed. The problem is that both projects and writing styles differ, so there is no single recipe for success. The research topic, methods, supervisors and your own way of working are all key aspects of developing a high quality document that will be assessed against the kinds of criteria set out in Appendix 2.

The purpose of this chapter is to highlight a few key points about the process of writing up your research project, as distinct from the process of doing the research itself, and offer some advice on writing effectively. Though obviously interrelated, it is worth teasing these two tasks apart since it can make the whole process more productive. The chapter begins with a look at mapping out your writing, before offering suggestions on how to find your focus and maintain it. The chapter then looks at overcoming writer's block, rewriting and editing, and the use of technology. This is followed by a series of writing tips, before the chapter concludes with some practical advice on the relationship between you and your supervisor.

Getting started

At some point, you will find yourself facing a blank page. More accurately, it will likely be a blank screen since almost everyone writes via a keyboard, screen and word processor today. Finding a way to get started is often the first challenge. You may have had to put a research proposal together before starting the dissertation proper. If so, then you will have an outline structure from which to work. A sensible first step is to create a contents page, which sets out those aspects of a research project that are commonly recognised such as an abstract, introduction, literature review, etc. Appendix 3 sets out some examples of typical project structures and includes details of indicative word count for each section. Whilst not cast in stone, these are a helpful guide and can offer you a way of gauging progress. Many students begin with the anxiety that they cannot imagine finding enough to write about. In practice, the reverse is often true, and finding a way to compress your project is more of a problem than the lack of words available.

Take each of the chapter headings from your contents page and break them down into subsections. For example, the methods chapter might open with an overview of the nature of knowledge claims, before moving on to the range of possible choices that you considered for your own research project. A justification for the methods that you have chosen might follow, then a detailed account of how you will operationalize these methods in the research that you conduct. The structuring of each chapter in your dissertation is determined by your own writing style, however appendix A3 provides an example of the common elements that normally appear within each chapter and a rough estimate of how many words each theme or subsection might require. The order and titles of these sections and subsections are likely to change as your project progresses, yet producing this map of your dissertation will allow you to see where you are headed, and what you need to do to get there. Writing the content is a slightly more involved undertaking, and the following observations and exercises are designed to simplify that process, and encourage you to write regularly.

Writing as thinking

"With the door shut, downloading what's in my head directly to the page, I write as fast as I can . . . If I write rapidly [then] I find that I can keep up with my original enthusiasm and outrun the self-doubt that's always waiting to settle in."

Stephen King (2002, p. 210)

The language we use when we talk about our interests and goals is typically much less formal than that which we use when writing the same things down, yet informal writing can actually be a very helpful way of thinking through ideas. When there is nobody else there to listen or read, use the blank page to communicate with yourself. Using the first person, write down what it is you want to look at, what you want to find out, and what you want to say now, what you want to write about next, what you don't want to look at and why you are explicitly setting your boundaries. Try to write for a few minutes without thinking about the rules of language, or deleting or editing anything. Ignore your internal critic, and allow yourself to write freely. You can use as many or as few words as you like, and if you get stuck then you can just start a new line. The aim of this exercise is to relax, make a record of your ideas, and work your way up to writing formally for an audience. Rowena Murray (2006, p. 89) notes that this 'freewriting' technique can help writers "work out their relationship to knowledge [and] help us test how much we have actually understood." Over time, you may find this practice of 'writing as thinking' offers a quick way of bringing your aims into focus and kick-starting your writing sessions.

Murray (2006, p. 104) offers the following seven prompts, which can help refine your thoughts into more formal language. By completing these sentences, you will develop a set of statements to keep you focussed as you write your dissertation. You will likely revise and clarify these statements several times throughout the duration of your project, so do not feel you have to get this right first time.

- My research question is . . . (50 words)

- Researchers who have looked at this subject are . . . (50 words)

- They argue that . . . (25 words) Smith argues that . . . (25 words) Brown argues that . . . (25 words)

- Debate centres on the issue of . . . (25 words)

- There is still work to be done on . . . (25 words)

- My research is closest to that of X in that . . . (50 words)

- My contribution will be . . . (50 words)

12

Although you will probably find it helpful to return to these exercises as you progress through your dissertation, it is important to remember that these are designed to stimulate your writing sessions, and should not be seen as a substitute for regular, formal written work. The key to completing a dissertation on time and to the best of your ability is getting into the habit of writing every day.

Making writing a habit

"You might not write well every day, but you can always edit a bad page. You can't edit a blank page."

Jodi Picoult (Charney, 2012).

By the time you come to write a dissertation, you will have been writing since childhood and will have accumulated years of experience of what works best for you. We each typically have habits and contexts which enable us to write. It may be that the library, your home or a coffee shop is your venue of choice. Most people who write professionally, e.g. novelists, journalists and playwrights, have an established writing routine. It is highly important for you to identify your writing routine and stick to it. Where you do not have a defined schedule for writing, ensure you write regularly. Remember that writing your dissertation is not the same as studying the literatures to develop your research ideas. After identifying when would be convenient for you to write, always remember to write and not study. Writing and studying at the same time would not only limit the amount of time you have allotted for writing but it might result in you constantly criticizing and editing what you have written.

Children's author Roald Dahl went to his 'writing hut' at the bottom of his garden and wrote for two hours in the morning, broke for lunch and wrote for another two hours in the afternoon. The ritual and routine of space and time can be an important enabler for writing. Some manage to write quickly. Others write painfully slowly. J. K. Rowling writes whenever and wherever the inspiration takes her, the names of the Harry Potter characters first drafted on an airsickness bag. Graham Greene would write meticulously neatly without crossing out anything, and in neat, square handwriting. His editor described this process as producing handwriting so tiny and cramped that it looked like an attempt to write on the head of a pin. Greene would write five hundred words exactly in a day and would stop for the day when he reached this target, even if he were in mid-sentence. Ernest Hemingway and Vladimir Nabokov wrote standing up, while Truman Capote wrote lying down. There is no way to tell what works for you but you should try to find the best time of day for you and stick to it where possible. It is important to schedule time for writing. You should also try to calculate how quickly you write and use this as a guide when working out how long it will take to complete individual chapters and the project as a whole.

Of course, today's technology allows us to write in a number of different ways. You can dictate, type or hand-write. You can write almost anywhere and at any time. One common experience, when tackling an extended piece of writing like a dissertation for the first time, is that ideas will strike you at the most unexpected of times. You may be in the midst of something completely unrelated when you realise that you need to connect some point from the literature review to some detailed point in your analysis. It is important to capture these moments and you may find yourself making notes, recording voice memos or using some other technique to capture your thoughts on the move.

Although it may seem peculiar at first, scheduling clear and manageable tasks every day will soon become as normal as checking your email. Speaking of checking your email, one tactic employed by many writers is to make writing their first task of the day, and to see any online social interactions as rewards for successfully completing their writing task. Unless there is a good reason for making contact with the outside world, you are eating into what may be the most productive hour of your day. Nathan Englander (Charney, 2013a) gives the following advice:

> *"Turn off your cell phone. Honestly, if you want to get work done, you've got to learn to unplug. No texting, no email, no Facebook, no Instagram. Whatever it is you're doing, it needs to stop while you write."*

At first, the time you spend away from social networks may only be 15-30 minutes each day, and this will probably feel like much longer. Although this will quickly become easier, and the length of time will naturally increase, you should maintain 15-30 minutes of writing time as a daily minimum. Once you are in the habit of writing, a common mistake is to try to block out whole days of writing time. In practice this rarely works as planned, and it may be more realistic to set yourself a more modest task e.g. write 300-500 words on the justification of your research techniques in a two hour window. By adopting this approach you are effectively taking one very large document and breaking it down into a series of smaller writing tasks. Not only does this make it less intimidating to write, it also makes it easier to schedule, since you can allocate shorter periods of time during which you will write shorter pieces of text. Furthermore, always remember to include a 'prompt' at the end of each writing section highlighting your research ideas for the next paragraph or section. Your prompt could start with 'what I want to write about in the next paragraph is…' It would enable you to link your research ideas and to be more productive with your allotted time for writing.

Remember to give yourself small rewards for sticking to your daily writing schedule (e.g. food, exercise, entertainment), take regular breaks, and don't write to the point of exhaustion. Hemingway (Plimpton, 1958) suggests that you "write until you come to a place where you still have your juice and know what will happen next". As such, a successful writing session is not necessarily one in which the tasks were completed to the highest standards, or even entirely

12

completed. James Joyce saw the composition of three sentences as a good day's work. While Joyce's satisfaction is perhaps characteristically unusual, Karen Russell (Charney, 2013b) nonetheless notes that

> *"You need to give yourself permission to write badly, just to get something down . . . if you can make peace with the fact that you will likely have to throw out ninety percent of your first draft, then you can relax and even almost enjoy 'writing badly'."*

Hopefully you will manage to retain more than ten percent of your writing from each session, but the general acceptance of one's writerly imperfections is a crucial stage of your academic development, and points to perhaps the most important principle of writing: **write first and edit second**. When you allow that internal critic to stop you from writing, you are interrupting the flow of thoughts both onto the page and within your head. It may well be that what you write is too simplistic or unclear, but getting these thoughts out as a first draft could lead you to conceive new ideas or forge unforeseen links between parts of your research. Rowling notes that in this respect writing is "like learning an instrument, you've got to be prepared for hitting wrong notes occasionally . . . or quite a lot."

Of course, it will not be long before you are sending your work to your supervisor for feedback. Although it may be tempting to ruthlessly cut all sentences that you do not consider suitably developed or relevant, there remains the possibility of your supervisor noticing something useful within these less certain notions. As such, you and your supervisor might like to agree upon a system that indicates your more tentative sentences and thoughts. For example, you could highlight in yellow those parts that you are unsure about, and highlight in red those parts that you really do not like. This extra level of communication about your writing will prevent you from losing potentially valuable ideas, whilst allowing you to show your supervisor that you are able to be self-critical.

For Russell (Charney, 2013b), the true measure of a good writing session is therefore a positive answer to the following question:

> *"Was I able to stay put and commit to putting words down on the page, without deciding mid-sentence that it's more important to check my email, or 'research' some question online, or clean out the science fair projects in the back of my freezer?"*

Writing is as much about discipline and practice as running a half marathon or learning to bake a soufflé, both of which make fine extracurricular rewards. Just as one would not succeed in either of these without first conducting considerable research, one cannot expect to perfect academic writing without first taking the time to read the writing of others.

Reading as writing

> *"The real importance of reading is that it creates an ease and intimacy with the process of writing . . . It also offers you a constantly growing knowledge of what has been done and what hasn't, what is trite and what is fresh, what works and what just lies there dying (or dead) on the page."*
>
> *Stephen King (2002, p. 145)*

At times, completing a review of the relevant literature may seem like a fairly mechanical task, particularly if you are diligent in the good practice of writing short summaries of robust articles and chapters as you find them. Yet the act of reading these pieces is also one of educating yourself about how to write to the highest academic standards. As you engage critically with the argument or approach of a publication, you should try to also engage with the language used to convey the points, and move between them. While you must never duplicate another person's work and present it as your own, the best way to get a working idea of academic writing conventions in your field is by reading highly regarded scholarship. You will notice certain words and phrases are frequently used by various authors in order to guide the reader through the structure of the piece. For instance, in *Social and Environmental Accounting Research*, Gray (2002) asserts that the social accounting project is not homogeneous but is the universe of all possible accountings, because it reflects different social, economic, environmental and political perspectives. These are key concepts that were reconstructed in numerous peer-reviewed articles. Consequently, take a note of the most commonly used concepts, examples and try using them at similar points in your own work.

At the same time as reading good writing motivates you to write well, discovering the scholarly positions and findings of other writers in your field will allow you to more clearly define your own critical voice. As such, you should note down your thoughts and any questions you think of as you read. As you may note above, several of Murray's (2006) seven writing prompts stem from your responses to the work of others. Reading and understanding the relevant literature will prevent you from spending time writing about that which has already been said, so making your writing sessions more efficient. Scheduled reading time is therefore crucial to the improvement of your writing. Stepping away from your dissertation to read is also one very effective way of tackling the dreaded writer's block, to which we now turn.

12

Writer's block

There is some disagreement about what exactly causes writer's block, but it is an experience that most writers experience or at least appreciate. This is something worth bearing in mind: everybody has to write several drafts before they get to the finished article. Murray (2006, p. 169) gives a number of reasons for experiencing writer's block:

- They think they must work out what they think – and what they want to say – before they can write . . . and get stuck at that point . . .

  . . . instead of using writing to sort out what they want to say.

- They struggle to work a point out logically, or scientifically or objectively . . . and get stuck at that point . . .

  . . . instead of working it out in words.

- They want to be sure before they write . . .

  . . . instead of writing when they are not sure.

- There is no end to the project in sight.

Thankfully, writer's block is a temporary and solvable problem, and by this point in the chapter you are already equipped with many of the tools to help you move past it. If you have tried all of the above and are still feeling unable to write about your dissertation topic, then simply try writing about anything that comes to mind. You might find it useful to write about why you feel unable to write, but even writing about what you had for breakfast and which will at least get some words on the page. Spend five minutes on this, and then try some freewriting around your research questions, before returning to the scheduled tasks. Remember to keep your aims clear, realistic, and flexible: you do not have to finish an entire section before moving on to another part of your dissertation.

Keep a list of less immersive writing tasks to carry out when you are feeling at your least creative, such as checking and adding missing references, writing transitional or linking sentences, or ensuring the contribution of each section to your overall argument is clear throughout. If you are able to reschedule your writing for a little later, then you may find that ten minutes of exercise helps to clear the mind. Haruki Murakami (2008) famously runs or swims every day, finding the routine of writing and exercise a crucial regulator of his productivity levels. Of course, you may have no inclination to run or swim, but even a short trip to the shops may deliver the change needed to get you writing; just make sure you do get writing!

General tips for better writing

- **Tell the reader what you are going to do and do it**. Write a paragraph that briefly guides the reader through what they are about to read. The body of the essay then follows this structural map. You will probably revise this paragraph, and the structure, several times.

- **Make your argument obvious**. As well as providing a paragraph explaining what you are going to do, explain to the reader the way in which the information presented and each point made contributes to your overall argument.

- **Stay on topic**. It's easy to drift off on a tangent when the ideas are flowing, and could be useful during the writing process, but be ruthless when it comes to editing. Save your cuttings though, as you might be able to use the less relevant ideas elsewhere.

- **Transitional or linking sentences are crucial.** They often serve a dual function in both linking one section to the next, and signposting why this transition contributes to your argument.

- **Write literally and be concise.** Avoid metaphors, appeals to common sense, sayings and stock phrases.

- **Read your work aloud.** This will help to show you where punctuation has been over or underused.

- **Take regular breaks.** Some suggest a break from writing every forty-five minutes, and the whole point of setting the daily writing tasks and targets above is to avoid the seriously harmful effects of a forty-eight hour break-free writing session towards the deadline.

- **Always be critical, but never be insulting.** In finding your own critical voice, you are likely to disagree with the work of other scholars. Be professional about this, and avoid value-laden terms that denigrate the work of others. Remember, if it wasn't for their work then you'd have nothing to disagree with.

- **Your conclusion must provide your answer to the research question**, by summarising your approach, findings, and discussion. Don't bring in any new material at this stage. If you find you wish to bring in some new theory here, then you must find a place to introduce this much earlier in the piece.

- **When proof-reading** a draft, do something to **distance yourself from your work**. This might be to print it out in a different font, or in booklet form. This will give you a fresh perspective on your work, closer to that of an outside reader.

12

■ **Most importantly: write first and edit second!** If you can write three to five hundred words every day then you will feel like you have mastered the art of writing. Don't let your editorial voice steal the spotlight!

(re)Writing skills and sub-editing

"Easy reading is damn hard writing. But if it's right, it's easy. It's the other way round, too. If it's slovenly written, then it's hard to read. It doesn't give the reader what the careful writer can give the reader."

Maya Angelou (Charney, 2013c)

It is worth noting that academic writing is quite different to other kinds of writing. The relationship between writing and academic writing is akin to the relationship between writing a novel and writing a legal document. The former is aimed at a general audience whilst the latter is aimed at a specific and targeted audience familiar with jargon, linguistic conventions, etc. One of the key differences is the need to cite the work of others when reviewing concepts, theory and literature. This tendency to "write with brackets" is one of the most obvious signs that you are reading an academic document. From earlier assignments you'll have learned to use citations to demonstrate that you are familiar with the work of relevant scholars. You'll need to master the Harvard style or some similar citation protocol and it is worth checking the style specified for your dissertation. But that is just the basic grammar. Beyond this, you need to learn to summarise and critique other people's work and to write with an appropriate **citation density**. If you're not sure, pick up any peer-reviewed article from an Accounting and Finance journal such as *Accounting Organizations and Society or Journal of Corporate Finance*, squint your eyes such that the text is almost out of focus (or if you're of a certain age, just taking your glasses off achieves the same effect) then look at the pattern of the text. The ratio of words to citations (name, date) is critically important. Most good scholars have mastered the art of summarising the literature by using citations. They don't under-cite with only one or two citations appearing sporadically. Equally, they don't over- cite where every statement or claim is supported by dozens of citations. Instead, writing with the appropriate citation density is one of the things that marks out a well-researched dissertation. You should also avoid citing the same text book repeatedly, since this indicates a lack of background reading and a relatively poor grasp of the literature.

Bear in mind who will read your eventual dissertation. It would be safe to assume that the academics reading your dissertation are familiar with the process of reading research papers. It is unlikely that they are reading about the concepts or theories that you are using for the first time. Rather, assume that they are familiar with most of the literature that you have reviewed. To take one simple example, when you say that Modigliani and Miller's (1958) argued that the capital structure of a firm is irrelevant in determining the firm's value and does not affect the wealth of its shareholders because the value of the firm is determined by its real assets and not by the composition of its capital structure. You are assuming that the reader will have read and remembered the contents of *The Cost of Capital, Corporate Finance and The Theory of Investment* by Modigliani and Miller. If you want to make a more specific point, use a direct quotation.

Typically, textbooks assume that you are starting from scratch in an area of theory. Academic articles or literature reviews assume that you've read the original citation and that the author of the article is trying to help lead the reader through a particular take on the literature, or to synthesize it, or to develop a critique. As a result, most of the words available to the author are used to develop an argument, not to re-telling you what someone else said. Therefore, good academic articles tend to appear impenetrable to novice readers because they are not designed with that audience in mind. Gradually, as you spend time getting to know your own field of study, you will become familiar with this shorthand style of citation writing. You should then find yourself better able to emulate it, but bear in mind that the marking process also has realistic expectations. Scholars publishing in top-tier journals have typically spent many years studying, reading, writing and publishing research in their chosen field. The vast majority of people preparing a dissertation have not yet spent the same amount of time and you are not expected to attain such standards in your first piece of extended, research-based writing.

Returning to the theme of writing practice, it is also worth considering the relationship between the processes of writing, reading, rewriting and editing. The award winning novelist and screenwriter John Irving claims that he is a modestly talented writer but a dedicated editor of his own work. In his own words, he says, "I began to make progress as a writer once I began to take my own lack of talent seriously". Our strong advice would be to factor the process of (re)writing into your project plan. Many people find it helpful to write through a series of progressively more refined stages from rough notes and bullet points, to a rough draft supplemented by useful quotes from the literature, to a finished draft, to a final draft. Often the final drafting stage is helped enormously by stepping away from the original text for a short period. Zadie Smith suggests that whenever possible "leave a decent space of time between writing something and editing it." When the text has just been completed, we are often blind to everything from small typos to major sequencing or content

12

errors. Yet a few days later, we are able to read our own text afresh and spot these flaws. In many of the weakest dissertations, the first person to read the assembled dissertation is the person who will mark it. Your project plan should allow time for revising your own text either because of comments from your supervisor, or simply because of your own proofreading.

Finally, academic writing relies on a strong narrative thread just as any other form of writing does. Where a novelist may look for a story arc, a hook or an interesting situation, an academic writer looks for a strong research question to orient the reader. Ideally, research questions make it obvious why the research is being conducted and in what way the project will generate useful insights. Often a dissertation will run to thousands of words but the underpinning logic of the dissertation is embedded in a few sentences in and around the research question(s). It is therefore worth spending a disproportionate amount of time on producing a clear, concise and compelling research question. Relating each significant point back to this question will keep the reader engaged with and aware of the overall narrative.

Software issues

In the last ten years or so, it has become more commonplace to use software to structure the large amounts of information from articles, interviews, etc. Some people find 'mind-mapping' tools useful, others cannot stand them. Again, these can be based on specific software such as Inspiration, or utilising MS Word. For managing the literature, that you will be reading you may wish to use software such as Endnote, Reference Manager or Mendeley. Independent of what type of literature, e.g. books, industry reports or journal articles, we would advise you to consider using referencing software. Spending a little extra time on this during your project could save you days of work at the end. Finally, there are software packages that help with the analysis of data. Some packages (such as SPSS) are helpful for quantitative datasets others (such as NVivo) are especially designed to help with qualitative data. As with our earlier recommendations, you may find that other packages suit your needs.

Of course, you will also need to type your project up and, these days, it would be almost impossible to find someone who did not routinely use a word processing package to do this. You may wish to create a document template at the outset that manages all of the details of page layout, formatting, font type and size, page margins for binding, etc. Again, check the departmental guidelines on these conventions, and if possible then look at some well-regarded examples. While the careless use of irregular fonts and the online thesaurus can ruin otherwise good writing, the sensible use of technology to manage your project can save a considerable degree of stress and frustration. If in doubt about any aspect of your dissertation then ask your supervisor, with whom you should regularly communicate. The next section offers advice on keeping this unique relationship productive.

Managing feedback from your supervisor

Managing feedback from your supervisor is critical to successfully completing a research project. If students expect to create a successful research project, obtaining feedback should not be left to chance. There are a number of proactive strategies that students should employ to manage the feedback they obtain from their supervisors.

First, students should organize regular meetings to discuss their research projects with their supervisors. Some degree programmes stipulate that supervision sessions be logged with agreed actions and a summary of key discussion points. This is a sensible approach, which is often overlooked. Typically, supervisors expect to meet with their research students every four to six weeks. Of course, this may vary depending on the research project's stage of development. For example, in the initial stages of the dissertation, weekly or fortnightly meetings to determine its scope and purpose may be required; on the other hand, during its write-up few if any meetings are needed. Frequent meetings provide opportunities for students to address problems and then modify their work for further consideration by the supervisor. Without frequent feedback, understanding of key topic ideas and issues can be forgotten.

Second, in order to get the best out of your supervisor it is important that you allow sufficient time between setting-up a meeting and its actual date. Sometimes students forget that their supervisors need time prior to a meeting to think about their student's research, and to read anything that he or she has sent to them in advance. It is important to show that you are aware of these things and appreciate the hidden time and effort that your supervisor gives to you. Therefore, if you want to enhance the opportunity of receiving high-quality feedback you should allow your supervisor sufficient time to think about your research work. It is a good strategy to agree dates for the next meeting during the course of the current one.

Third, it is a good idea to actually turn-up at the agreed time and date. If you turn-up late to a scheduled meeting it will probably be cut short and mean the opportunity to gain insights from your supervisor's feedback is lost. In addition, even if a student still manages to obtain a meeting after being late, it will

12

be likely that the supervisor will be worrying about other work that he or she should be attending to, but which is being neglected because of the time given to you. Therefore, being late increases the likelihood of lowering the quality of feedback received from your supervisor. Meetings not only provide valuable feedback, but also help to establish what kind of student-supervisor relationship you are going to have. If you cancel a meeting at short notice, the time and thought that your supervisor had already invested in it is wasted. Lateness and missed meetings have a negative impact on the future relationship between supervisor and student. Certainly, it will harm the degree of seriousness and commitment with which the supervisor approaches future meetings.

By respecting your supervisor's time and other commitments, you are encouraging them to take you seriously. In a positive way, you are demonstrating to your supervisor that you expect meetings to be well prepared and treated with respect. Some students even phone or e-mail a day or two before the planned meeting to confirm with their supervisor that everything is okay and whether there is anything else they should be thinking about or preparing that may not have been mentioned previously.

Fourth, students should always present work to a high standard of presentation, i.e. it should be logically structured and not contain proofreading errors. A high standard of presentation is important as it enables the supervisor to focus his or her energy on evaluating the quality of your ideas presented rather than struggling to decipher it due to awkward structuring and/or proofreading errors. High standards of presentation allow the supervisor to maximize his or her time with you during meetings by discussing substantive issues and making suggestions rather than wasting time highlighting grammatical issues. Therefore, taking the time to present ideas in a readable format pays dividends, as it ensures more of your supervisor's time is focussed on the quality of the ideas presented. Moreover, a positive aspect of proofreading is that it strengthens your overall writing skills. Proofreading your work will also make it look more professional and accomplished. Many writers spend more time editing and proofreading than they do on the actual creative process. The overall feel of the finished product lies within how well your work has been proofread and edited. As stated above, your supervisor will appreciate the effort. Therefore, having the discipline to ensure that all written work given to your supervisor is of a high standard is a necessary activity and good practice for the future.

It may seem an obvious observation but supervisors expect students to follow the advice given. It is surprising how often advice is disregarded. If you disagree with the feedback provided then it is important that you confront the issue with your supervisor rather than ignore him or her and continue to write what you think is right. Disagreement is nothing to worry about, as long as you can defend your position through reason and argument. Your supervisor will accept that your views differ from his or her own. Nevertheless, you should listen to what your supervisor says to you. Remember, he or she will have considerable experience and broad knowledge of your discipline. In some cases, disagreements can prevent successful cooperation, which can again harm the feedback received.

Moreover, it is essential that students be enthusiastic and excited about their work. Enthusiasm and excitement works to the advantage of the student, as it will encourage your supervisor to produce high quality feedback. When students are excited about what they are doing, it stimulates those around them. If you succeed in maintaining your enthusiasm, it will make your research project enjoyable for your supervisor. Certainly, students will be investigating subject areas in the normal course of events that enable them to gain more depth and detailed knowledge on a topic than their supervisor. Therefore, it is no exaggeration to state that your supervisor will expect to be intermittently surprised by new information, evidence and ideas that you are able to supply. Accordingly, supervisors benefit from having a research student as a means of keeping them up-to-date with new developments and at the forefront of knowledge in their field. Gaining new information and evidence will enhance your supervisor's enjoyment and encourage them to spend additional time reading and thinking about your topic area. In other words, enthusiasm and surprises will inspire your supervisor to commit more time and energy into the feedback he or she provides.

One way to improve the quality of feedback you receive from your supervisor(s) is to take some responsibility for the content of your supervisory sessions. It is advisable that students enter a meeting with a proposed list of topics or questions for discussion. Preparing a list of topics or questions serves a number of purposes: it provides a basic itinerary for the meeting; it forces the student to clarify issues that may remain vague; and it prevents the accumulation of a number of small issues becoming a single insurmountable obstacle.

It is hoped that the suggestions and exercises above will promote good writing practices for those undertaking their first major writing project. While there is no guidance that can guarantee dissertation success, and no approach that cannot be compromised by careless writing and research methods, daily writing and regular communication with your supervisor will give you the best chance of producing your strongest work.

12

References

Charney, N. (2012). Jodi Picoult on Writing, Publishing, and What She's Reading. Retrieved 1 June, 2015, from http://www.thedailybeast.com/articles/2012/04/03/jodi-picoult-on-writing-publishing-and-what-she-s-reading.html

Charney, N. (2013a). How I Write: Nathan Englander. Retrieved 1 June, 2015, from http://www.thedailybeast.com/articles/2013/03/27/how-i-write-nathan-englander.html

Charney, N. (2013b). Karen Russell: How I Write. Retrieved 1 June, 2015, from http://www.thedailybeast.com/articles/2013/02/06/karen-russell-how-i-write.html

Charney, N. (2013c). Maya Angelou: How I Write. Retrieved 1 June, 2015, from http://www.thedailybeast.com/articles/2013/04/10/maya-angelou-how-i-write.html

Gray, R. (2002). The Social Accounting project and the Accounting Organisations and Society: Privileging engagement, imaginings, new accountings and pragmatism over critique? *Accounting Organizations and Society, ***27**(7), 687-708.

King, S. (2002). *On Writing*: Pocket Books.

Modigliani, F. and Miller, M.H. (1958). The cost of capital, corporate finance and the theory of investment. *The American Economic Review*, **48**(3), 261-297.

Murakami, H. (2008). *What I Talk about When I Talk about Running*: Vintage.

Murray, R. (2006). *How to Write a Thesis*: McGraw-Hill Education.

Plimpton, G. (1958). The Art of Fiction XXI: Ernest Hemingway. *Paris Review*, **5**(18), 68.

A1 Time Management and Planning Your Research Project

John Sanders, Vera Tens and Robert MacIntosh

Managing a research project is similar to managing any other type of project: following some basic rules minimises the chances of things going wrong as well as making the whole process more enjoyable and productive.

Project planning: Phases, tasks and milestones

One of your first activities should be to map out the key phases, tasks and milestones that will make up your research project. Combined, these three items form the basis of the project plan.

Phases tend to be interpreted by many researchers as groups of activities. Listed below is one view of the key phases in your research project.

1 Establishing your topic

2 Building an understanding of the literature

3 Choosing your method(s)

4 Gathering data

5 Doing the analysis

6 Writing and re-writing

7 Formatting and submission

There may be small variations based on the type of qualification that your dissertation sits within. For example, research-based degrees such as a PhD or MPhil typically incorporate an oral defence of the thesis whereas this only occurs in very rare circumstances in a taught programme. Similarly, in some degree programmes, topics are assigned rather than chosen. Nevertheless, this list of key phases, or a close variant of it, offers the first building block with which you can prepare a project plan. A simple first step is to check the submission date and work backwards from there, allowing time as you see fit for each of the phases that are as relevant to your project.

Tasks are those activities that go to make up an individual phase. Tasks are therefore shorter, more precise, and should be described in a level of detail that would make it clear to anyone reviewing your project plan what is going on and when. Task descriptions should not be long sentences or even paragraphs, but key points that identify necessary activities. For example, phase 2 listed above suggests that you will need to develop a solid grasp of the key literatures pertaining to your chosen topic. This phase will be made up of a number of specific tasks, often stated in the form of a list, using some form of numbering or similar as identifier. For example:

Phase 2: Building an understanding of the literature (see Chapter 3)

Tasks

2.1   Identify key concepts

2.2   Identify seminal authors and contributions

2.3   Identify key journals

2.4   Agree search terms and the boundaries of a structured review of the literature

2.5   Summarise key debates and points of agreement/disagreement

2.6   Establish a research question

Depending upon your own preferences, tasks may contain subtasks and can be broken down into a sensible number of sub-levels. Whilst this level of detail is partly dependent upon your choices it also relates to the nature of the research project. The example given above is typical in that tasks are ordered in sequence that they will likely occur over time, e.g. the first task that is to be executed appears at the top of the list, and the last one at the bottom. Bear in mind that tasks or subtasks may overlap and that some iteration will probably occur between tasks.

Finally, milestones are events that usually attached to a particular deadline such as a submission date, or the point by which ethical approval must be secured. In many cases, milestones are linked with finishing a phase. To some degree, they can be regarded as objectives, and one of their key purposes is to allow you to monitor whether the project as a whole is on time or not. Milestones often indicate that a new task or phase can or should be started. Identifying milestones is just as subjective as the process of identifying tasks and subtasks. Our strong advice would be to discuss phases, tasks and milestones with your supervisor(s) to strike an agreement over the way in which your project will be delivered.

Even the simple process of identifying phases, tasks and milestones in list format is a big step in the right direction. It creates a rudimentary project plan and it is worth noting that experience suggests that students following a rudimentary project plan tend to be better organised and achieve better outcomes than those who approach their project informally. From here, we will refer to this basic project plan as 'Plan A'. A student following Plan A has a clear view of what they should be doing, by when, in order to complete their research project in time and to a high standard. This can be regarded as approaching your project in an organised manner. That said, no project plan is static, and most projects of this scale and duration experience setbacks and unexpected delays. Tasks which at first appeared sequential in nature may in fact need to be done in parallel and vice versa. A common experience for students is that the start of one task is put on hold until other tasks in the project plan progress or even finish. But sometimes data collection takes longer than expected, analysis is more challenging or ethical approval slows things down.

We have given an example of a dissertation project plan below. We would stress that this example is not definitive; rather it is one of many possible project plans. It does however demonstrate the general point that research projects can be divided into phases, tasks and sub-tasks.

Plan A: Tasks

1. Project organisation/planning
    1.1.   Identify your research area
    1.2.   Identify your research question
    1.3.   Identify tasks and milestones
    1.4.   Identify resources, e.g. time, financial, etc.
2. Literature
    2.1.   Search the literature
    2.2.   Review the literature
    2.3.   Search and review more literature

A

3. Data

   3.1. Research approach

      3.1.1. Review research philosophies

      3.1.2. Identify philosophical stance

      3.1.3. Identify research method and methodology to be used

      3.1.4. Get ethical approval for planned data collection

   3.2. Data collection

      3.2.1. Identify potential samples, i.e. people or organisations

      3.2.2. Identify ways of accessing samples, e.g. interviews face-to-face, interviews via Skype, field work etc.

      3.2.3. Data collection according to research method(ology)

   3.3. Data evaluation

      3.3.1. Validity and reliability

      3.3.2. Triangulation

      3.3.3. Comprehensiveness

   3.4. Data analysis

      3.4.1. Document data collection process

      3.4.2. Document data collected, e.g. transcribe interviews, etc.

      3.4.3. Analyse data collected, e.g. use statistics software, content analysis or similar

4. Writing

   4.1. Writing requirements

      4.1.1. Word count

      4.1.2. Page layout

      4.1.3. Font type and size

      4.1.4. Referencing style

      4.1.5. Other

   4.2. Write literature review

   4.3. Write research methodology

   4.4. Write discussion and conclusion

   4.5. Write other necessary chapters

   4.6. Write the introduction

5. Review and revise

    5.1.   Revisit earlier tasks as often and when necessary

    5.2.   Edit written chapters and sections

    5.3.   Check references, citations and quotes

    5.4.   Check formatting, spelling, grammar

    5.5.   Re-read and re-write sections and chapters

6. Submission of report/thesis

The milestones that you set for your research project will obviously vary with the topic, but will also be based on the views of both you and your supervisor(s). For illustrative purposes, we have translated the example above into milestones.

Example milestones and timeline

1 Identify research area and topic and prepare project plan (3rd year, 2nd semester)

2 Provide an extended research proposal to supervisor (4th year, by week 4 of 1st semester)

3 Discuss literature review findings with supervisor (ongoing until submission, starting as early as possible)

4 Provide first draft of literature review chapter to supervisor (no later than week 4 of 1st semester in year 4)

5 Prepare first draft of research methodology chapter (4th year, by week 8 of 1st semester)

6 Submit on-line Research Ethics Approval form (4th year, by week 8 of 1st semester)

7 Prepare first draft of data collection and analysis chapter (4th year, no later than week 1 of 2nd semester)

8 Prepare first draft of discussion and conclusion chapter (4th year, no later than week 4 of 2nd semester)

9 Prepare first draft of dissertation (4th year, no later than week 8 of 2nd semester)

10 Submit final version of dissertation (4th year, by week 12 of 2nd semester)

No matter what your own plan and milestones look like, it would be wise to remember that they are not set in stone.

A

Managing resources

Developing the initial project plan, Plan A, is the first step into managing the research project. However, every project also requires the identification, allocation and management of resources.

Resources can be related to time, people, finance, knowledge and skills or others. They may be required or provided by the researcher and/or another party such as supervisors or other third parties. It is always useful to identify resources for each task and to keep information relating to these resources in a single overview document rather than having them stored in different forms or locations.

Perhaps the single biggest resource at your disposal is time. Your project will require you to identify and allocate your time wisely, e.g. who is executing which tasks and how long are they likely to take. The identification and allocation of time to each task in the project plan is critical if you are to avoid the experience of cramming too much activity into too little time close to the submission deadline. In project management terms, time allocation can be done 'forward', where there is no existing deadline, or 'backwards' where a specific and known time constraint is in place.

Forward planning means that time is allocated to each task at the lowest level; the sum of each task on that level will define time for the higher level task, and so forth. This forward planning process allows the creation of a finish date for the project. It may be useful to allow for overrun on some tasks and therefore push the finish date out a little.

The backward planning approach is used when a deadline, i.e. a time constraint such as a submission deadline, already exists. Some projects have a number of externally driven time constraints, e.g. a date by which a draft literature review must be completed, a final submission date for the project as a whole, etc. In such circumstances you will have to work backwards by dividing up the available time between the tasks required to ensure that you meet the final deadline and any interim deadlines that you face. Using this approach, it is necessary to start at the highest task level or even phase and then work downwards to the lowest level of task.

Examples for each using some of above Plan-A tasks and milestones are shown below.

Task #	Task	Est. duration	Start date	Est. finish	Comments
1	Project organisation/ planning				Requires info from all subtasks first
1.1	Identify your research area	2 days	Day 0	Day 2	
1.2	Identify your research question	5 days	Day 2	Day 7	Assumes tasks are done in sequence
1.3	Identify tasks and milestones	10 days	Day 7	Day 17	Assumes tasks are done in sequence
1.4	Identify resources, e.g. time, financial, etc.	15 days	Day 17	Day 32	Assumes tasks are done in sequence
1	Project organisation/ planning	32 days	Day 0	Day 32	Once all subtasks are identified, the sum will define the task duration and estimated end date

N. B. It is good project management practice to allow for overrun, e.g. in above example for instance to allow for an additional 3 days for Task 1.

Figure A1.1: Forward planning

Milestone 7 "Submit on-line Research Ethics Approval form" has to be done in 4th year, by week 8 of 1st semester. In order to fill in and submit the on-line form, it is necessary to be clear about the research methodology to be employed though.

Milestone 5 "Prepare first draft of research methodology chapter" would have to be finished before this milestone is reached. Furthermore, additional time maybe required as your supervisor might want to read and comment on the methodology. Assuming that this will require 4 weeks, it thus means that Milestone 5 has to be done by week 4 of 1st semester in year 4.

Figure A1.2: Backward planning

▪ Other approaches to planning

A project plan need not be restricted to the two approaches described above. It is possible for some tasks to be time constrained, whereas others may not. Milestones in general tend to be linked with a deadline, and thus are most likely to require the backward planning approach. In addition, time constraints by, for example, third parties will add to the complexity of the planning and managing process and needs to be reflected in the project plan.

A

As with any other project, research projects may also require financial resources. These can be related to the purchase of data, costs of travel, accommodation, transcription or having to pay for access to specific books or literature. It is therefore good project management practice to plan for financial expenditure by developing a project budget, which also identifies where the finances are likely to come from.

Another crucial type of resource of any research project is literature (see Chapter 3). Access to project relevant literature is a basic requirement and therefore needs to be considered at the start of each project.

Overall, no matter how detailed or crude a project plan is, it should always be revisited as the project itself unfolds. Furthermore, it is good management practice to get the buy-in from everyone who will be involved in the project. Giving early notice of any requests for people's time is always a good idea, e.g. interviews that you wish to schedule, requests for feedback on written drafts from your supervisor(s), etc.

■ Useful resources

People manage projects of all kinds across almost every industry, geography and size of organization. As a result, there are a plethora of helpful tools available to anyone looking to manage a project. Academic research projects are, in principle at least, no different and you may well choose to use software or other specialist project management resources to help you manage your work.

You may already know one particular type of project planning software, in which case use what you already know and spend the time you would have invested in learning the software on completing your project. If you have never used project management software you might find that the time invested up front more than repays itself when you come to execute the project plan. One commonly used example is Microsoft's Office Project. This has the advantage of being relatively easy to use, but, whilst those managing complex industrial projects may need specialist features, the less experienced project manager will find that the basic functionality of something like MS Excel is sufficient. To a certain degree, it comes down to personal preference. The timing of a project is often visualised by using a Gantt-chart, which is built into MS Project already. A simple example – using MS Excel – may look similar to the below table using data from above example of Plan A tasks.

#	Milestone	Week 1	Week 2	Week 3	Week 4	Week 5
1	Project organisation/planning	███	███	███		
1.1	Identify your research area	▓▓				
1.2	Identify your research question		▓▓			
1.3	Identify tasks and milestones			▓▓		
1.4	Identify resources, e.g. time, financial, etc.			▓▓		
2	Literature				███	███
2.1	Search the literature				▓▓	▓▓
2.2	Review the literature					▓▓

Figure A1.3: Project planning using a Gantt chart

Contingency planning: when Plan A goes astray

It would be a mistake to assume that Plan A will come together exactly as formulated. Indeed, experience indicates that each phase, task or milestone usually takes longer than planned. This can have a profound effect on student motivation, as what once seemed an achievable and highly manageable plan of action can start to seem hopelessly optimistic given the time remaining. Below are a number of common challenges encountered with suggested contingencies.

Challenge #1: Employment

Before accepting, or extending, any work commitments, you should consider the total demand which it will make on your time. Essentially the most important determinant of the amount of part-time employment or outside activity in which you can safely engage is your ability to organise your own time effectively. There are students who manage a substantial part-time commitment to research whilst at the same time being employed. In contrast, many students find it difficult to organize their time effectively even on a single task such as a research project. Therefore, you must make a realistic personal assessment of what you can and can't do. If you feel that you have overcommitted yourself, then take immediate action to remedy the situation. The worse thing to do is to hesitate and let the stress of over-commitment force you to miss deadlines. This is where a project plan is useful. A project plan at least alerts you to where you are in relation to both self-imposed and externally imposed deadlines.

A

Challenge #2: Unforeseen illness

Perhaps because research projects can be time-pressured, you can find that exhaustion makes you prone to illness. Whether the illness is relatively minor or something more significant, it can affect your ability to complete the project. Equally, the illness of a close relative can detract from your ability to focus on your research work. Generally universities are very sympathetic towards students who suffer from medically certified illnesses. If an illness is starting to affect progress this should be notified to the university as soon as possible. The worst thing to do is nothing, as the longer the notification is left the more difficult it becomes for the university to reconstruct timings and dates for later evaluation. The decision becomes even more difficult if shorter periods of illness are involved when there may be a preference to absorb the time lost and at the same time maintain any grant payment. If illness is going to cause long-term problems it is much better to make a decision about suspending studies earlier rather than later.

Challenge #3: Motivation

What may have seemed a fascinating or exciting project can quickly become dull or difficult as you face the reality of writing an extended piece of work. While it is difficult to make a contingency plan for a loss in motivation, it is important to realize that it will happen. Conducting a research project can be an extremely arduous process and no student can maintain the same level of enthusiasm for it throughout his or her studies. Perhaps you can set current tasks to one side and switch attention to another element of the research study. Possibly you can focus on the initial reasons for choosing the topic and remind yourself why it seemed interesting, or maybe you need to accept that it isn't as exciting as you first thought and focus instead on the role this project plays in reaching graduation.

Challenge #4: Feasibility

Whether it is a lack of access, or the quality of the data that you eventually capture, there can be the gradual realization that the planned conclusions cannot be drawn from the available data. You may discover that the envisioned relationships between variables are unclear or do not exist; an outcome which would be judged unacceptable. Alternatively, the promises of interviews or focus groups may fall through and you are left with either no or limited data. In these circumstances, early advice from your supervisor can help you to reframe your research to design research aims and objectives that remain achievable.

Challenge #5: Computing difficulties

Most of us rely, most of the time, on computers to create documents, capture and analyse data, communicate, etc. Computer problems can also cause considerable delays and problems to researchers. Alarmingly computer software related problems occur at the most inconvenient of times. It goes without saying that maintaining up-to-date backups of all data and word processing files is a sensible precaution especially given the scale of the writing task.

References

Easterby-Smith, M., Thorpe, R., & Jackson, P. R. (2008). Management Research. 3rd edition. London/ UK: Sage Publications Ltd

A

A2 Evaluating Your Research Project

Nigel Caldwell and Robert MacIntosh

Whilst each individual college or university will have its own particular marking process and criteria, there are large areas of common ground when it comes to the assessment of research projects. We have studied an extensive set of marking guides and combined features of these to produce three fictitious examples (which we refer to here as universities A, B and C). Our purpose in doing this is to illustrate some key points about assessment. These marking guides are reproduced in Table A2.1 below. It is worth noting that we are examining general principles, not specifics, since these would vary with the nature of the particular programme of study. A very sensible next step would be to find and read the specific equivalent from the course handbook of the programme that you are studying.

Table A2.1: Anonymised research project marking guides

Guide A	Guide B	Guide C
Identification of the research area, aim, objectives and/or research questions [20%]	How well chosen and well justified are the research methods employed in the project ? [25%]	Is the purpose of the research clear, justified and achievable? [30%]
Does the literature review inform the research? [40%]	Literature or body of knowledge has been thoroughly investigated, understood and incorporated [45%]	Technical content including use of literature and methods [30%]
Is the chosen methodology appropriate? Are valid and reliable analysis methods used? [30%]	Initiative, originality, imagination and skill in construction and execution [10%]	Evidence of the effort involved and of originality [30%]
Writing style and presentation: (English grammar, reporting style, presentation of tables, figures, equations, etc.) [10%]	Presentation of relevant and well-founded conclusions and recommendations [20%]	Implications for practice, for theory and limitations to the work [10%]

Of course, what interests you as an individual student is the mark that you will eventually obtain for your research project, and how that mark is constructed. The primary concern of those doing the marking of your research project is ensuring fairness and consistency in the allocation of marks. Consider for a moment a cohort of 100 students, each working on a research project in their final year of study. Naturally, the 100 projects will vary in terms of topics, methods, types of data, etc. From the university's perspective, marking 100 research projects is qualitatively different from marking 100 exam scripts, because of the inherent variations from one project to the next. To deal with this, most universities involve multiple markers to ensure consistency. First, your research project will likely be marked by your supervisor. Then, typically, a second copy of your project is given to an independent second marker who forms their own view of the grade in relation both to the kinds of criteria set out in Table A2.1 *and* to more generic grade descriptors that set out the characteristics of an A, B or C grade piece of work (see Table A2.2).

Table A2.2: Indicative grade descriptors

A Grades [typically 70%-100%]	Exceptionally good work that is distinctive and goes beyond run of the mill. Rich in conceptual sophistication, independent insight, pertinent information or understanding of relevant issues. Demonstrates an easy familiarity with concepts and sources.
B Grades [typically 60%-69%]	Very good standard of work demonstrating an obvious and consistent understanding of the topic or problem at hand. A convincing grasp of relevant literature combined with effective use of evidence and argumentation. Some indication of critical scrutiny and independent thinking, and a high standard of presentation.
C Grades [typically 50%-59%]	A good performance, offering an accessible and well structured discussion of relevant issues or arguments, suitably illustrated with original or appropriate secondary source material. Presentation will be coherent, well structured and literate, with accurate and effective referencing of the material used.
D Grades [typically 40%-49%]	Competent work offering a routine treatment based on limited reading or a heavy reliance on lecture notes. Though a basic understanding will be apparent, the work may lack depth, breadth, clarity or focus. Communication may be hampered by a poorly structured presentation.
E Grades and below [typically 39% and below]	Submissions showing some awareness of the topic under investigation, yet with limited conceptualisation, discussion and/or articulation. May not distinguish between relevant and irrelevant material and tends to be superficial in the treatment of both concepts and data. Poorer work may be plagiarised, inaccurate or misleading.

A

Where the marking guide sets out weightings for individual aspects of the project, each aspect would be graded individually then weightings applied to arrive at an overall grade. Once both markers have arrived at an independent assessment of the project, their written comments are compared. The second marker role is a safeguard against bias (positive or negative) from the first marker. Where there is agreement the mark is confirmed. Where the first and second markers disagree, a third marker is usually asked to offer an opinion, often with sight of the written reports from the first and second markers. This process is time consuming but helps ensure that there is a consistent standard such that all distinction or first class projects are of a comparable standard, and all fails are confirmed as deficient in relation to the grading scheme, etc. All of this occurs within the university and is then endorsed by an external and independent examiner from another university. Typically, a representative sample of all research projects are considered by the external examiners alongside a statistical analysis of the spread of marks, standard deviation, comparison with previous years, etc. External examiners are appointed for a fixed period of 2 or 3 years and cannot fulfil the role of examiner indefinitely, to ensure that there is always a fresh perspective on the marking process.

From your point of view, it pays to realise that whilst your supervisor will usually have some expertise or interest in the specific topic of your research project, very often the second marker will not. Also, whilst your supervisor will have helped in the evolution and shaping your research project by offering comment and advice, the second marker will come to the project cold. The document must stand on its own merits with no prior assumptions or knowledge on the part of the reader. Rather than being a disadvantage, this aids the objectivity of the marking process. The processes described above occur at what are variously called assessment, award or exam boards that take place after the degree programme or course has completed.Securing the agreement of the external examiners is a necessary pre-condition to confirming the award of individual marks, degree classifications, etc. All universities have an appeal process in place but typically such appeals centre on the process rather than the academic integrity of the grades awarded.

Why should you care about the assessment process, beyond a vague sense of reassurance that consistency and fairness is built into the process? Well reading about this 'backstage' process should help you with understanding the challenge you face in writing a research project. Try to keep in mind that there is a wider audience for your study, that it will be read and the mark validated by someone who will have little or no contact with you, your work or your topic, and that this internally validated mark then has to be validated by an external authority. Understanding this process should make you put a premium on clarity – being able to clearly explain what you are proposing to study and why, what the relevant literature tells you and what it doesn't, the way you approached the research in terms of any methods used, clear presentation of any data collected and analysis and conclusions that are patently linked to the original research questions or issues. Whilst you cannot fully predict the outcome of the marking process, there are things that you can do to get feedback. Your supervisor should be your primary source of feedback (as discussed in Chapter 12) but you can also test out the sense of the project by asking someone else to read either a complete draft or a sample section/chapter. If they struggle to see the purpose of the project, find it too dense or too obtuse, then it is likely that your markers will too. Typos don't materially influence the overall grade but they do create an impression that little care was taken in the production of the project. The best projects are those which are easiest to read and follow, they offer the reader clear signposting about the journey ahead of the reader, the route the research will take them on, and where the research – and reader – will end up.

Example marking guides

The point that clarity is central brings us to the first issue in assessment, that the research problem being addressed is an appropriate level of challenge. Whilst many students start their research project with lofty ambitions, there is no requirement to change the world. Marking guidance often asks whether the student has designed a study with enough challenge to be interesting but also do-able within the time frame and available resources? Guides A and C explicitly mark against this theme, though the weightings applied vary. Framing your project is important and choosing a topic which is too diffuse has negative knock on effects throughout the development and writing of your project. Chapter 2 offers clear guidance on shaping a suitable project.

The quality of the literature review is assessed explicitly in all three guides. Note that the emphasis on the *use* made of the literature; it has to *guide and inform* the dissertation. There is therefore an obvious link between the extent to which a clear brief has been specified (see previous paragraph) and the extent to which a precise and detailed literature review has been conducted. The literature review represents the largest portion of the overall grade in guides A and B. Guide C combines what is described as the "technical content" including literature and methods, whilst guides A and B separate out the choice of methods as a separate theme for assessment. The originality of the work attracts 30% of the grade in guide C, only 10% in guide B and doesn't feature as an explicit criterion in guide A.

A

Presentation is mentioned in guides A and B but it is worth observing that many students write research projects in a second, or even third language and any critique of your grammar would be placed in that context. Guides B and C draw specific attention to conclusions reached, with guide C focusing particularly on implications for both theory (linking back to the literature review) and practice.

Our point in dissecting both marking guides and grade descriptors is twofold. First, it establishes that whilst each individual marking guide or set of grade descriptors is different, there are certain common themes which tend to recur in most universities or colleges. This is understandable given that the process of arriving at judgements of quality occurs in all universities and colleges. Within the wider curriculum, research projects are commonly used to provide a detailed analysis of your individual ability to think and write coherently, to draw together insights from the literature and to work with data to develop findings. How you develop a research design, link this to the literature, gather and analyse data and present findings are the underlying features of all research projects. Our second purpose in examining three different marking guides is to encourage you to find the specific guide that your research project will be assessed against. Whilst it is tempting to focus on the need to press ahead and meet the deadline, looking at assessment criteria should be one of the first things that you do. Indeed, it can be done before you reach the research project since marking guides are available in advance. At the very least, you should be paying attention to any explicit signals about the relative weighting associated with individual aspects of your research project by those doing the assessment.

A3 Project Structure and Word Counts

Kevin O'Gorman

The following table offers a suggested structure and approximate word counts for dissertations, relative to the degree being pursued. This is designed to be altered according to the needs of the researcher, and the stipulations of their supervisor and institution. It is important to understand that the table is offered here only as a set of non-specific suggestions for your (hopefully!) very specific project. All dissertations are different, and your supervisor is the best person to talk to about your specific institutional, school, or college requirements, which may vary quite significantly. Creating your own outline through discussion with your supervisor gives you both a sense of where you are in the process and what needs to be done, whilst also functioning as a reference point when completing smaller intermediary targets. The examples below illustrate a general principle of successful research espoused by this book: a larger project becomes much more manageable when broken down into smaller, clearly defined sections. This approach is likely to prove helpful even beyond PhD level, when writing papers for publication in academic journals, for instance, or even when completing a new edition of a textbook!

Section	Word Count			
	Hons Dissertation	MSc Dissertation	MPhil	PhD
Introduction	**1500**	**1500**	**5000**	**8000**
Pre-theoretic overview	500	500	1000	1500
Why this is interesting?	100	100	500	500
Research purpose	600	600	1500	2000
Aim and objectives	300	300	500	500
Something	0	0	1500	1500
Something else	0	0	0	2000
Literature review	**3000**	**3500**	**12000**	**23000**
Historical overview (of theory)	500	500	1000	8000
Contemporary review of theory	1500	2000	7000	10000
Context for study	1000	1000	5000	5000
Methodology	**2000**	**2000**	**6000**	**17000**
Philosophy	500	500	1000	3000
Methodological options	0	0	0	4000
Data collection technique	600	600	2000	4000
Sourcing and selecting data	200	200	500	750
Research ethics	200	200	500	750
Data analysis tool(s)	500	500	2000	5000
Empirical material	**2000**	**2500**	**6000**	**12000**
Presentation of data	500	750	1500	3000
Analysis	1000	1000	3000	6000
Findings	500	750	1500	3000
Discussion	**2000**	**2500**	**6000**	**12000**
Discussion	1800	2000	5000	8000
Theory development	200	500	1000	4000
Conclusion	**1500**	**2000**	**5000**	**8000**
Reviewing the aim and objectives	300	500	1500	2000
Contribution - theory				2000
Contribution - context	300	500	1500	
Contribution - method				1000
Contribution - management practice				
Methodological review	300	300	500	1000
Limitations and further research	300	300	1000	1000
Overall conclusion	300	400	500	1000
Total	**13000**	**15000**	**40000**	**80000**

A4 Information and Consent

James Richards, Lakshman Wimalasena and Gavin MacLean

Sample information sheet

> Thank you for showing interest in taking part in my dissertation. The information below provides details of what my study is about and your potential role in my study.
>
> The aim of my project/dissertation is to [*provide concise and jargon free details of your study*].
>
> Participation in my study involves [*include details of what this involves plus an estimation of the time required of the participant*].
>
> The benefits of taking part in my study include [*provide a range of benefits that relate to both you and the participant*]. The study, however, comes with minor risks [*if applicable, state what these may be for the participant*].
>
> Information provided by you will only be used for my university project/dissertation. The information you provide will be kept secure [*provide details*] and the information will not be used in a manner that will reveal your identity [*where there is a possibility of partial identification you should detail what this may involve*]. Only my project/dissertation supervisor and I will have access to such information in its original format. All such information will be destroyed one year after the completion of my dissertation.
>
> Participation in this dissertation is completely voluntary and you have the right to withdraw at any time without any prejudice or negative consequences.
>
> This study has been approved by [*insert details of research ethics committee at your institution*].
>
> If you have any questions or queries about my study please contact me through the details below.
>
> [*Name, telephone/email address*]

Sample consent form

Title of project/dissertation: [*insert the title of project/dissertation here*]

I have been informed of and understand the purposes of the study.

I have been given an opportunity to ask questions about the study.

I understand that I can withdraw from the study at any time without prejudice or negative consequences.

Any information which might potentially identify me will not be used in the final report/dissertation.

I agree to participate in the study outlined to me.

Name of participant:

Signature of participant:

Date:

Index